THE SPIRIT OF THE LAWS

War and Genocide

General Editors: Omer Bartov, Brown University; A. Dirk Moses, European University Institute, Florence/University of Sydney

There has been a growing interest in the study of war and genocide, not from a traditional military history perspective, but within the framework of social and cultural history. This series offers a forum for scholarly works that reflect these new approaches.

"The Berghahn series Studies on War and Genocide *has immeasurably enriched the English-language scholarship available to scholars and students of genocide and, in particular, the Holocaust."*—**Totalitarian Movements and Political Religions**

For a full volume listing, please see back matter

THE SPIRIT OF THE LAWS

The Plunder of Wealth in the Armenian Genocide

Taner Akçam and Umit Kurt

Translated by Aram Arkun

berghahn
NEW YORK · OXFORD
www.berghahnbooks.com

Published by
Berghahn Books
www.berghahnbooks.com

Turkish-language edition
©2012 Iletişim
Kanunların Ruhu: Emval-I Metruke Kanunlarında Soykırımın Izini Sürmek

The Jerair Nishanian Foundation
generously supported and financed the
translation of this book.

Library of Congress Cataloging-in-Publication Data
Akçam, Taner, 1953-
[Kanunlarin ruhu. English]
The spirit of the laws: the plunder of wealth in the Armenian genocide / Taner
Akçam and Ümit Kurt; translated by Aram Arkun.
    pages cm.—(Studies on war and genocide; volume 21)
Includes bibliographical references and index.
ISBN 978-1-78238-623-0 (hardback: alkaline paper)—ISBN 978-1-78238-624-7
(ebook)
    1. Armenians—Turkey—History—20th century. 2. Armenians—Legal status,
laws, etc.—Turkey—History—20th century. 3. Armenian question. 4. Arme-
nians—Relocation—Turkey—History—20th century. 5. Forced migration—Turkey—History—20th century. 6. Pillage—Turkey—History—20th century.
7. Turkey—History—Mehmed V, 1909-1918. I. Kurt, Ümit. II. Title.
    DR435.A7A53513 2015
    956.6'20154--dc23
                                                                2014033521

British Library Cataloguing in Publication Data
A catalogue record for this book is available from the British Library.

Printed on acid-free paper

ISBN: 978-1-78238-623-0 hardback
ISBN: 978-1-78238-624-7 ebook

Dear Hrant,[*]

Years ago during an interview you said, "What happened to the civilization, the wealth, created by a thousands-of-years-old society [i.e., Armenian]?"

Interviewer: To whom did it go?
Hrant Dink: To whom did it go. . . . This, as a matter of fact, is one of the basic issues about which Turkey cannot talk. The question of Armenian properties is truly at this point Turkey's most demonic, most frightening issue concerning the future. In my opinion, Turkey took a legal step in the past against the demand for compensation that could come from the Armenians. Because a law called "abandoned properties" was issued. A deadline was given to the Armenians. It was said, "Let them come; we will give [them] their goods." The goods of the Armenians who did not come within the prescribed period of time went to the Treasury. Such laws were issued; implementation took place. Turkey took its step legally. Anyway, in this country it is harder to talk about the survivors than the deceased.
Why?
Because unbelievable injustices are going to come to light. . . . If it is asked, "To whom were the belongings remaining from the Armenians apportioned; what happened to [the properties] and to whom [were they given]," this creates a very great shock. Because a history dictated to a country will collapse. The thought will spread among people that if this history was incorrectly explained, then other things also are incorrectly explained. An important transformation is going to take place in Turkey.
(Interview with Neşe Düzel in *Radikal*, 23 May 2005)

We only cracked the door open slightly with the hope of making a small contribution to the shock and transformation, which you awaited, predicted, and hoped for. . . .

Taner Akçam and Umit Kurt

---

[*]. Editor of Armenian Turkish Newspaper AGOS, assassinated 19 January 2007 in Istanbul.

CONTENTS

⚜

Introduction   **1**

**Chapter 1. The Laws and Decrees of the Committee of
Union and Progress Period**   **19**
The Decrees and Regulations of 17, 30, and 31 May 1915   20
The Regulation of 10 June 1915   22
The Temporary Law of 26 September 1915 and the
     Regulation of 8 November 1915   24
A Brief Evaluation   29

**Chapter 2. The Armistice Period and the Returning
Armenians**   **34**
The First Ones Returning from Deportation   34
12 January 1920: The Ittihadist Laws Are Annulled   38
A Brief Evaluation   40
The Treaty of Sèvres of 10 August 1920   40
The Prohibition against the Return of Greeks and
     Armenians Staying Outside of Turkey   42
The Articles of Law Used to Prevent Their Return   43
Policies to Obstruct Repatriation   46
The Prohibition of Domestic Travel and Migration   48
A Brief Evaluation   50

Chapter 3. The Turkish Republic Prior to Lausanne   **58**
The First Laws and Regulations of the Turkish
     Grand National Assembly   58
The 20 April 1922 Abandoned Properties Law   60

The Regulations of November to December 1922   61
Regulations Relevant to Istanbul   61
The 14 September 1922 Abrogation of the Property
    Regulation   63
Why Was There a Return to the Ittihadist Laws of the
    Genocide?   64
The Plunder of Izmir and the Independence Tribunals   66
Return to the Ittihadist Mentality: The 15 April Law
    and 29 April Regulation of 1923   69
A Brief Evaluation   71
Abandoned Properties and National Tax Obligations
    (Tekalif-i Milliye)   72

Chapter 4. The Treaty of Lausanne: A Turning Point   **78**
The Abandoned Properties Question in the
    Negotiations and Treaty   79
Mass and Individual Repatriations and the Armenian Homeland   79
A Plan to Expel the Armenian Population   84
The Question of the Belongings That Were Left Behind   85
The Amnesty: Draft Proposal and Final Form   88
The Lausanne Regulations: The Question of Nationality   90
The Lausanne Regulations: Property, Rights, and Interests,
    or, The Issue of Compensation   94
A Brief Evaluation of Lausanne   98

**Chapter 5. After Lausanne: The Armenians Remaining
Outside of Turkey**   **104**
The Treaties of Alexandrapol (Gyumri), Kars, and Moscow   106
Turkey-France: A Pair of Treaties   107
The 25 October 1934 Turkey–United States Compensation
    Treaty   114
An Interim Note on the U.S. Compensation Treaty   119
The International Commission and Mixed Arbitral Tribunals   121

**Chapter 6. Turkey after Lausanne: Raising a Virtual
Wall around Its Borders Like a Fortress**   **132**
Armerican Armenians Are Not Permitted to Enter Turkey   134
The Return of the Armenians: A Question of the Honor and
    Pride of the State   136
"To Allow Their Return Means to Waste . . . the Blood
    We Spilled"   142
The Legal Vacuum Created by Lausanne on Repatriation   144
The Travel Regulation: Bans on Entry into the Country and
    Domestic Travel   149
Prohibitions on Domestic Travel   152

Passport Laws   155

**Chapter 7. Domestic Legal Regulations during
the Republican Period**   164
    The First Adjustments   165
    The 13 June 1926 Regulation   168
    1928: The Distribution of Title Deeds and the Transfer of
        Revenue to the Treasury Begin   169
    The 22 April 1963 Constitutional Court Decision   172
    The Citizenship Laws of 1928 and 1964   175
    Those Removed from Citizenship and the Liquidation of
        Their Properties   178
    The Abandoned Properties Laws and the Present Situation   180
    The 1983 and 2001 Circulars of the General Directorate of
        Land Registry and Cadaster   182
    Profound Fear: Title Deed Registries   184

Conclusion   191

Bibliography   195

Index   203

INTRODUCTION

On 27 May 1915 the Ottoman government, using the ongoing world war as a pretext, made the decision to deport its Armenian citizens to the regions of Syria and Iraq, which at that time were Ottoman provinces. However, the true aim was not to change the locations of the Armenians, but to annihilate them.[1] This deportation and destruction also gave rise to an important question: What was going to happen to the properties the Armenians left behind? How would they be administered?

A series of laws and decrees were issued in order to deal with this question. The main idea was that the state should take over these properties and liquidate them based on certain priorities, including their distribution among the Muslim population. Since the entire operation was portrayed as an "involuntary deportation" by the state of a certain group of citizens, their rights to their properties were not completely eliminated and the principle of providing them with the equivalent values of their seized properties was accepted.

In 1918, while the Ottomans were losing the war, some Armenians who had managed to survive the Genocide began to return to their homes and demanded their belongings back. It became necessary to make a series of revisions to the laws and regulations that had been issued. However, during the years following 1918, the country fell into complete chaos. The Armenians who had survived the wave of genocide from 1915 to 1917 and were returning home were forced to leave the country. As a result, a new series of laws and regulations were issued concerning Armenian properties. Even though a final decision

concerning Armenian properties was made in the 1923 Treaty of Lausanne, the administration of these properties continued to remain a serious legal issue; throughout the entire period of the Turkish Republic
new laws and regulations continued to be issued about them.

The goal of the present volume is to attempt to understand the spirit
of all of these laws and statutes, which were known as the Abandoned
Properties Laws.[2] The central thesis of this work is that these laws
were a structural element of the Armenian Genocide of 1915 as well as
of today's Turkish legal system, and yet, paradoxically, they continue
to this very day to protect the rights of the Armenians to their properties. Even when these properties were sold or transferred to others, the
government continued to act on the principle that it was administering
them in the name of the original owners.

The majority of the relevant laws and regulations were issued in
the Republican period. The Republic of Turkey and its legal system
were built, in a sense, on the seizure of Armenian cultural, social, and
economic wealth, and on the removal of the Armenian presence. In
Turkey today the Directorate of Religious Affairs and the army are
usually considered the two most important institutions of the Republican regime. A third such institution would be the General Directorate of Foundations, a continuation of the General Directorate of Pious
Foundations of the previous period. It was established on 2 May 1920
as a separate ministry; and on 3 March 1924 was turned into a directorate affiliated with the office of the prime minister. One of its most
important tasks was to administer the properties of Christians (mainly
Armenians) who were exterminated or forced to leave Turkey at different periods.

In 1914 approximately one fourth of the Ottoman population were
Christians. If we consider that Christians do not form even 1 percent
today, we can begin to realize the importance of this institution. The
great majority of the deported and annihilated Christians were Greeks
and Armenians. A set of treaties and regulations were conducted with
the Greek government concerning the properties left behind by the Ottoman Greeks. Consequently, most of the properties administered by
the General Directorate of Foundations belonged to Ottoman Armenians, as well as Orthodox Syrians (Assyrians). Based on this fact, the
present work argues that the Republican legal system institutionalized the Armenian (and Assyrian) Genocide of 1915–17.

The Abandoned Properties Laws are perceived as normal, common-
place laws in Turkey. Their existence has never been questioned in this
regard. Their consideration as natural is also an indication of why the

Armenian Genocide was ignored throughout the history of the Republic. This commonality is equivalent to considering an issue nonexistent. Turkey was founded on the transformation of a presence—Christian in general, Armenian in particular—into an absence.

* * * * *

Today, the problems that Christians and Jews have been facing in Turkey are usually discussed and studied under the heading of minority issues. It is accepted that these groups possessing different ethnic, religious, and cultural identities, and being numerically in the minority, face a series of issues in connection with the society of the majority, so their discussion takes place within the framework of minority rights. This approach is quite problematic: the republic was essentially founded on the basis of the destruction of the Christian communities which formed at least 25 percent of the population.

Consequently, it is incorrect to look at the issues of Christians in general (including the Greeks and Assyrians), or Armenians in particular, as the minority of the Republic—it is more complex than that. It is necessary to discuss the topic directly as a question connected to the existence of Turkey. The Turkish Republic is a construction based on the transformation of Christian existence to absence—or, more rightly, on the negation of an existence. This is the reason why the topic, which is called the Armenian Question in Turkey, is basically discussed as a national security issue. Bringing it up, or even just calling for an open discussion, is perceived as a threat to national existence and national security.

In 2006 the Turkish National Security Council decided that making land records covering the 1915 period available to archives and researchers was contrary to national security and prohibited it.[3] The fundamental motivation behind the assassination of the outspoken Turkish-Armenian newspaper editor Hrant Dink and the killings of three Christians in Malatya in 2007[4] was anxiety about national security. It was not a coincidence that Ergenekon[5] suspect İbrahim Şahin, former executive director of the Special Forces Department, labeled a group of intellectuals proposing an open discussion of the Armenian issue as "threateners of national security" in 2009.[6] The Istanbul Second Criminal Court of the First Instance, which sentenced Arat Dink (son of Hrant Dink and owner now of Dink's newspaper *Agos*) and Sarkis Seropyan (a journalist with *Agos*) to prison for having used the word "*soykırım*" (genocide), considered the use of this word to be a threat to national security.[7] The truth revealed by these examples is very simple: because Turkey founded its existence on the absence of the other, every conversation on the other's existence inspires fear and anxiety. The chief difficulty in speaking on the Armenian issue in Turkey lies in this existence-absence dilemma.

The institutionalization of the elimination of the Christian-Armenian presence was fundamentally realized, along with many other things, through the Abandoned Properties Laws. These laws are structural components of the Armenian Genocide and one of the elements connected to the basis of the legal system of the Republican period. In this way, the Republic adopted genocide as its structural foundation. This is a cue to take a fresh look at the relationship between the Republic as a legal system and the Genocide. This is what is done in this work.

* * * * *

Raphael Lemkin introduced the concept of genocide for the first time in 1944 in his book entitled *Axis Rule in Occupied Europe*.[8] The book consists of a compilation of 334 laws, decrees, and regulations connected with the administration of seventeen different regions and states under Nazi occupation between 13 March 1938 and 13 November 1942. Lemkin did not introduce the concept of genocide together with barbaric practices like torture, oppression, burning, destruction, and mass killing observed in all genocides, but rather through a book quoting and analyzing legal texts. Could this be a coincidence?

Given its importance, it is necessary to stress this one more time: in the year that Lemkin completed the writing of his book, 1943, he already knew of all the crimes perpetrated by Nazi Germany. However, he did not present the concept of genocide in a framework elucidated by these crimes. On the contrary, he introduced the term through some laws and decrees proclaimed by the Nazi Regime to administer occupied territories that perhaps in the logic of war might be considered normal. This situation is not in accordance with our present way of understanding genocide. The general perception is that genocide is the collapse of a normally functioning legal system; it is the product of the deviation of the system from the so-called normal path. In this point of view, genocide means the institutions of civilization are not working and are replaced by barbarism. Lemkin, however, seems to be saying the complete opposite of this: that genocide is embedded in ordinary legal documents. By doing this, it is as if he is telling us not to look for the traces of genocide as barbaric manifestations, those that can be defined as inhuman, but to follow their trail in legal texts.[9]

Genocide as a phenomenon operating as an integral part of the legal system—this is an interesting definition. And this definition is one of the central theses of this work. Therefore, the Armenian Genocide does not just exist in the displays of barbarity carried out against the Armenians, but is may also be hidden in a series of ordinary legal texts.

Genocide does not just mean physical annihilation. Going even further, physical annihilation is only one detail of the process. How many Armenians died during the course of the deportations or destruction, or how many remained alive—as important as this is on the human level—is just a secondary issue from a definitional point of view; what is important is the complete erasure of the traces of the Armenians in their ancient homeland. Interior Minister Talat Pasha's 30 April 1916 telegram sent to the governor of Syria and commander of the Fourth Army, Cemal Pasha (both were members of the governing Committee of Union and Progress Party triumvirate), in connection with the Armenian Catholicate in Sis is the clearest expression of this policy: "Essentially the goal of the abolition of the Sis Catholicate and, at the first opportunity, the expulsion of the Catholicos from there aimed at completely eliminating the existence of this place which possesses a very great historical and national value in Cilicia for Armenians and is presented by them as supposedly the final seat of an Armenian government."[10]

In Talat Pasha's expression, everything was arranged in a way suitable for "completely eliminating the existence" and place of the Armenians. In this understanding, genocide is not a deviation from the normal operative legal system. It is in itself a product of the legal system, and has been implemented by means of this system. Hasan Fehmi Bey, the first secretary of the treasury of the Turkish Republic, on 15 April 1923 while discussing the new Abandoned Properties Law, spoke about "splitting a hair into forty in legal theory," and said, "It has been two or three years since we here set out to take into consideration the [20 April 1920 dated] Law of Abandoned Properties as one of the most delicate and fine points of our legal bases." Through these words he demonstrated the extremely crucial relationship between law and the regime of genocide.[11]

* * * * *

Genocide is defined in Lemkin's work *Axis Rule in Occupied Europe* as "a coordinated plan of different actions aiming at the destruction of essential foundations of the life of national groups, with the aim of annihilating the groups themselves."[12] The expropriation of the property of the groups being annihilated varies from genocide to genocide.[13] The Ottoman experience naturally also has some unique elements compared with other examples. First, during this process it was not only the properties of Armenians that were seized. Other Christians were also subjected to the same procedure. Second, the properties of Armenians who were not deported were not seized. Confiscation was confined only to the properties of those Armenians who were deported.

During the 1913 to 1918 period, the properties of two large Ottoman communities, Greeks and Armenians, were seized through special laws connected to a central policy that removed these people from their homes.[14] The policies carried out against each of them did have some differences. However, these dissimilarities were not formulated within the framework of ethnic and religious differences but were determined by the changing policies followed by the Committee of Union and Progress government in different periods and circumstances. Careful distinctions were made through laws and decrees not only between Greeks and Armenians, but also within each of these communities.

As an example, the two categories pertaining to Greeks in the 1913 to 1918 period can be mentioned. The first category includes the Ottoman Greeks who were the subject of a population exchange program between the Ottoman Empire and Greece at the beginning of World War I. The exchange of Greek property was to be administered according to the principle of reciprocity. Although this agreement did not enter into force because of the war, the seizure and use of the properties of Ottoman Greeks falling into this category was still different from that of the remainder of the Greek masses in the Empire. The second category includes Greeks deported to internal regions from coastal areas during the later years of the war.

In this way there were two separate political practices enacted toward the Ottoman Greeks. On the one hand there were the Greeks forcibly deported to Greece, and on the other hand there were those driven from coastal cities to interior regions. In order to rectify the resultant confusion, the regulation called Directive on the Manner of Filling Out Tables on the Exchange of Migrants[15] was created to specify the two groups of Greeks, the differences in the administration of their goods, and the amount of consideration necessary.

The administration of Armenian goods confiscated as a result of the deportation law of 1915 was treated as a matter distinct from the administration of the aforementioned Greek properties. In government correspondence with the provinces it was specifically requested that authorities pay attention to the differences.[16] The most important one was that the Greek goods were not subject to certain liquidation. Orders to the provinces emphasized this point.[17] The government's aim was to exchange the properties left behind by the Greeks going to Greece with properties of Muslims coming from Greece. Additionally, it was expected that the Greeks deported to internal Ottoman districts for military considerations would eventually return, so their property was not liquidated.

Similar developments were observed at the end of 1919. Among the Greeks distinctions made were between those subject to the 1923 Turkish-Greek Population Exchange Convention and those who were not subject to it. While Istanbul Greeks were not subject to the exchange, the situation of many Greeks who settled in Istanbul and its environs from Anatolia in the 1918–22 period, on the other hand, was different. The people who came to Istanbul later were included among the Greeks subject to the exchange (which created the possibility of seizing their goods). The government attempted to clarify any confusions that might arise in the situations discussed above through special decrees.[18]

* * * * *

In the case of Armenians during the period of deportation: only the belongings of Armenians who were being deported were subject to liquidation. The property of the Armenians who were not being deported was not confiscated. In various telegrams sent to the provinces it was distinctly specified that only the goods of people being expelled should be liquidated: "The non-Muslims who are not being transported [continue to] possess their movable and immovable properties. The property of Armenians . . . being transported and the other non-Muslims who were being deported together with them at that time [is] subject to liquidation."[19] In addition, if Armenians who stayed in the places where they were located and were not deported had properties in other regions, those properties were not touched. This occurred, for example, with Armenians living in Istanbul.[20]

Second, because the confiscation of the Armenians' property did not take place on the basis of a racist ideology, unlike the case of the Jews in Nazi Germany, no discussion of removing the citizenship of the Ottoman Armenians took place during the deportations and genocide. Moreover, if Armenians did not have their citizenship removed specifically by a decision of the Council of Ministers or through their own individual resignations, their citizenship was preserved until as late as 1964.

Third, while the material wealth of the Armenians was being seized, it did not take place in the form of a simple appropriation, or irreversible plunder; that is, it was not said that the goods or their equivalent values would not be returned to their owners. On the contrary, it was stated that the goods, or their value, would be administered by the state in the name of their owners. Everything was organized around the idea that the goods or their equivalent worth would eventually be returned to their true owners—though when this would actually occur was uncertain. The decision to do this was based on the way the Genocide was structured and its ideological justifications. This approach made it difficult for the government to simply confiscate the properties without addressing ownership rights. Moreover, the forcible seizure of goods not in the form of appropriation or plunder, but through the preservation of the rights of the Armenians to their ownership, created internal tension and contradiction. Again, the state accepted that the true owners of the properties taken were the Armenians, and adopted the principle that the equivalent values of these properties would be given to the latter. In the post-genocidal period, even the right of restating the ownership was accepted, which created serious and complicated legal problems for the state. The tension or contradiction mentioned is this: on the one hand, there is a state that does not wish to be accused of appropriating goods by force, and the language of the Abandoned Properties Laws was set accordingly; however, on the other hand, the same state wished to destroy the bases of existence of the Armenians, and institutionalize and render official the appropriation. The present legal system was founded on this tension and contradiction.

The debate in a November 1922 secret session of the Turkish Grand National Assembly between the deputy for Kırşehir Yahya Galip Bey and Treasury Secretary Hasan Fehmi Bey showcased this contradiction very well.[21] The treasury secretary criticized Yahya Galip Bey for saying that the abandoned properties henceforth must be known as the property of the state because they had passed into the state's hands.

> Hasan Fehmi Bey: Yahya Galip Bey asked how the property of the state will be administered. It is not the property of the state; it is abandoned property.

Yahya Galip Bey: It is not abandoned property. They all fled; it is the property of the state.

Hasan Fehmi Bey: This is the law that we have for abandoned property—the Abandoned Properties Law. It consists of income being registered in a current account that is going to be opened and managed in the *name of people who have disappeared.*

Yahya Galip Bey: It is not so, it is not so.[22] [italics are ours]

The tension and contradiction mentioned continued to exist throughout the entire period of the Republic, whether at the negotiations for the 1923 Treaty of Lausanne with the Allied powers victorious in World War I or during the development of the laws of adjustment issued in the 1920s, and even with the 2001 circular of the General Directorate of Land Registry and Cadaster. They still are present today and form the foundation of the Turkish legal system.

* * * * *

The law was used in a dual manner for the removal of the economic foundations of the survival of the Armenians. First, in 1915 the Armenians were legally forbidden the right to any arrangement over the goods they left behind. Second, although the law formally granted them the right to the value of their properties, not a single step was taken to reimburse them. None of the promised laws and regulations were issued.

In the entire era of the Ottoman Empire and the Republic of Turkey, the laws and decrees issued in connection with abandoned properties have been infused with the principle that these goods or their values should be given back to the Armenians. However, on the other hand, this procedure of restitution was not arranged in any manner, and the same legal system also followed the principle of not ceding even a single step to the Armenians. Especially in the Republican period, in the rare case when some Armenians who somehow survived or their heirs were able to ask for their properties or their equivalent values, they only ended up lost in the corridors and passages of the existing legal order. There are a multitude of cases today that are dragging on in similar circumstances.

The argument that the Abandoned Properties Laws and decrees basically do not deny the rights of the Armenians to their property has a special significance for the present debate on the question of compensation and reparation. The existing Turkish laws and decrees cannot be used as the reason for the Armenians' irreversible loss of all rights to their properties. On the contrary, it can easily be claimed that the existing laws and decrees can be used as the basis for the thesis that the Armenians are still the true owners of these goods and it is imperative that those goods or their equivalent value be returned to the Armenians.

The Committee of Union and Progress government was aware that this was the situation too. A report prepared by an interministerial commission in February 1918 stressed that the rights of the Armenians to their properties remained in tact. As this historic report stated, "Although the Armenian abandoned properties have been designated for legal liquidation, [and] while, as required by law, the remittance of the equivalent values is required to be given to the owners of the properties transferred to the pious foundations treasury and the treasury [proper], they are not being given until now," it was clearly accepted that the equivalent values of Armenian properties had not been given until that date. Furthermore, it emphasized "the fulfillment and consummation of the phases of the procedures shown by the law as soon as possible being essential because of the elimination of the right of ownership for people whose properties are subject to liquidation also in accordance with the provisions of the aforementioned law, on condition of the payment of their equivalent values as required by law; and because while the aforementioned properties are being impounded, it will not be suitable not to take into consideration the rights of the owners in connection with them and their appeal concerning the selection of this right." [23]

The meaning of the report is clear. By February 1918 the equivalent value of the Armenians' properties had still not been given to them. The report asked for the fulfillment of the requirements of the law as quickly as possible, and that, taking into consideration the rights of the property owners, the equivalent value of these properties be given to them.

During the peace negotiations in Lausanne, the Turkish government expressed similar views. When the victorious Allied powers of World War I—especially Great Britain, France, Italy, and Greece—learned that Turkey had issued on 15 April 1923 another Abandoned Properties Law (about liquidation) they forcefully protested, in particular because it was applicable to their own citizens. İsmet Pasha, who reported the situation to Ankara on 22 June 1923, received the following response, which must be considered of historical import, on 26 June: "In the Abandoned Properties Law, prepared and put into effect by the Turkish Grand National Assembly, our government's sole point of consideration being directed toward the protection of citizens' assets and the law, for the purpose of the protection from damage of the abandoned properties of those fleeing or absent, their sums are to be registered in their own current accounts [held by the Finance Ministry], and in this respect whatever is required for the safeguarding of laws will also be assured."[24]

The government repeated that the Armenians are the true owners of the properties, and in order for the goods and possessions of the citizens of the state not to be destroyed, it took the goods and possessions of the citizens for purposes of protection, and registered them in the citizens' names. For this reason, it is extremely difficult to point to the Abandoned Properties Laws and say that the Armenians cannot receive their goods or their equivalent values.

The examples cited show that both the Ottoman and Republican governments openly repeated the principle that the Armenians possessed rights to their goods. This point is crucial to the reparations question.

* * * * *

In order to understand how the laws and decrees concerning abandoned properties were constructed as an important element of the Armenian Genocide, it is necessary to study their connection to three different issues. First, which principles were going to be used to determine how the deported Armenians would be settled in new places? Second, were the goods they left behind, or their equivalent values, given to them—and if they were then how would this take place? Third, who used the properties that had been left behind, and how?

When we examine the laws and decrees in this fashion, we are confronted with an interesting picture. Concerning the first issue—that is, the topic of how the Armenians were going to be settled in their new locales—the laws and decrees play almost no role. This issue was dealt with only in one decree issued at the very beginning of the deportations, in an extremely limited matter. It was as if such an issue did not exist. As for the second issue, a general principle was only repeated several times—that is all. It was accepted that the true owners of the properties were the Armenians and the state was administering these properties in their names. However, when and how these properties or their equivalent values would be given to their true owners was not discussed in any way, and no arrangement was going to be made concerning this issue.

The absence of the first two issues shows us something: the Ittihadists in their mental world and practical politics believed that the Armenians ceased to exist from the moment they were deported from their homes. And making any sort of arrangements for a community considered nonexistent was unnecessary. With such characteristics, these extant laws are the best evidence to refute the official Turkish state thesis concerning the Armenian deportations, and implicate them otherwise. According to the official thesis, the aim of the Armenian deportations was to settle the Armenians in a new region and give the equivalent value of the goods left behind to them. If there was such a goal, then there would have also existed laws and regulations reflecting it. Indeed, the February 1918 report cited above openly accepted that the equivalent value of the goods was not given and no arrangements had been made in this regard.

A similar situation existed for the period of the Republic. Of course problems pertaining to the first issue of the relocation of the Armenians were absent. The Armenians had been to a great degree annihilated; those surviving (if not assimilated in Anatolia) remained outside of the borders of the new state. As far as the second set of issues was concerned, the laws and decrees issued were like those of the Ittihadist period, repeating the same general rule. The true owners of the properties were Armenians; the properties or their equivalent values would be given back to the latter. The state was administering these properties or revenues in their names only because of the absence of the Armenians. Nevertheless, in order to be able to give back the goods, the Armenians had to be present together with their properties as of 6 August 1924. This was the principle accepted in the Lausanne Treaty.

From Turkey's point of view, what would happen if the surviving Armenians wanted to return, or if their heirs tried to ask for their goods back, constituted a serious problem. This has been the fundamental issue to be solved in the Republican period. In order to prevent the Armenians from taking back their belongings an elaborate legal system was formed, with all the details thought out and any holes or gaps coming to view filled in, similar to the refinement of a silkworm spinning its cocoon.

The biggest goal of this system was to erect a barricade in front of the Armenians who might enter the country en masse or as individuals and demand their properties. There were some situations where it would be impossible to prevent their entry legally. In these instances there was no hesitation in transgressing the law. The internal tension and contradiction of laws and decrees could be observed throughout the Republican period. Examples of this situation will be discussed throughout this work.

While the first two aspects are absent legislatively, the main topic of the laws and decrees of the Ottoman and Republican eras is connected with the third aspect: how will the Armenian movable and immovable properties that were left behind be liquidated? If they are sold, how will they be sold? If they will be distributed, to whom and according to which rules will they be distributed—and how should they be registered? The primary goal of the laws and decrees, by seizing all the movable and immovable property of the Armenians, was to eliminate the physical foundations of Armenian existence in Anatolia. Thus, the removal of the physical and cultural existence of the Armenians was intrinsic to the Turkish legal system. This is why we call the system a genocidal regime.

The secret of why Turkey followed such an aggressive policy of genocide denial, both domestically and internationally, lies in the realities discussed above. The Turkish state knew that it was very difficult to prevent the return of the Armenians' goods through the logic of the existing legal system. If it said, "These properties do not belong to the Armenians and will not be returned," it would have accepted that a crime was committed. It would be forced to accept the fact of their appropriation because not a single cent was paid in exchange for the Armenian goods. This aside, the Abandoned Properties Laws already constitute a crime according to the existing Turkish constitution. According to the principles of international law, they are a clear violation of human rights.

On the other hand, if Turkey says, "The owners of the properties are the Armenians," the means would have been available for the goods or their equivalent values to be returned to their owners. Unable to say either of the above alternatives openly, only one choice remained—obstinacy and taking an aggressive stance on the topic. Putting aside the fact that Armenian properties were seized by force and plundered, the law is a face-reddening moral crime, and Turkey is belligerent because it knows that it committed this offense.

* * * * *

The last point necessary to add is that even though there is a direct connection between the Abandoned Properties Laws and the issue of indemnity, it is necessary to discuss them as two separate issues. The

Abandoned Properties Laws, as in the examples of the treaties of Sèvres and Lausanne, whether on the international level or in the Turkish legal system, basically were understood as a mechanism for paying the equivalent values of the goods of the Armenians who survived the Genocide. The Armenians who ended up outside of Turkey, whether as survivors of genocide or as a result of the clashes of 1919–22, sought compensation for their losses in accordance with their rights born from treaties by applying to the governments of the countries in which they later lived—the mixed arbitral tribunals established pursuant to the Treaty of Lausanne, or to the League of Nations. A similar process took place in Turkey, and if Armenians were present in Turkey as of 6 August 1924, the date on which the Lausanne Treaty entered into force, they could ask for the return of their properties.

However, as is known, the issue of compensation is not only limited to the request for the return of properties of Armenian survivors of genocide or their heirs, but also is a question of the destruction of the economic, social, and cultural existence of the Ottoman Armenian community and of compensation for this mass crime. Consequently, it is not right to discuss this issue as if it is only limited to whether properties confiscated by the Abandoned Properties Laws or from individual Armenians should be returned to their owners.[25]

* * * * *

The present volume is an attempt to understand the dominant logic of the laws, decrees, and regulations concerning the abandoned properties, which are related to the Armenian Genocide. As historians we tried to read and understand the laws and decrees in question from a social science perspective. We are not in a position here to develop legal arguments or propose legal theses. The legal meanings and interpretations of the extant laws and decrees in and of themselves form a separate topic for discussion, which falls outside of the field of our expertise. No matter how much we attempted to refrain from making any type of legal interpretation, we still apologize for any errors we may have made in this vein. One of the greatest difficulties we encountered during the preparation of this work was the lack of relevant serious legal studies. We hope that our work will encourage young legal scholars to pursue this issue.

We wish to repeat our belief: no matter what type of legal interpretation is carried out concerning this topic, we believe that in the end it is not a legal question, but a moral one. The topic we are confronting is very simple. As Ahmet Rıza, president of the Ottoman parliament of the time, said in December 1915, when the Abandoned Properties Law was being discussed in the parliament, the essence of the matter "is an oppression." He continued: "Hold me by my arm, throw me out of my village, then sell my goods and property later; this is not lawful at any period of time. Neither Ottoman conscience or law accepts this." Ahmet Rıza Bey rightly said that the goal of this law was the completion of plunder as soon as possible. He added, "The goods of the Armenians were partially plundered. Nothing will be left by the time the legislative power rejects the law."[26] Indeed, it took place likewise.

How and to what extent these laws were applied, or the issues encountered while they were being applied, are not part of the topic of this volume. Moreover, the events of the time concerning these laws and decrees are only dealt with in an extremely limited manner. Another topic outside the scope of this work is the question of the possessions of the pious foundations of the minorities during the Republican period. This issue hurt, and still continues to hurt, Turkey a great deal during its process of achieving full membership in the European Union. The reason why this is not discussed here is that we believe that this issue is a byproduct of the Armenian Genocide of 1915–17. Moreover, several studies have been carried out on the issue. Insofar as we are able to see, the most important defect of these studies is that they do not at all discuss the connection of these issues of the minority pious foundations with the Genocide.[27] It can be said that the present work fills this gap.

A final word of thanks: this work could not have been realized without the valuable contributions of many people. In particular, Professor Dr. İştar Savaşır and lawyer Cem Murat Sofuoğlu were kind enough to assist us in the interpretation of the laws of the Republican period. There is no need, of course, to add that full responsibility for the views expressed here lies with us.

The opinions articulated in this work must be understood as a part of the effort to confront Turkish society with the reality that it was founded on an immense crime against humanity: genocide. We hope that our writings will contribute in a modest way to the efforts to create a democratic society freed from the destructive influences of genocide and able to fulfill its moral responsibilities concerning this issue.

Notes

1. There are many works on the Armenian Genocide, which took the lives of approximately 1 million human beings: Raymond Kevorkian, *The Armenian Genocide: A Complete History* (New York: I.B. Tauris, 2011); or Taner Akçam, *A Shameful Act: Armenian Genocide and the Question of Turkish Responsibility* (New York: Metropolitan Books, November 2006) are good starting points for readers.
2. The term used at the time, "abandoned properties," is used in this work for ease of reference, but of course it embodies a falsehood since the deportees did not willingly "abandon" their properties but were forced to leave them behind.
3. *Hürriyet*, 19 September 2006, http://www.hurriyet.com.tr/gundem/5109117_p. asp and *Radikal*, 20 September 2006, http://www.radikal.com.tr/haber.php? haberno=199165; in addition, see http://bianet.org/bianet/bianet/85432-osmanli-arsivleri-acilirsa-resmitez-zayiflar.
4. Hrant Dink was assassinated in Istanbul in front of his office on January 19, 2007; three Christians in Malatya were killed in their office on April 18, 2007. It became evident from the investigations conducted after each crime and the testimonies of witnesses and supporting evidence obtained in the lawsuits initiated afterwards that these crimes were prepared by the Special War Department connected to the Office of the Commander of the General Staff in Ankara. When these lines were written, the lawsuits were still in progress.
5. Ergenekon is the name of a clandestine, secularist ultra-nationalist terror organization in Turkey with ties to Turkish military and security forces. In 2008 an investigation was launched against this organization and close to 300 people were arrested. There were several trials, which ended with verdicts on August 2013. The defendants were sentenced to heavy penalties. For more detailed information about Ergenekon, see İhsan Bal, "Ergenekon Case in Turkey," *USAK Yearbook of International Politics and Law* (3/2010): 489–4950.
6. *Radikal*, 11 February 2009; *Milliyet*, 19 February 2009.
7. Şişli Second Criminal Court of First Instance of the Republic of Turkey, File E: 2006/1208, K: 2007/1106, T: 11.10.2007.
8. Raphel Lemkin, *Axis Rule in Occupied Europe: Laws of Occupation, Analysis of Government, Proposals for Redress* (Washington, DC: Carnegie Endowment, 1944).
9. It is difficult to find the exact distinction made here between civilization and barbarism in Lemkin's works. Lemkin in essence is more disposed to see genocide in the classic framework of civilization vs. barbarism. For more information on this topic see Michael Freeman, "Genocide, Civilization and Modernity," *The British Journal of Sociology* 46, no. 2 (June 1995): 207–23; Dirk Moses, "Toward a Theory of Critical Genocide Studies," ed. Jacques Semelin, Online Encyclopedia of Mass Violence, http://www.massviolence.org/IMG/article_PDF/Toward-a-Theory-of-Critical-Genocide-Studies.pdf.
10. Ottoman Prime Ministry Archives [Başbakanlık Osmanlı Arşivi henceforth BOA], Cipher Office of the Interior Ministry [Dahiliye Nezareti Şifre Ofisi henceforth DH.ŞFR] 68/215, Directorate of Public Security of the Interior Ministry cipher telegram to Fourth Army Commander Cemal Pasha, 7 October 1916.
11. Türkiye Büyük Millet Meclisi [henceforth TBMM], *TBMM Zabıt Ceridesi*, Period 1, Assembly Year 3, Vol. 29 (Ankara: TBMM Matbaası, 1961), 161.
12. Raphael Lemkin, *Axis Rule in Occupied Europe: Laws of Occupation, Analysis of Government, Proposals for Redress* (Clark, NJ: The Lawbook Exchange, 2008), 79.

13. For a general summary of the process during the Jewish Holocaust, see Peter Hayes, "Plunder and Restitution," in *The Oxford Handbook of Holocaust Studies*, ed. Peter Hayes and John K. Roth (Oxford, New York: Oxford University Press, 2010), 540–59.

14. Documents could not be found among the laws and decrees specifically concerning the Assyrians (or, to use a broader term, Syriac Christians). What happened to the properties of the Assyrians is not clear, at least from Ottoman laws and decrees, so this topic is not covered in the present study. It is most probable that their goods met the same fate as those of the Armenians, and the same laws were applied to them, but this is a topic requiring more research.

15. For the exact text of the regulation, see BOA, Third Department of Public Security of the Interior Ministry 2/26-A, 14 October 1914.

16. On the differences in administration of Armenian and Greek properties during the war years, see Taner Akçam, *Ermeni Meselesi Hallolunmuştur: Osmanlı Belgelerine Göre Savaş Yıllarında Ermenilere Yönelik Politikalar* (İletişim Yayınları: Istanbul, 2008), 127–29. For a more detailed work on this subject, see Ahmet Efiloğlu, Raif İvecan, "Rum Emval-i Metrukesinin İdaresi," *History Studies* 2/3, 2010, 125–46.

17. As examples, the reader can examine the following documents: BOA/DH.ŞFR72/229, 73/69, 74/69, and 89/113.

18. The report prepared by the Office of Tribal and Immigrant Settlement of the Interior Ministry [Dahiliye Nezareti İskan-ı Aşair ve Muhacirin Müdüriyeti henceforth İAMM] dated 29 January 1917 and titled "Memorandum about People Being Transported to Other Places Due to Extraordinary Conditions and Necessities and Their Abandoned Properties" discussed in detail the various policies the Committee of Union and Progress regime implemented concerning the properties of different groups. The report discusses four different groups: Armenians, Greeks, Syrian families (Arabs), and Bulgarians, and summarizes the different practices concerning their goods (BOA/Sublime Porte Documents Office [henceforth BEO] 4505/337831).

19. BOA, Cipher Office of the Interior Ministry, Office of Tribes and Immigrants of the Interior Ministry [Dahiliye Nezareti Aşair ve Muhacirin Müdiriyeti Umumiyesi; henceforth AMMU], cipher telegraph to Diyarbakır Province, 23 November 1916. Another telegraph sent to Sivas said, "The property of those exempt from deportation due to conversion to Islam or other reasons and being kept in their places is not subject to liquidation" (BOA/DH.ŞFR, 61/253, Interior Ministry Directorate of General Security, cipher telegram to Sivas province, 9 March 1916).

20. The fourth article of the Regulation dated 13 June 1926 concerns only this topic, and is connected to the ruling that the belongings in other regions of people not being removed from their homes cannot be touched. The article specifically mentions Istanbul. Thus, there is a decision of the Council of Ministers of 1 August 1926 that declares that the property of Istanbul Armenians "not fleeing and disappearing in any direction" who are in places like Kartal and Pendik outside of the borders of the city of Istanbul should not be seized as abandoned properties, and if they have been, this seizure was illegal (Prime Ministry Republican Archives [henceforth BCA]/General Directorate of Land Settlement Archive [henceforth TİGMA] 030_0_18_01_01_020_49_014). The authors owe special thanks to Sait Çetinoğlu for directing their attention to the documents in the Republic Archives, which are used in this work.

21. On 16 March 1920, the capital city of the Ottoman Empire, Istanbul, was occupied by the victorious Allied Powers (Great Britain, France, etc.). The sultan officially disbanded the parliament on 11 April 1920. The same parliament, with some newly elected deputies, resumed its work in Ankara on 23 April 1920. The parliament

elected a "temporary" council of ministers, which was the beginning of the Turkish Republic.

22. *TBMM Gizli Celse Zabıtaları*, Period 1, Assembly Year 3, Vol. 3 (Ankara: Türkiye İş Bankası Kültür Yayınları, 1985), 1139–40.

23. BOA/BEO 4505/337831 Prime Ministry Office to Justice, Treasury Ministry and Interior Ministry, 28 February 1918.

24. Bilal N. Şimşir, *Lozan Telgrafları II* (Şubat-Ağustos 1923) (Ankara: Türk Tarih Kurumu, 1994), 473–74, 494.

25. For a general introduction to this topic, see Henry Theriault, "The Global Reparations Movement and Meaningful Resolution of the Armenian Genocide," *Armenian Weekly* (6 May 2010), http://www.armenianweekly.com/2010/05/06/reparations-2/.

26. *Meclis-i Ayan Zabıt Ceridesi*, Period 3, Assembly Year 2, Vol. 1, 13 Dec. 1915 session (Ankara: TBMM Basımevi, 1990), 133–35.

27. The following works can be consulted on this topic: Yuda Reyna, Ester Morenzo Zonana, *Son Siyasal Düzenlemelere Göre Cemaat Vakıfları* (Istanbul: Gözlem Gazetecilik Basın ve Yayın A.Ş., 2003); Dilek Kurban, Kezban Hatemi, *Bir 'Yabancılaştırma Hikâyesi: Türkiye'de Gayrimüslim Cemaatlerin Vakıf ve Taşınmaz Mülkiyet Sorunu* (Istanbul: TESEV, 2009).

CHAPTER 1

THE LAWS AND DECREES OF THE COMMITTEE OF UNION AND PROGRESS PERIOD

⸙⸙⸙

The Ottoman government, which was under control of the political party of the Committee of Union and Progress, published a law with four articles known as the Deportation Law (Tehcir Kanunu) on 27 May 1915.[1] The law gave authority to the army corps, division commanders and their representatives, and commanders of fortified posts to take preventative measures immediately, and with military force in the most severe manner, to completely destroy aggression and confrontation in any sort of situation of armed opposition or resistance to government orders, as well as to implement and regulate the defense of the country and protect public order.

Though the seizure of Armenian properties began after the decision on this date, in fact the deportations and the confiscation of goods had begun much earlier. The first deportations began in the months of February and March 1915, and Armenians from areas such as Adana, Iskenderun, and later Marash were sent straight to the interior of Anatolia. Beginning on 24 April, the direction of the deportations was changed toward the deserts of Syria and Iraq. The systematic confiscation of Armenian properties began on 17 May.

The Decrees and Regulations of 17, 30, and 31 May 1915

The first decrees on the systematic confiscation of the goods left behind by the deported Armenians were not issued, as is still claimed today, on 30 May 1915. But we have established that those decisions were made a good deal earlier, on 17 and 23 May.

> The first decree issued on 17 May was limited to those who left the country or were military deserters and their families; it ordered that the same procedure be applied to them as was done to the Ottoman Greeks forcibly expelled to Greece in 1913 to 1914. A secret communication sent from the office of the prime minister to the War Ministry stated, As the abandoned properties of Armenians who, because of the shameful acts and oppressions they perpetrated during the occupation against Muslims, fled to foreign countries during the retreat, and still have not returned, and are still associated with the military, are administered by relatives or representatives, their [the aforementioned properties'] impoundment by the government in the name of the Treasury [a department of the Finance Ministry], like the properties of the Ottoman Greeks, and their administration [was decided. The expectation of the government] especially if the properties of Armenians who during the period of military service fled and were deserters are going to be confiscated by the government [was to decrease military desertion].[2]

The first systematic step concerning what would be done about the entirety of the properties the Armenians left behind did not take place on 30 May, as has been claimed, but on a date prior to 23 May. On 23 May 1915 the Interior Ministry officially wrote to the command of the Fourth Army, reporting in detail which areas would be emptied of their Armenian populations and where the latter would be settled. It concluded with the note: "The Armenians being transported can take with them all their movable properties and goods. Detailed instructions concerning immovable properties are ready for notification." In other words, a directive about what was to be done with the belongings left behind by the Armenians was ready to be sent to the provinces at this date.[3]

The best-known regulation on the topic is the comprehensive one of the Council of Ministers dated 30 May 1915. The Directorate of Tribal and Immigrant Settlement of the Interior Ministry sent it the following day to relevant provinces organized in fifteen articles.[4] It provided the basic principles in accordance with which all deportations and resettlements would be conducted, and began with the listing of the reasons for the Armenian deportations. The most important provision concerning Armenian properties was the principle that their equivalent value was going to be provided. According to this decree, "properties and land are going to be distributed to them [the Armenians in their newly resettled areas] in proportion to their previous financial and economic situations. The state is going to construct houses for the needy, distribute seeds to farmers, [and] distribute tools and implements to those with professions who need them. The things and goods which remain in the places they left or their equivalent values will be given to them in the same form."[5]

Two procedures would be applied to goods left behind. First, "immigrants and tribes" would be settled in the Armenian villages being emptied and, after the value of the land and property there was determined, it would be distributed to the new settlers. In cities and towns, "immovable property belonging to people who are being transported . . . after its type, value and quantity are determined," will also be distributed to the settlers. Second, "properties which produce income such as olive, mulberry, grape, and orange orchards, and stores, factories, inns and warehouses, which remain outside of the scope of the work that they know and do . . . through being sold in public auction or being rented, their total equivalent value *will be placed temporarily in accounts of local treasury directorates* [*mal sandıkları*] *in the names of their owners so that it be given to the latter* [italics are ours].[6]

In order to implement these procedures, three-person commissions were to be formed with a chairperson and one member each from the Interior Ministry and Finance Ministry. These commissions, which were going to be sent to various regions for their work, would have the authority, if necessary, to establish subcommissions or appoint officials. In regions where there were no commissions the work would be conducted directly under the highest local administrative authority (governor, provincial district governor, etc.).[7]

The general principles mentioned above infuse the fifteen-article regulation of 31 May 1915, but this new set of instructions essentially concerns the steps to be taken during the deportations and how the Armenians would be resettled. It repeats the principle that "land [will be given] in a sufficient quantity to each family being deported, taking into consideration its previous economic situation and present needs."[8] In addition, this regulation discusses topics such as the characteristics of the new settlement areas, that they must be twenty-five kilometers from railway lines, how the Armenians would be registered in the population ledgers, and the prohibition of travel. It states that *göçmen komisyonları* (immigration commissions) would be formed to arrange all settlement matters. The regulation does not mention anything about what would happen to the properties that were left behind.[9]

The importance of the decree of 30 May and the regulation of 31 May lie in the following: the publication of a series of laws and decrees was necessary in order to implement the general principles that were announced in connection with the settlement of the Armenians and the provision of the equivalent values of their goods. This was something that would never be done in any manner whatsoever. Instead, laws and decrees began to deal with only one topic: the confiscation of the properties left behind by the Armenians.

The Regulation of 10 June 1915

This thirty-four–article ordinance regulated in a detailed manner how the property and goods the Armenians left behind would be impounded by the state.[10] The first ten articles pertained to the method to be followed during the process of impoundment, while the eleventh and twenty-first articles explained to whom these properties should be given and the principles according to which this should be done. Article 1 announced that "committees formed in a special manner" were going to be created for the administration of the "immovable property, possessions and lands being left belonging to Armenians who are being transported to other places, and other matters."[11] The most important of these committees were the Abandoned Properties Commissions. These commissions and their powers were regulated by Articles 23 and 24. The commissions were each going to be composed of three people— a specially appointed chairperson, an administrator, and a treasury official—and would work directly with the Interior Ministry.

Their first task was to affix their seals to goods and buildings belonging to those being transported and place them under the protection of an official or special committee found suitable by the commission. After the kind, quantity, and estimated value of the goods being taken under protection were registered in a detailed fashion together with their owners' names, they were transferred to places like churches, schools, or inns suitable for use as storehouses. Record books indicating their places of safekeeping were to be prepared.

After this procedure, animals and things that might spoil among the movable goods at hand were to be sold at public auction by a committee created by the commission, and their equivalent value be surrendered to the accounts of the *mal sandığı* (local treasury directorate) in the name of their owner when this could be ascertained, or, if not, in the name of the village or town where the goods were found. The type, quantity, value, original location, purchaser, and sales price of the goods being sold were to be registered in detail in special record books.

Articles 10 and 22 are the most important for this study. Article 10 prohibited any transactions concerning the properties, even if a power of attorney existed. All procedures concerning the properties would have to go through the Abandoned Properties Commissions, which were to be established. Here it is possible to ask some extremely simple and ordinary questions. If what was taking place was an ordinary relocation, why were the Armenians prohibited the right of disposal over their goods? Why should an Armenian not have been able to administer his properties while on the road or from the place to which he was sent through a power of attorney or similar means? Why, for example, could he not himself sell his belongings or transfer them to somebody else? It is difficult even today to answer these questions. Only one answer exists: the desire to completely destroy the Armenians' economic and cultural existence. This will become more apparent through a discussion of Articles 6 and 22, combined.

In these articles, the principle that the equivalent values of the properties of the Armenians would be given to the latter in the places to which they had gone was repeated. Article 6 concerned the decree that the "existing objects, pictures and holy books" in churches would be surrendered to the people of the village in which the church was found at their new location of settlement. Article 22, after stating that the revenues obtained from Armenian properties sold in public auctions or rented out are going to be left "to the accounts of the local treasury directorate in the names of their owners in trust," added, "they are going to be given to the owners according to an announcement which is going to be made later."[12]

However, this giving "to the owners" procedure never took place. The reason is that the Armenians were going to be considered nonexistent. The issues of their settlement and the presentation of the value of their properties or their revenues ceased to be topics of laws and decrees and never again were going to be dealt with. There is no obstacle to reading the 10 June 1915 regulation as the basis for the creation of a legal system suitable for the elimination of the material living conditions of the Armenians, as it took away from the Armenians any right of disposal of their own properties.

The Temporary Law of 26 September 1915
and the Regulation of 8 November 1915

The most important steps toward the appropriation of Armenian cultural and economic wealth were the 26 September 1915 law of eleven
articles[13] and the twenty-five-article regulation of 8 November 1915[14]
on how the aforementioned law would be implemented. It is helpful
here to broadly summarize some of the articles of the temporary law
and the regulation in order to demonstrate how the political authority,
that in this manner was targeting the cultural and economic wealth of
the Armenians for seizure, organized even the smallest details. Many
matters were covered in a detailed fashion in the law and the regulation, including the creation of two different types of commissions with
different tasks called the Committees and Liquidation Commissions
(the differentiation was made in a separate decree); the manner in
which these commissions were to be formed; the conditions of work,
including wages; the distribution of positions and powers among these
commissions and various departments of ministries and the state; the
documents necessary for applications by creditors to whom Armenians
owed money; aspects of the relevant courts; rules to be followed during
the process of liquidation of properties; the different ledgers to be kept,
and how they were to be kept; and examples of relevant ledgers.

   This characteristic of the aforementioned law and regulation is the
most important indication of the desire not to return their properties,
or their equivalent value, to the Armenians. The reason is that if the
desire to return property or provide compensation existed, it would
have been necessary to apply the same diligence and detailed arrangements to this process, too.

   The Temporary Law of 26 September is also known as the Liquidation Law. Its chief goal was the liquidation of Armenian properties.
According to its first article, commissions were to be established to
conduct the liquidation. These commissions were to prepare separate
reports for each person about the properties, receivable accounts, and
debts "abandoned by actual and juridical persons who are being transported to other places."[15] The liquidation would be conducted by courts
on the basis of these reports.

   The second article explained at which institutions the properties
would be registered. In order to be liquidated, places like income-
producing houses, inns, and stores, as well as revenue-producing
properties of pious foundations would be registered in the name of the
Pious Foundations Ministry, while the remaining properties would be

registered in the name of the Finance Ministry. After properties were liquidated—that is to say, after the procedures concerning debts and receivable accounts were concluded—whatever remained was to be returned to the original owners. Another important issue treated in this article is that if lying, fraud, and collusion occurred in property transfers transacted more than fifteen days prior to deportation, the transfers would be annulled. In fact, the relevant decision was taken much earlier and put into practice. The first task of the committees to be founded with the goal of the liquidation of properties, would be to produce a list of all transactions conducted after, as well as up to, fifteen days prior to the deportations.

The other articles of the temporary law discussed the stages of the liquidation procedure and the details of how it would be conducted. They stated that the commissions would carry out procedures such as the collection of receivable accounts or the payment of debts, for each person or for the payment. It was possible to apply to the courts concerning these above-mentioned procedures. After all transactions were completed, properties that were not the subject of a lawsuit would be sold by auction and the resulting funds would be placed in the account of the local treasury directorate in the name of their true owner. Detailed records would be kept for all of these procedures.

The fifth article of the law is important. It stated that the courts' "verdicts were not protestable, refundable, contestable or appealable."[16] In other words, the decision of a court on the credits and debits of accounts could not be changed. The purpose of the article can be better understood after realizing that no deported Armenian could be present at any of these courts.

The temporary law also declared that a regulation would be promulgated about the formation of the commissions and described how the provisions of the law would be applied. This regulation, which was agreed on to 8 November 1915, regulated in a detailed fashion the protection of the movable and immovable property of Armenians who were being deported, the creation of new committees for liquidation issues, and the working principles of the commissions. The two-part regulation with twenty-five articles, moreover, included explanatory information on what had to be included in the record books to be kept during the liquidation process, and how these record books were to be used.

The regulation stated that two bodies would be created, one a committee and the other a commission, and defined their tasks and powers in detail. The first three articles concerned these committees and their duties. The day after this regulation was officially announced every district where the Armenians were deported a committee was to be established with one official, each chosen by the highest-ranking civil service official from the tax, title deed, and civil registry offices, and, if it existed locally, the Pious Foundations Office. The committee chair would report to the highest-ranking finance official of that locality.

This committee would first prepare a record book within a period of three days by using the minute books in the title deed registry. All sales transactions conducted in a period of fifteen days prior to the date of transport of the abovementioned individuals or after the communication of the order for transportation would be included. This book would be given to the Liquidation Commission. Article 13 regulates the work of the commission on these transactions, and clarifies that the commission should prepare reports for the courts for the annulation of sales transactions indicated as fraudulent and contrived.

Moreover, in accordance with the second article of the regulation, the committee would prepare two copies of a record book about the various types of real estate, including those of foundations, belonging to deportees by means of a comparison of tax and title deed registry documents. After determining the location, street, and document number of each immovable property, this information, along with the total number of properties and their total value, must be registered in the names of their owners in the record books. In the case of houses for which the owners are not known, information will be obtained by asking elderly people in that area or trustworthy individuals. One copy of the record books will be given to administrative councils for study, and a second to title deed registry directorates to be available to any interested parties.

According to the third article, the administrative councils would conducting investigations and ascertain the value of each approved immovable property according to its cadastral records and tax valuations. The councils would also prepare two reports on this, and send one copy each to the Pious Foundations Ministry and Finance Ministry, and inform the Liquidation Commissions. As for the fourth article, it stated that, in accordance with the law of 26 September 1915, fees and taxes were not to be taken for immovable property documents recorded in the name of the pious foundations and finance treasuries.

The majority of the remaining articles of the regulation concern the establishment, duty, and authority of the Liquidation Commissions. These commissions were going to be composed of a chairperson appointed by the Interior Ministry and one person appointed each by the Justice Ministry and Finance Ministry. In places where there would be few procedures, the work would be transferred to the geographically closest commission. The commission chairpersons were to be paid wages of 1.5 liras each, and the members 1 lira each.

The commission chairperson would distribute the work to the members in accordance with their areas of specialization. The commissions would keep tabs on the money of people being transported, abandoned movable property, the sum of money on deposit and receivables, restitution, collection and if necessary the initiation of lawsuits, the sale through auction of abandoned goods when there is no opposition, and other matters within their purview, and make any necessary decisions concerning payments.

All documents and transactions regulated and conducted by commissions[17] established through the 10 June 1915 regulation prior to these new rules coming into effect would be transferred to the Liquidation Commissions.[18] After their deficiencies were corrected and they began work, these commissions would accept petitions from those making claims about loans, debts, and abandoned properties. Those who claimed to have money owed to them by deportees were obliged to add to their petitions receipts and other documents they possessed, the power of attorney in the case that the application was made by proxy, or certified copies of the aforementioned documents. Moreover, these petitions had to include how much and what kinds of debt owed were being claimed and the place of original residence of the deportee. Later the commission would give to these people a receipt with the date of their application. People with claims could apply to a court with a document demonstrating that they carried out all these procedures concerning their claimed debts.

The tasks of the commissions included confiscation of the money and goods taken under guard by the government from the people being deported, and all the rest of their belongings. In addition, the commissions would ask banks, other institutions, and individuals for the accounts of money and properties left by people being deported. All those being asked were required to immediately provide the accounts, and, if necessary, documents, receipts, and letters to substantiate them. In this way, the government also was able to seize the belongings the deported Armenians had left to others. These belongings later would be sold by Liquidation Commissions in public auctions.

According to the regulation, all the goods, pictures, and holy books in churches would be registered in books and preserved. Later they would be sent to the place the people of the relevant village or quarter settled. The right of use of any type of building or object connected to education, like schools or monasteries, that were left from the Armenians would be given to the Education Ministry.

The other important articles of the regulation were that on the demand of the chairperson of the commission the government would send police officers and gendarmes for the accomplishment of the tasks of the commission; the work of the commission would be conducted under the supervision of the government; and the members of the commission would be held financially responsible for damages caused by any negligence, laxity, and delay shown in their duties.

The regulation notes that of the two different record books to be kept by the commission, one would be the principal book and the other the accounts book. The first book, specified as the Principal Record Book of the Abandoned Properties Liquidation Commissions, separately treats the classification of abandoned properties, expenses, and revenues from their sale in fourteen distinct sections. There is a detailed section at the end of the regulation called the Principal Record Book Sample, which gave examples of the forms of these books, on how and where to write information.

The second book was called Record Book of Current Accounts of Abandoned Properties. Detailed information on its recording and use were given. Every page of the book was to be divided into four tables. After the neighborhood or county of the person being transported together with his name and the number of the dossier kept by the commission were noted, the record book could be used. The regulation gave an explanation of the tables in a detailed form. After the publication of the regulation, Liquidation Commissions were going to be established in various places of Anatolia, and the regions for they were going to be responsible would be specified.[19]

Some changes were made to the temporary law and the regulation in the period until 1918. For example, on 5 October 1916 this phrase was added by a law: "this much that in the places where the aforementioned people being transported to other places are settled, to the degree that it can assure their subsistence with overnight stays and dwellings, assistance may be given by providing real estate, land transferred to the Treasury, and habitation and land at no charge from the land of the Treasury."[20]

The second important change took place in May 1916, and all transactions of the Abandoned Properties Liquidation Commissions commencing from this date became connected with the Finance Ministry.[21] Some further limited changes were still going to be made, as in the example of the Regulation on the Manner of Renting for Immovable Property in the Charge of the Treasury of the Department of Finance[22] of 27 May 1917, but these are not very important for this study.

A Brief Evaluation

As can be understood from the broad overview above, nothing exists in laws or regulations on how the equivalent values of the Armenians' properties was going to be paid beyond the repetition of the general principle in the 30 May 1915 regulation of the Council of Ministers and the 10 June 1915 ordinance. In the second article of the temporary law, the principle was merely reintroduced that "after liquidation the remaining quantity would be given to their owners" of the revenue and value of the properties.[23] In addition, Article 17 of the decree says only, "the value of properties the owners of which are not known . . . [will be sent] later by the government to the neighborhood in which the people of the aforementioned village or neighborhood will be settled."[24]

Two points are extremely important about this law and regulation that do not include even a single regulatory provision concerning how the equivalent value of the Armenians' properties would be paid. First, the extent of the properties and wealth which were to be confiscated was widened. This was done in three ways: (1) It was announced that any type of transaction conducted up to fifteen days prior to the Armenians' deportation pertaining to their goods and wealth could be annulled. (2) If any type of sequestration decision had been taken by courts previously concerning the property of Armenians, it would be annulled and the property would pass to the state. (3) If there was money owed to Armenians by others, it was decided that the state would collect this debt directly itself. In this way, the possibility of the Armenians to collect what was owed them from other channels was blocked by the law. The second point is that it was announced that the debts owed by Armenians to local and foreign people and organizations would be paid. In this way, any possible intervention of foreign powers, especially Germany, would be prevented. Moreover, and perhaps most importantly, the legal paths for the Armenians to act against these official decisions were completely closed down.

It is worth discussing one additional important matter here. Long before the publication of the law and the decree, the points discussed here were already put into practice. For example, the government began months earlier through various orders sent to the provinces to attempt to have a complete inventory made of the properties to be confiscated and prevent the Armenians' belongings from being transferred to others. A telegraph of 11 July 1915 sent to Trebizond can serve as an example of this. It asked that all receipts concerning the debts owed to Armenians be collected and recorded. Moreover, the telegraph stated that permission was not given for the transferal of Armenian properties to others or their sale to foreigners.[25]

On 10 August 1915 the Office of Tribal and Immigrant Settlement of the Interior Ministry announced that a regulation was about to be issued concerning how the Armenians' debts and money owed them would be settled, and that for now these should be recorded in special record books.[26] On 11 August 1915 the same office stated that it had been ascertained that the properties of the Armenians were being sold to foreigners in particular at cheap prices. It asked that all these sales be annulled and the foreigners wandering about the provinces immediately be removed.[27] In a telegraph sent on 28 August 1915 to nearly all provinces, the office asked that within three days a list of the buildings and lands belonging to Armenians in the province that had been sold to foreigners as early as eight days before the deportations began or during the deportations, and transferred to others, be prepared and sent to the central government.[28]

In summary, through the laws and regulations issued during the period of the Union and Progress government, a very detailed action plan was presented about what should be done with the properties left by the Armenians, but no legal arrangements were presented as to how the values of these properties should be given back to the Armenians. In the eyes of the Ittihadists, from the moment Armenian citizens were deported, they no longer were alive. Consequently, it is not at all surprising that in a report prepared in February 1918 it was admitted that the equivalent value of the Armenians' properties was not paid.

Notes

1. *Takvim-i Vekayi* No. 2189, 1 June 1915. The precise name of the law is Vakt-i Seferde İcraat-ı Hükûmete Karşı Gelenler İçin Cihet-i Askeriyece İttihâz Olunacak Tedâbir Hakkında Muvakkat Kanun [Provisional law on steps to be taken militarily concerning those who during campaigns oppose the actions of the government].
2. BOA/BEO 4355/326591 Private Secretariat of the Office of the Prime Minister, confidential, to the War Ministry,17 May 1915.

3. BOA/DH.ŞFR 53/94–1, Interior Ministry Public Security Directorate [henceforth EUM] cipher telegram to Fourth Army Command, 23 May 1915.

4. BOA/Minutes of the Council of Ministers [henceforth MV] 198/163, 30 May 1915 quoted in Azmi Süslü, *Ermeniler ve 1915 Tehcir Olayı* (Van: Yüzüncü Yıl Üniversitesi Rektörlüğü, 1990), 112, 115; Genelkurmay Başkanlığı, *Arşiv Belgeleriyle Ermeni Faaliyetleri,1914–1918*, Vol. 1 (Ankara: Genelkurmay Basım Evi, 2005), 131–33, 427–38.

5. Başkanlığı, *Arşiv Belgeleriyle Ermeni Faaliyetleri, 1914–1918*, Vol. 1, 131.

6. Ibid, 131–32. The italics are ours.

7. Ibid, 132.

8. Ibid.

9. Ibid.

10. Ibid., 139–42 for the text of this regulation, formally entitled "Ahval-i Harbiye ve Zaruret-i Fevkalade-i Siyasiye Dolayısıyla Mahall-i Ahire Nakilleri İcra Edilen Ermenilere Ait Emval ve Emlâk ve Arazinin Keyfiyet-i İdaresi Hakkında Talimatname [Regulation on the condition of administration of property, possessions and land belonging to Armenians whose Transportation to other places is being conducted due to the conditions of war and extraordinary political exigencies]."

11. Ibid.

12. Ibid., 141.

13. *Takvim-i Vekayi* No. 2303, 27 September 1915. The full name of the law was Ahar Mahallere Nakledilen Eşhâsın Emvâl ve Düyûn ve Matlûbât-ı Metrûkesi Hakkında Kanun-ı Muvakkat [Temporary law on the abandoned possessions and debts and abandoned debts of persons transported to other places].

14. *Takvim-i Vekayi* No. 2343, 10 November 1915. The full name of the decree was Âher Mahallere Nakledilen Eşhasın Emvâl ve Düyun ve Matlubat-ı Metrukesine Mütedair 18 Zilkade 1333 Tarihli Kanun-ı Muvakkatin Suver-i İcraiyesi Hakkında Talimatname [Regulation on the manners of execution of the temporary law dated 18 Zilkade 1333 concerning the possessions and debts and abandoned debts of persons tranposted to other places]. For the original texts of some laws and decrees relevant to the topic of the present volume, see also T.C. Maliye Vekâleti Milli Emlak Müdürlüğü, *Milli Emlak Muamelelerine Müteallik Mevzuat* (Ankara: Başvekâlet Matbaası, 1937); Salâhaddin Kardeş, *"Tehcir" ve Emval-i Metruke Mevzuatı* (Ankara: T.C. Maliye Bakanlığı Strateji Geliştirme Başkanlığı, 2008).

15. *Takvim-i Vekayi* No. 2303, 27 September 1915.

16. Ibid.

17. Internal correspondence of the Interior Ministry dated 6 November 1915 reveals that these commissions were called Abandoned Properties Commissions, while the commissions to be established through the new regulation were to be called Liquidation Commissions (BOA/Legal Counsel Office of the Interior Ministry [henceforth DH.HMŞ]) 12/31, Note dated 6 November 1915 written by the vice undersecretary in the name of the interior minister.

18. Orders were issued in various telegrams sent to the provinces in accordance with this regulation for the creation of a commission composed of officials from the Treasury and civil service. For one example, see BOA/DH.ŞFR 54/226 İAMM Interior Ministry cipher telegram to Kayseri provincial district government 28 June 1915.

19. On the commissions that were going to be established and their regions of authority, see BOA/Record Office of the Public Security Directorate of the Interior Ministry, 73/43 List prepared by the Interior Ministry dated 1 January 1916 showing the places where the Abandoned Properties Liquidation Commissions were located. According to it, in Istanbul the commission was at the capital of the province. In

Edirne, at Tekfurdağı. In Adana province, including Adana and Mersin, the commission was in Adana. In Cebel-i Bereket, the commission was in the provincial district center. In Kozan, the commission was in the provincial district center. In Erzurum, the commission was in the provincial capital. In Hüdâvendigâr province: [illegible] and Karacabey, the commission is in Bursa; for Kirmastı, the commission is in Bursa; for Gemlik and Orhangazi, the commission is in Gemlik; for Ertuğrul with its surroundings, the commission is in Bilecik. In Ankara province: for Yozgat, Kırşehir, and Boğazliyan, the commission is at Yozgat; for Ankara, Keskin, and Çorum, the commission is at Ankara. In Trebizond province: for Bafra, Termen, and Çarşamba, the commission is in Samson; for Ünye, Fatsa and Tirebolu, the commission is in Ordu; for Trebizond, the commission is in the capital of the province. In Sivas province: for Amasya and Gümüşhacıköy, the commission is in Sivas; for Merzifon and Havza, the commission is in Merzifon; for Tokat, it is in Tokat. In İzmit provincial district: for İzmit, Karamürsel, and Yalova, the commission is in İzmit; for Adapazarı, Kandıra, and Gemlik the commission is in Adapazarı. In Eskişehir provincial district: for Sivrihisar and Mihalıççık, the commission is in the provincial district capital; for Eskişehir, it is in the provincial district capital. In Kayseri provincial district: for Kayseri, the commission is in the provincial district capital; for Develi, the commission is in the county center. In Aleppo province: for Aleppo, the commission is in the provincial capital; for Maraş, it is in the provincial district capital; for Antakya, it is in the provincial district capital. In Konya, Bitlis, Mamuretülaziz, and Diyarbakır, the commissions are in the respective provincial capitals. In Niğde, Karahisar-ı Sahib, Urfa, and Karesi, the commissions are in the respective provincial district capitals.

20. Kardeş, *"Tehcir" ve Emval-i Metruke Mevzuatı*, 37. The full name of the law is 26 Eylül 1915 Tarihli Kanunun İkinci Maddesinin Birinci Fıkrasına Ek İbare Hakkında Kanun [Law on the supplemental phrase to the first paragraph of the second article of the law dated 13 September 1331].

21. BOA/Foreign Affairs Ministry Political Division [henceforth HR.SYS.], 2873/3–35, AMMU to the Foreign Affairs Ministry 13 May 1916. On the procedure of transference as of 23 May 1916, see BOA/DH.HMŞ.1–1/6–26, HMŞ communication dated 20 July 1917.

22. *Düstur*, Series 2, Vol. 9, Reference No. 3334, cited in Mehmet Hakkı Sağlam, *II. Tertip Düstur Kılavuzu, Osmanlı Devlet Mevzuatı (1908–1922)* (Istanbul: Tarih Vakfı Yurt Yayınları, 2006), 400.

23. *Takvim-i Vekayi*, No. 2303, 27 September 1915.

24. *Takvim-Vekayi*, No. 2343,10 November 1915.

25. BOA/DH.ŞFR 54/393, İAMM cipher telegram to Trebizond provincial government, 11 July 1915.

26. BOA/DH.ŞFR, 54-A/368, İAMM cipher telegram to Erzurum, Adana, Ankara, Aydın, Bitlis, Aleppo, Hüdavendigâr, Diyarbakır, Suriye, Sivas, Trebizond, Mamuretülaziz, Musul and Van provinces, and Urfa, İzmit, Canik, Zor, Karesi, Kayseri, Karahisar-ı Sahib, Maraş, Eskişehir, and Niğde provincial district governments, dated 10 August 1915.

27. BOA/DH.ŞFR, 54-A/388, İAMM cipher telegram to the Erzurum, Adana, Ankara, Aydın, Bitlis, Aleppo, Hüdavendigâr, Diyarbakır, Suriye, Sivas, Trebizond, Mamuretülaziz, Musul and Van provinces; the Urfa, İzmit, Canik, Zor, Karesi, Kayseri, Karahisar-ı Sahib, Maraş, Eskişehir and Niğde provincial district governments; and the Adana, Aleppo, Maraş, Diyarbakır, Sivas, Trebizond, Mamuretülaziz, Erzurum and İzmit Abandoned Properties Commission Chairmanships, 11 August 1915.

28. BOA/DH.ŞFR 55/280 İAMM cipher telegram to the Erzurum, Adana, Ankara, Bitlis, Aleppo, Hüdâvendigâr, Diyarbakır, Sivas, Trebizond, Mamuretülaziz, Van and Konya provinces; Urfa, İzmit, Canik, Karesi, Kayseri, Karahisar-ı sâhib, Maraş, Eskişehir and Niğde provincial district governments, and the chairmanship of the Aleppo, Adana, Sivas and Trebizond Abandoned Properties Administrative Commissions, 28 August 1915.

CHAPTER 2

THE ARMISTICE PERIOD AND THE RETURNING ARMENIANS

⌒⊙ⴟⴟ⌒

After the disastrous conclusion of World War I, the Union and Progress government resigned on 8 October 1918. The first new cabinet was established by Ahmet İzzet Pasha on 11 October 1918, and from then until 4 November 1922 eleven governments in all held office.[1] Among the first actions of these governments were the initiation of legal proceedings against the members of the Committee of Union and Progress,[2] and the granting of permission for the surviving Armenians to return.

The First Ones Returning from Deportation

In fact, permission began to be granted for the return of deportees to a limited extent during the period of the Committee of Union and Progress regime from the start of 1918. The first order found on this topic is dated 28 February 1918, and concerns the granting of permission to return to Arab women and children under the age of sixteen who were deported from Syria to the interior of Anatolia.[3] Later, through a decree of 4 April 1918, Arabs over the age of sixty and who need assistance were also permitted to return,[4] and the provinces were requested to prepare lists of people over this age.[5] On 21 July 1918, the practice was expanded, and "among those being deported from the region of the Fourth Army, for those who repent but are not condemned by a court-martial verdict, permission to go to their homelands" was granted.[6] However, permission was still not being given for the return of many families who were punished by the court-martial or who were found suspect from the point of view of security.[7]

The second group allowed to return was the Muslim (primarily Kurdish) refugees. In April and May 1918, first permission was given to Muslims who would not constitute a financial burden to the state to return to their former places.[8] Starting from the end of summer, similar decrees began to be taken for Greeks deported from the coasts to interior regions. It was communicated to the provinces that "no inconvenience was seen in the return of Greeks from among the people of the province who were taken to the interior for military reasons,"[9] and it was asked that "there not be any obstacle to those who want to go to their homelands from among them, and during the time of their return, provision of their protection" be arranged.[10]

During the period when limited permission to return began to be granted to Arab, Greek, and Muslim (Turkish and Kurdish) refugees, strict controls were still continued for Armenians. Telegraphic orders were sent to the provinces along the line that without consent from Istanbul, even for "Armenians within the province/provincial district," "permission does not exist for journeys and voyages."[11] It was asked that special lists be prepared about Armenians trying to go to other places.[12]

News that Armenians were going to be permitted to return and that decrees were going to be issued about this began to be heard in the summer months.[13] On 5 August 1918, the newspaper *İkdam* reported that, according to rumors, the return of the Armenians was going to commence.[14] On 21 August 1918, the newspaper *Sabah* reported that "news about the government having decided on the return of Armenians deported to other places to their homelands [was greeted with joy] among the Armenians found in the provinces." Gradually many letters were published in the Armenian newspapers on it, so that *Sabah* published details from these letters.[15] In the following days, statements were published in the press that through Enver Pasha "instructions were given where necessary and [the Armenians] gradually are going to return to their homelands in order to reside in places which have no disadvantages from a military point of view," and the Istanbul Armenian Patriarchate expressed its thanks for the granting of permission for Armenians to return to their homes.[16]

At first, the issue did not concern permission to return home, but permission for travel to Armenians wanting "to go from one place to another in a province/provincial district" after "being investigated by the security forces."[17] Consequently it can be understood from telegrams such as the following that permission was decided separately in each circumstance. It was written to Erzurum on 8 August 1918 that "the return of Armenians in the Caucasus to their villages at the present is not suitable." A telegram to Bursa of 1 October 1918 declared that "unless the return of the people removed from their places by military decision is permitted by the military, the return of people such as these to their aforementioned places cannot be lawful."[18] On the other hand, a telegram sent to Adana on 16 October 1918 gave permission for the dispersal and settlement of "Armenians declared to have been removed from their work on the Amanos railway line to the villages."[19] A telegram of 19 October 1918 sent to Mosul declared that "permission for the departure of applicants to the places they want is suitable."[20] It is necessary to add that in this period, the return of Armenians fleeing from the places in which they had been settled was also an issue.[21]

The first official step concerning mass returns was taken on 18 October 1918, and it was communicated to all provinces that "permission for the return to their places of all people removed from one place and deported to others due to conditions of war by military decision" was given. The safe travel of those returning, and "evasion and delay in the application of the order not being allowed to happen in the least" were desired.[22]

On 19 October 1918 Ahmet İzzet Pasha announced in the government program being read in parliament that a "decision for our compatriots who due to war conditions and necessity were moved and deported from one place to another within the homeland gradually to return to their old homes" was made and began to be carried out. In İzzet Pasha's words, "the movable and immovable properties of these children of the homeland subject to extremely great distress for the last year or two will be returned to them, and the equivalent value of their belongings which have been sold will also be paid to them."[23]

After the reading of the program, on 21 October 1918 the order giving permission for deported Armenians and Greeks to return was sent to all relevant provinces.[24] On 22 October the removal of the system of travel with travel documents was being considered, and it was asked what sort of harm might come of this.[25] On 23 October 1918 it was requested that the necessary steps be taken for Armenians and Greeks who had been deported to be able to return to their homes safely. It was proclaimed that those officers who commit mistakes in this respect would be punished.[26]

Later orders continued to be sent to the provinces for the precise and orderly realization of the return process. These orders asked that Armenians and Greeks be allowed to travel without travel documents; the assignment of special trains to them; the provision of their needs including food, drink, and travel expenses; and their secure arrival in the places to which they were going.[27] According to figures reported on 20 November 1918, 7,163 Armenians, and a total of 10,601 people returned.[28] On 21 December 1918, it was announced that 2,552 Muslims, 19,695 Greeks, and 23,420 Armenians returned. The minister, who made the announcement in the parliament, also said that these people had been resettled.[29]

The most important step on this issue was taken on 4 November 1918, when the temporary law of 27 May 1915, known as the Deportation Law, was found to be contrary to the constitution, and rescinded.[30] On 21 October in accordance with the consent of the Armenians they were left free to return to their prior religions, and on 5 November 1918 it was announced that this permission was limited to people over twenty years of age and older. On 8 February 1919 this attitude changed, and it was requested that since the religious conversion of Armenians less than twenty years old could not be accepted, those less than this age should be given Armenian identity documents too.[31]

The biggest question encountered concerning the repatriates was how the movable and immovable property left by the Armenians should be returned to them. A detailed circular was prepared on this topic on 18 December 1918 and sent to the provinces. The circular asked for the return of the confiscated properties of the Armenians and the most rapid evacuation of their homes by officials, police, and other individuals who might be living in them.[32] The Armenians' houses and lands were to be surrendered to the former. Immigrants and refugees living there had to vacate them; in cases where this was impossible, however, several families would be given shelter together in appropriate houses, and those remaining homeless would be settled in immigrant villages. In a communication dated 22 December 1918, the interior minister declared that a law was quickly being prepared that would provide for the "complete and whole return" to the owners of "properties and claims" that had been subject to liquidation in accordance with the temporary law of 22 September 1916.[33]

As a result of the delay of this proposed law, government attempted to solve questions pertaining to the return of goods and properties and settlement issues primarily through telegrams sent from the capital. One of the noteworthy issues was that it had been decided that "abandoned movable and immovable properties" could not be given to proxies or guardians, but only to the actual owners of the properties,[34] but this was changed by the 12 January 1920 decree, which allowed proxies and guardians to also take the properties.

Attempts to solve these issues through instructions from the capital continued throughout 1919. For example, on 19 February 1919, a circular sent to all provinces requested that properties transferred temporarily from abandoned property warehouses to government offices be returned to their owners.[35] Similarly, on 19 March 1919, the Interior Ministry instructed that Armenians and Greeks subjected to deportation be exempt from some taxes.[36] However, the government opposed some requests coming from the provinces concerning abandoned properties on the grounds that such issues were being discussed in the Council of Ministers, so that it would be better to wait.[37]

Reports in the newspapers of the period make it evident that the removal of those who had settled in Armenian homes was a serious issue. According to a report of 27 March 1919, Muslims who had settled in vacant Armenian and Greek houses established an organization called the Society of Refugees. In a statement, they explained that "upon their [the Armenians and Greeks'] return, Muslim refugees who had settled in their places, being taken out from those places, [became] utterly homeless." The Society estimated that there were "approximately 150 thousand" Muslims left without homes.[38] In order to understand some of the problems being encountered, the government summoned the refugee directors of the provinces to the capital and asked questions like, "How many [Muslim] refugees remained homeless upon the return of the Armenians and Greeks to their places of origin? Of these [Muslims], how many today require housing? Where are they? Is land suitable for the settlement of the [Muslim] refugees available? If it exists, how much is it and where would the settlements [be]?"[39] The government was trying to find a solution for these problems.

12 January 1920: The Ittihadist Laws Are Annulled

The anticipated regulation concerning the return of abandoned properties was finally issued on 12 January 1920. It contained thirty-three articles and delimited in a detailed fashion how Armenian properties were to be returned. Its thirtieth article revoked the Liquidation Law of 26 September 1915 and the Regulation of 8 November 1915.[40] The most important point of the regulation is that in accordance with the law of 26 September and the regulation of 8 November, immovable properties impounded by the state and registered in the names of the treasuries of the Finance Ministry and Pious Foundations Ministry were to be immediately returned to their original owners. If these owners were not alive, then the properties, regardless of whether they were registered in the names of the aforementioned ministries, would be immediately surrendered to heirs and registered in their names. If no heirs were alive, the properties would remain with the state. Furthermore, if the original owners of the properties did not accept the first sales conducted by the Finance Ministry and Pious Foundations Ministry, then the owners could get their properties back.[41]

The revenues from properties of deported people while these properties were in the hands of the state would be given to the original owners after the deduction of taxes or any other item specified in the law. The government would also pay compensation for any damage to the properties.[42] The regulation stipulated that the money amassed by the Liquidation Commissions would be paid with interest. If the original owner of the property did not accept the rental agreements made by the treasuries of the Finance Ministry or Pious Foundations Ministry with new tenants, it was decreed that within a period of ten days after the original owner applied to the government, the renters had to be expelled and the property returned to the owner.[43]

The following important matters were also arranged by the regulation: The councils of elders would distribute the equivalent values of properties registered in the name of villages or neighborhoods to the people of the village or quarter entitled to them. If there were no heirs to properties that were sold, the equivalent value of the immovable property would be given to spiritual leaders for distribution to orphans of that community. There were some cases with additional complications. For example, in some places the government or new owners made some changes such as adding buildings, trees, or other things to the property, which was controlled by the treasury, sold, or abandoned. If the value of these additions were equal to or less than that of the real estate on which they were located, an agreement could be attempted between the original owner and those who made the additions. If successful, the original owner would pay the value of the additions in installments over a period of three years and the property, together with its additions, would be his again.[44]

A Brief Evaluation

With the Vahdettin Regulation[45] of 12 January 1920, all the practices of the Union and Progress period concerning Armenian properties were revoked and the return of usurped Armenian properties began. There are two important aspects of the period encompassing the 1918 regulation and the Vahdettin Regulation, which must be emphasized. First, starting in October 1918 while the properties left behind by the Armenians were being returned, no indication of any kind is encountered indicating that any type of payment of the equivalent values of these properties had been made earlier. In other words, the information conveyed in the report of February 1918 mentioned above that the equivalent value of the Armenians' properties was not being paid is confirmed by the practices of this entire period.

Yet, as is well known, for years Turkish governments and some historians were claiming that "the equivalent values of the properties being sold [were] sent to the owners by the Abandoned Properties Commissions," and they even alleged that "the refugees arriving at the settlement places established businesses with this money which was transferred to them and [had] adapted to the area."[46] Through these documents, which we have published, this lie, which has been repeated for decades, has been deciphered.

The second aspect of this period is the relationship between the Turkish Republic and the Genocide. As we will discuss later in greater detail, the legal system of the Republic of Turkey was founded on the annulation of the Vahdettin Regulation and the reacceptance of the 1915 genocide regulations. For this reason, in the case of the abandoned properties, we can say that the Republican regime institutionalized the Genocide through its legal system. The secret of the emancipation of Turkey from the status of a regime, which legally institutionalized genocide rests in the Vahdettin Regulation. In our opinion, in order to achieve this objective it is necessary to cleanse the legal system of the laws of the Genocide and their consequences and again turn toward the sensibility of the Vahdettin Regulation.

The Treaty of Sèvres of 10 August 1920

The return of the Armenians and the restoration of their properties were a topic of the peace negotiations after the Ottomans' defeat in the world war, and consequently these topics were treated in the Sèvres treaty. They were discussed in Articles 140–51 in connection with the safeguard of minorities. Article 141 defined the Ittihadist regime as terrorist, and annulled all conversions of religions conducted after 1 November 1914. Article 143 resolved that as compensation for the harm it caused during the massacres, the Turkish government must mobilize all the means it possessed and work to find the people who disappeared, who were forcibly deported, or who were imprisoned after 1 November 1914.

Article 144 made arrangements concerning the abandoned properties. When the provisions of the article are studied, the parallels with the Vahdettin Regulation become apparent. According to this article, the Ottoman government accepted as unjust and invalid the Abandoned Properties Law of 1915 and the other legal arrangements supplementing this law. Decrees taken in line with the Abandoned Properties Law and other laws connected to the latter were considered invalid in connection with both the past and the future.[47]

Again according to this article, the Ottoman government officially pledged to ensure the return to their native lands and jobs of the surviving Ottoman citizens who were not Turks and who were being killed or forcibly deported after 1 August 1914. The movable and immovable properties belonging to the aforesaid subjects and their communities, which could be obtained again (no matter in whose hands they were found), were going to be immediately returned to their owners. Such properties would be exempt from any kind of tax, and when they were returned to their former owners the latter would not have to pay any sort of compensation. Their rights of initiating lawsuits against those who used their properties would be preserved.

The Ottoman government accepted the formation of arbitration commissions by the Assembly of the League of Nations in every place seen as appropriate. Each of these commissions would be composed of a representative of the Ottoman government, the person claiming injury or an agent from the community representing that individual, and a chair person appointed by the Assembly of the League of Nations. The arbitration commissions would investigate all applications and carry out the decisions made concerning their demands. The commission would decide the removal of every person who was proven after investigation to have actively participated in killings and deportation or who was the cause of such actions, and the steps to be taken concerning the property of such a person. All assets and real estate belonging to a member of a community who after 1 August 1914 died without an heir or who disappeared was to be transferred to the community to which the property owner was affiliated instead of to the government of the place where the assets and properties were located.[48]

All legal procedures carried out concerning immovable properties after 1 August 1914 were going to be annulled. The Ottoman government would provide restitution for all properties, but this could not be an excuse for delays. Consequently the Ottoman government would both return immovable property to its original owners and pay compensation for the damages to this property. Moreover, if the person in possession of the immovable property undertook some expenditure on it, the arbitration commission had the authority to make reimbursements in a just fashion. The Ottoman government pledged not to oppose but to carry out as far as possible the decisions taken by the commissions.[49]

In sum, the provisions of the Treaty of Sèvres were openly supportive of the 12 January 1920 Vahdettin Regulation and supplementary to it. Some of the matters treated here, such as compensation for the damages suffered by citizens of the signatory parties based on the principle of reciprocity, or the establishment of joint arbitration commissions, were going to be reiterated in the Treaty of Lausanne.

The Prohibition against the Return of Greeks and Armenians Staying Outside of Turkey

In spite of the fact that permission was given to the surviving Armenians who had been deported to return starting on 18 October, this process was not carried out without problems. The Ottoman government, and later the nationalist movement that was established in Ankara, worked to prevent the return of Armenians and Greeks remaining outside the borders drawn by the Mudros Armistice through several measures; on 30 October 1918 this was signed on between Great Britain and Ottoman Government to end the war. It is striking that both Istanbul and Ankara adopted a similar position on this topic.

In order to understand the issue of returning refugees to their homes, it is necessary to divide the process into two periods. The first period is from October 1918 through November 1922. In this period there was a still a government functioning in Istanbul. The second period begins after November 1922, with the transfer of control over Istanbul to the Nationalist government in Ankara and the Lausanne negotiations. Essentially, it continues through the rest of the 1920s. During this second period 6 August 1924, the date the Lausanne Treaty entered into force, must be considered an important turning point.

In the first period the issue of returning refugees was extremely complicated for a number of reasons. First, although World War I had ended, in Anatolia fighting was continuing on several fronts, and breaking out on new fronts. Depending on the course of the fighting, the Muslim and Christian masses fled the war regions insofar as possible. Second, different regions were under the control of different political and military forces. The Turks were still divided. They were being governed by two different political centers, which sometimes supported each other but at other times were in conflict. For this reason, when examining the prohibition on returning during the 1918 to 1922 period, it is necessary to distinguish the practices of the Ottoman government in Istanbul from those of the Nationalist government in Ankara. Even if in the end similarities may be seen, these were decisions taken by two different political centers.

It is also necessary to add that in this period parts of Anatolia were under the control of occupation forces such as those of the British, French, or Greeks. The disorder in the Caucasus would continue until the beginning of 1921. Consequently, it is a serious question as to what extent the policies expressed in certain laws and regulations were actually implemented. Nonetheless, it is important to know about these laws and regulations at the least in order to understand what the goals of those in power were.

Another point that should not be forgotten is that people who had survived large-scale massacres were not that enthusiastic about returning for reasons of security. When they were able to return, the evacuation of Muslim refugees who had settled in their homes was a serious problem. Moreover, the great powers, which were expected to provide the most aid to the returning Christians, particularly the Armenians, gradually began to perceive the problems of these people as a burden.

The Articles of Law Used to Prevent Their Return

The most important of the laws used to prevent the Armenians and Greeks from entering the interior was the 1869 Law of Citizenship. The fifth and sixth articles of this law regulate the principles of how Ottoman citizens can acquire the citizenship of another country, and are extremely important. According to Article 5, it was only possible for an Ottoman citizen to acquire a different country's citizenship with the permission of the Ottoman government. Without this permission, such a procedure would be considered invalid. The person concerned would continue to be considered an Ottoman citizen and would be treated accordingly. According to the sixth article, a person acquiring the citizenship of another country without permission could, if the state wished, be removed from Ottoman citizenship and prohibited from entering the Ottoman state.[50] The November 1918 passport law added that those who attempted to enter the country would be punished with prison sentences.

It is useful to note that the 1869 Law of Citizenship was issued for a very specific purpose. Throughout the nineteenth century, the Great Powers were granting Ottoman Christians citizenship by means of their consulates in the Ottoman Empire, so that these people were able to make use of the treaty rights known as the Capitulations.[51] The 1869 law was issued in order to prevent this common practice. During the period under discussion, that law was used to prevent the return of the Armenians and Greeks who had been forcibly removed from their homes and to stop them from regaining their properties.

This practice became much more common after 1923. When states such as Great Britain and the United States, relying on the provisions of the Treaty of Lausanne, asked for indemnification for the properties of Armenians who had adopted their own citizenships, the Turkish authorities informed these states that this right would only be recognized for people who had informed the Ottoman state before adopting other citizenships. People who had not obtained this permission would still be considered Turkish citizens according to the 1869 law, and therefore claims of foreign states would be rejected. However, if these people who were still considered Turkish citizens by Turkey wanted to come to obtain their properties in person, they would be told that because they adopted other citizenships without giving any notice, according to Article Six of the 1869 law, they could not reenter the country.

The other laws frequently referenced in this period are the Passport Laws of 1911, 1915, and 1918. While the 1911 law was rescinded with the 1918 law, it is still useful to closely examine the former in order to understand the importance of the changes made in 1915 and 1918. According to the regulations in the fourth section of the law, a person who does not have an Ottoman passport and cannot prove that he is an Ottoman citizen cannot enter the country. The eighteenth article indicates that the possession of passports of other countries is not sufficient by itself to solve the issue of citizenship.[52] There is no other provision relevant to the present book in this law. It appears to be a very normal and understandable law. This situation will help illuminate the changes that were made in the later passport laws.

Some very important restrictions were introduced in the 1915 Temporary Passport Law. According to its third article, some people would be forbidden to enter the country "even if they were bearers of passports in due form." It declared that even if they owned normal passports, any vagabonds, people expelled from the country indefinitely or who have not yet completed their sentence, those seen as suspicious due to activities against the state, those who in a manner contrary to the rules and laws in effect left the homeland without obtaining permission from the government, and those whose entry into the country was prohibited because their citizenship had been annulled would not be permitted into the country.[53] The most important relevant change appears in Article 23. It states, "An Ottoman subject entering the Ottoman domains bearing a foreign passport will be imprisoned for six months to two years."[54]

These articles were later identically repeated in the Passport Law of November 1918, which replaced the 1911 law. A minor change in the language of the third article in this new law is extremely understandable and important. In the original article, "Those who emigrate without obtaining official permission from the exalted government in accordance with observed custom and current decisions," the phrase "those who emigrate" is changed to "arriving refugees." It is very clear that all the changes were made in reference to the Armenians. The Temporary Passport Law keeps Article 23, concerning the arrest of Ottoman citizens who come with foreign passports, unchanged.[55]

These changes to the 1911 law introduced in March 1915 and November 1918 are quite meaningful. The fact that a law created by the Ittihadists was reissued by others after the Ittihadists lost power demonstrates continuity in policies. The goal was to obstruct the entry into the country of people who had been forcibly deported and who survived, ending up outside the borders of the state that were later delimited. It must be accepted that this is evidence that the lawmakers knew very well what they were doing when they prevented these people from re-entering the country on the grounds that they did not leave the country with an appropriate document from the Ottoman Turkish state.

The new articles of the Passport Law were to be used against the Armenians who wished to return to their homes after the Ittihadists lost power. For example, a telegram sent to Erzurum on 4 May 1919 declared that the entry into the country was prohibited for "those whose entry into the Ottoman dominions was forbidden in accordance with the third article of the Passport Law" of those Armenians "who flee to Russia and other foreign countries," along with those who would disturb the security of the country.[56] We see in a 28 May 1919 telegram sent to Trebizond that the same procedures were conducted concerning the Greeks. It informed that "the return to the Ottoman dominions of those who went to foreign countries without obtaining permission in accordance with the third article of the Passport Law [was] forbidden," and demanded the immediate expulsion of those who did enter the country contrary to the law.[57]

The use of citizenship and passport laws in order to prevent Armenians and Greeks from reentering the country became more systematic over time. Instructions sent to the provinces openly stated that "as a general rule, due to the special provisions of the passport and citizenship laws, the return to Ottoman domains of those who without obtaining permission from the government emigrate, and in the same way those who without obtaining permission from the government change their citizenship in foreign lands, is prohibited."[58] Passport laws were also used in the Republican period as an important means of preventing repatriation.

Policies to Obstruct Repatriation

The first efforts at preventing repatriation after October 1918 were directed against Greeks who "fled." A telegram of 7 November 1918 communicated to relevant places the nonacceptance in Ottoman territory of "Greeks who fled to Greece or other places due to various crimes which they committed."[59] As the number of such repatriations was increasing, the Ottoman government applied to the representatives of foreign governments in Istanbul and asked that they not assist in the mass repatriation of Greeks.[60] These efforts were renewed at the start of April,[61] and the result of discussions with British and French diplomats was an understanding concerning the nonacceptance of Greeks who fled and cut off their ties with the Ottoman state.[62]

There were a variety of reasons why the Ottomans attempted to prevent the return of the Greeks. First, both during the Balkan Wars and from 1913 to 1914, many Ottoman Greeks were expelled to Greece and Muslim immigrants from Greece were settled in their places. The Ottoman government wished to solve this issue through negotiations with Greece. Second, there was the concern that Greece was taking advantage of the situation to create a Greek demographic majority in various parts of Anatolia.[63] Thus, on 11 April 1919, the Council of Ministers made the decision to prevent "Greece and Bulgaria taking advantage of the present situation, making increases in the population [of their conationals] in some places and settlement efforts."[64]

An important step in the prevention of repatriation was taken on 16 April 1919, when the Council of Ministers issued a four-article decree concerning those who would be given permission to enter the country. The entry of anyone in a situation conflicting with the Passport Law and the decree of the Council of Ministers was not desired.[65] Various communications written to frontier districts stated, since, "as previously communicated, the non-acceptance of Greeks who flee to foreign lands being . . . required by a decision of the Council of Ministers, not giving any opportunity at all for the entry of such fugitives, and the immediate expulsion outside of the borders of those whose positions and situations are seen as suspicious among the ones who have come up until now" were requested.[66]

Attempts were made throughout an entire summer to prevent the reentry of Greek refugees. For example, on 4 June 1919 a telegram sent to Trebizond, "On the non-entry of runaway Greeks to the Ottoman domains," recalled that the 16 April 1919 Council of Ministers decree was circulated, and repeated that "the resolution of the exalted government about the non-acceptance of such people who fled to foreign countries or Greece in the Ottoman domains is absolute." Moreover, it asked for "the immediate expulsion of those whose circumstances and behavior attract suspicion from among those who came up until the present."[67]

Communications sent to the provinces throughout August 1919 repeated that an understanding was reached with British and French representatives concerning the necessity to fully prevent the return of Greeks who had emigrated during the Balkan Wars or World War I and who had cut off their ties partially or fully with Turkey. The prohibition of their entry into the empire was requested.[68]

The restriction of entry from abroad was not limited to Greeks; in time it was extended to include Armenians. On 28 April 1919 the War Ministry prepared a list "of who might be acceptable to enter the country among the Armenians who fled to Russia and foreign countries during the period of the world war in order not to leave room for error."[69] Later a regulation was prepared and on 4 May 1919 was sent to all border gates.[70]

The regulation placed a number of conditions on the granting of permission for the entry of Armenians from border gates. Among these were not having committed any crime during the deportations or during the world war, not having conducted any activity disturbing the public order of the country, and not having committed any of the violations stipulated in the third article of the Passport Law. Moreover, the third article of the regulation stipulated that Armenians who were not Ottoman citizens would not be allowed to reenter the country.

A gendarme and two police officers would be placed at each border gate for the reception and registration of Armenians who had been given permission to return. These registration records would include information such as the names of the members and heads of families of the accepted Armenians; the Ottoman village, township, and county in which they used to reside; and what types and quantities of goods, animals, and tools they had with them. The Armenians would be resettled in the villages to which they were affiliated.[71]

Directives were sent to the provinces analogous to this regulation indicating that Armenians who had fled to Russia and committed crimes during the world war, those who disturbed the order of the country, and those whose entry onto Ottoman soil was prohibited in accordance with Article Three of the Passport Law should not be let into the country, but the acceptance of other Armenians was necessary.[72]

The Prohibition of Domestic Travel and Migration

However difficult it may be to separate the following two topics from another, it is necessary to discuss each one individually. The first topic consists of domestic travel in general during the 1918 to 1923 period and its prohibition, while the other is the prohibition of the travel of certain groups, in particular Armenians, and their migration from one province to another. With the growing strength of the Turkish Nationalist movement, the greater part of Anatolia passed under its control, so that it was mostly the government in Ankara that was making decisions on domestic travel and migration. War and security were the main problems. As Ankara was battling on the eastern front with Armenians and western fronts with Greeks, it was forced to limit wandering around. In the first circulars on this point there was no distinction between Muslim and non-Muslim.

We can give the decree of 7 October 1920, number 260, as one example on this topic. The decree said that each person who would travel "in the Ottoman domains" was required "to obtain [a] travel document." The seventh article is significant: travelers "coming from Istanbul, foreign countries or similar varied places" will be asked at the first place they appear about the reason for their travel; "those whose circumstances appear somewhat suspicious will be placed under surveillance or observation according to their situations." Information about such individuals will be obtained from the Interior Ministry and action will be taken accordingly.[73]

The procedure for non-Muslims was a little different. "The acceptance and non-acceptance of non-Muslims" coming from the abovementioned places was completely within the power of the Interior Ministry so that permission had to be obtained from the latter. Article 12 prohibited the travel of all foreigners, with the exception of those who obtained special permission.[74] A 26 November 1921 decree, number 1218, introduced an important change. After this date, identity documents were considered sufficient for Muslims, who no longer had to obtain travel papers.[75]

We can say that all these prohibitions were directly connected to the war. After informing the government that foreign forces were obtaining military intelligence from civilians freely traveling from Istanbul to Anatolia, the military chief of staff in a communication of 11 March 1923 asked that the movements of "Muslims also who are going to be traveling to the war zone" be subject to serious investigation.[76] Another communication of 15 March stated that "upon the announcement being given to the newspapers by the Istanbul police directorship that Muslim and non-Muslim travelers with the citizenship of the Turkish Grand National Assembly will be able to travel to Anatolia," people began to enter the war zone. The army's general headquarters was not happy with this announcement: for people "to enter the zone of war operations in an unrecorded and unconditional manner" created an extremely dangerous situation for the army, and it demanded "speedy efforts for the immediate prevention of the situation."[77] On 16 March it asked that the travel ban be reintroduced at least for Trakya (Thrace).[78]

In this period, aside from such military measures, there were also special steps taken to forbid the domestic migration of Armenians. The governments of Istanbul and Ankara worked in harmony on this issue. It first appeared on the agenda in the Erzurum and Sivas Congresses of the Turkish Nationalist movement in 1919,[79] with the consideration of "places the possibility of occupation of which by the enemy are greater." It was decided that the Representative Committee of the Nationalist movement had to give permission for people to migrate to a place.[80] The Erzurum Congress decreed that "migration without notification being made by the Representative Committee through [local] committee centers is prohibited."[81] Article 5 of the principles adopted by the Anatolia and Rumelia Defense of Rights Association at the Sivas Congress reiterated this prohibition.[82]

Domestic migration began to constitute a serious problem as the course of the war of independence progressed. In particular, it was feared

that Armenians, as they grew numerous in certain areas, might demand
certain rights. The immigration of some Armenian families from different parts of Anatolia who did not feel secure to the region of Çukurova
or Cilicia, then under French control, was interpreted in this way. Arch-
bishop Zaven Der Yeghiayan, the Armenian patriarch of Istanbul, declared in a newspaper interview that this emigration was due to fear of
the Nationalist movement. On 20 October, Mustafa Kemal responded to
Patriarch Der Yeghiayan and declared that these migrations to Cilicia
were conducted upon "the instigation of the Armenian [revolutionary]
committees and the [Armenian] Patriarchate itself in order to form a
majority in Adana and its environs, and in a future Armenia."[83]

The Istanbul government also took up this issue, and on 26 October
1919 made the decision to halt migration from the interior of Anatolia
to Cilicia. On 13 November 1919 this decision was expanded to encom-
pass Greeks with the decree that "the giving of permission [to Greeks]
who want to go to Izmir and other places is not lawful."[84] Later, many
telegraphs were sent to the provinces to prevent Armenians from assembling in Adana and its environs.[85]

After Istanbul was fully occupied by the Allied forces on 16 March
1920, one of the first acts of the newly created government in Ankara
was to prohibit the rights of Armenians to travel freely. A decree issued on 18 June 1920 instructed the provinces that "freedom of place
and travel [is] not seen as appropriate for any of . . . the Armenians
found in the interior." The signatures of all the ministers, including
most notably that of Mustafa Kemal, were placed under the decree.[86]
A similar decree was made on 4 December 1921, and again the council
of ministers led by Mustafa Kemal forbade the travel of Armenian orphans in Konya to Istanbul.[87]

A new policy began after the victory in the war against the Greeks, and
difficulties for those who wanted to go were removed. First, on 29 October
1922 the prohibition "on going outside for those who want it from the
non-Muslim elements" was lifted for the period of a month.[88] Then on 14
December 1922 the decision was made to "give permission for an indefi-
nite period of time for non-Muslims to go outside of the country."[89] Having won the war, Turkey wanted all non-Muslims to leave the country.

A Brief Evaluation

At the same time as the intensification of the war against the Greeks
in the west and against the French in the south, the return of those
deported during World War I stopped, and instead a new wave of

migration began. The Greeks and Armenians of western Anatolia fled or were forcibly expelled to Greece, while with the retreat of French forces from Cilicia, Syria became the destination of the Armenians in the south.[90]

The question of refugees during World War I and after 1919 was a fundamental issue for the League of Nations, created through the Treaty of Versailles. The League began to be involved with the return of prisoners of war and refugees to their homes in the spring of 1920. On 27 June 1921 the High Commission of Refugees was founded in the framework of the League of Nations and Fridtjof Nansen was entrusted with this work.[91] One of Nansen's first tasks was to organize the return of more than 1 million Greek and Armenian refugees who had been forced to leave Turkey. In October 1922 he came to Istanbul and after a series of meetings learned that Turkey would not give permission for even a single refugee to return to their home.[92]

It is very difficult to estimate how many Armenians were able to return to their homes after 1918 and how many of these were able to take back their properties. In a report prepared by the Ottoman Interior Ministry, after complaints by the occupying forces that insufficient aid was provided to returning refugees, the number of those returning was given as 232,679.[93] According to news that appeared in Ottoman newspapers of the same period, 118,352 Greeks and 101,747 Armenians returned and were resettled.[94] Damat Ferit Pasha, prime minister of the Istanbul government, in a 17 June 1919 report given to the British High Commissioner in Istanbul cited a figure of 276,015 returning Armenians and Greeks.[95] On 3 February 1920 newspapers quoted the figure of 335,883 "Armenians and Greeks who by means of the government were able to return to their homelands since the armistice."[96]

How many of the returning Armenians were able to get back their properties? We do not have much information on this. However, Finance Minister Hasan Fehmi Bey, during the discussions in the Grand National Assembly about annulling the 12 January 1920 Regulation that we have called the Vahdettin Regulation, made an extremely important statement on 14 September 1922. He said, "The implementation of the regulation [of 12 January 1920] is one out of ten of the provisions existing in the law. That is to say that many articles were not implemented."[97] Apparently 90 percent of the abandoned properties had not been returned to their owners and, as a matter of fact, this was the reason for the desire to annul the 12 January 1920 Vahdettin Regulation. The Ankara government no longer wanted to return any property to the Armenians.

We can now take a closer look at the practices of the new parliament
formed in Ankara and the Republican regime.

Notes

1. On the periods in office of these governments, established by seven different grand
    viziers, see Tarık Zafer Tunaya, *Türkiye'de Siyasi Partiler, Cilt II, Mütareke Dönemi*
    (Istanbul: Hürriyet Vakfı Yayınları, 1986), 37.
2. In the 1919–22 period, the court-martial active in Istanbul in all tried sixty-three
    cases, and prosecuted approximately two hundred defendants. For more detailed
    information on this topic, see Vahakn Dadrian and Taner Akçam, *Judgment at
    Istanbul: The Armenian Genocide Trials* (New York: Berghahn Books, 2011).
3. BOA/DH.ŞFR, 84/187, cipher telegram to Edirne, Adana, Ankara, Aydın, Sivas,
    Kastamonu, and Konya provinces and Karahisar-i Sahib, Eskişehir, Kütahya,
    Maraş, Niğde, and Urfa provincial district governments, 28 February 1918.
4. BOA/BEO. 4511/338204, EUM cipher telegram to the Prime Ministry Office, 4 April
    1918. The provinces were informed of this decree in a cipher telegram sent on 7
    April (see BOA/DH.ŞFR 86/60). İ. E. Atnur, in his article "Osmanlı Hükümetleri
    ve Tehcir Edilen Rum ve Ermenilerin Yeniden İskânı Meselesi" (*Atatürk Yolu* 4,
    no. 14 [November 1994]: 121–39) incorrectly states that this decree included the
    Armenians and Greeks too.
5. BOA/DH.ŞFR 585/63. On Those Whose Age Surpasses Sixty among People Who
    Are Being Banished to the Interior of Kayseri through Expulsion from the Zone of
    the Fourth Army, 5 July 1918; and BOA/DH.ŞFR 58499, On the Names of Those
    Exceeding the Age of Sixty from Families in Ankara and Environs Who Are Being
    Expelled from the Zone of the Fourth Army, cipher telegram, dated 18 July 1918.
6. BOA/MV. 212/95, 1336 L 12.
7. Mustafa Özdemir, "I. Dünya Savaşı Sırasında Osmanlı Ülkesinde Yaşanan Göç
    Hareketleri," doctoral thesis, Dokuz Eylül University, İzmir, 2007, 198–200.
8. BOA/DH.ŞFR 86/195, AMMU cipher telegram to Mamuretülaziz province, 21 Nisan
    1918, and BOA/DH.ŞFR 87/166 AMMU cipher telegram to Erzurum and Van prov-
    inces, 16 May 1918.
9. BOA/DH.ŞFR 91/149, AMMU cipher telegram to Trebizond province, 14 September
    1918.
10. BOA/DH. ŞFR. 91/150, AMMU cipher telegram to Sivas province and Canik provin-
    cial district government, 14 September 1918.
11. BOA/DH.ŞFR 85/171, Cipher telegram to the Edirne, Adana, Ankara, Aydın,
    Beyrut, Aleppo, Hüdâvendigâr, Diyarbekir, Suriye, Sivas, Kastamonu, Konya,
    Mamuretülaziz and Musul provinces and Urfa, İzmit, Bolu, Canik, Çatalca, Zor,
    Karesi, Kale-i Sultaniye, Menteşe, Teke, Kayseri, Karahisar-ı Sahib, Eskişehir,
    İçel, Kütahya, Maraş and Niğde provincial district governments, 20 March 1918.
12. BOA/DH.ŞFR 87/74 EUM cipher telegram to Edirne, Adana, Ankara, Aydın, Aleppo,
    Hüdâvendigâr, Diyarbekir, Suriye, Sivas, Kastamonu, Konya, Mamuretülaziz and
    Mosul provinces; and Urfa, İzmit, Bolu, Canik, Çatalca, Zor, Karesi, Kudüs-i Şerif,
    Kale-i Sultaniye, Menteşe, Teke, Kayseri, Karahisar-ı Sahib, Eskişehir, İçel, Kü-
    tahya, Maraş, Niğde and Cebel-i Lübnan provincial district governments, 8 May
    1915.
13. The government was making some preparations on this issue, according to BOA/
    DH.ŞFR 90/51, EUM cipher telegram to Mamuretülaziz province 6 August 1918.

14. Quoted from *İkdam* of 5 August 1918 in Adem Günaydın, "The Return and Resettlement of the Relocated Armenians (1918–1920)," doctoral thesis, Orta Doğu Teknik Üniversity, Ankara, 2007, 12.

15. *Sabah*, 21 August 1918.

16. *Sabah*, 25 and 30 August 1918.

17. BOA/DH.ŞFR 90/176, EUM cipher telegraph to Edirne, Erzurum, Adana, Ankara, Aydın, Bitlis, Aleppo, Hüdâvendigâr, Diyarbakır, Suriye, Sivas, Trebizond, Kastamonu, Konya, Mamuretülaziz, Mosul, and Van provinces; and Urfa, İzmit, Bolu, Canik, Çatalca, Zor, Karesi, Kale-i Sultaniye, Menteşe, Teke, Kayseri, Karahisar-ı Sâhib, Eskişehir, İçel, Kütahya, Maraş, Niğde, Cebeli Lübnan, and Erzincan provincial district governments, 19 August 1918.

18. BOA/DH.ŞFR, EUM cipher telegram to Erzurum province 8 August 1918; and BOA/DH.ŞFR 92/03, AMMU cipher telegram to Hüdavendigâr province, 1 October 1918.

19. BOA/DH.ŞFR 92/153, EUM cipher telegram to Adana province, 16 October1918.

20. BOA/DH.ŞFR 92/170, EUM cipher telegram to Mosul province, 19 October 1918.

21. For an order concerning the deportation of Armenians fleeing Damascus back to where they came from, see BOA/DH.ŞFR 91/160, EUM cipher telegram to Adana province 15 September 1918.

22. Başbakanlık Devlet Arşivleri Genel Müdürlüğü, *Osmanlı Belgelerinde Ermenilerin Sevk ve İskânı* (Ankara: Osmanlı Arşivi Daire Başkanlığı Yayını, 2007), 396.

23. *Meclis-i Mebusan Zabıt Ceridesi*, Period 3, Assembly Year 5, Vol. 1,19 October 1918, (Ankara: TBMM Basımevi), 29.

24. Müdürlüğü, *Osmanlı Belgelerinde Ermenilerin Sevk ve İskânı*, 396.

25. BOA/DH.ŞFR 92/207, Cipher telegram to Edirne, Erzurum, Adana, Ankara, Aydın, Bitlis, Aleppo, Hüdâvendigâr, Diyarbakır, Sivas, Trebizond, Kastamonu, Konya, Mamuretülaziz, Mosul, and Van provinces; and Urfa, İzmit, Bolu, Canik, Çatalca, Karesi, Kalei Sultaniye, Menteşe, Teke, Kayseri, Kütahya, Karahisar-ı Sahib, İçel, Batum, Kars, Erzincan, Eskişehir, and Niğde provincial district governments, 22 October 1918.

26. Müdürlüğü, *Osmanlı Belgelerinde Ermenilerin Sevk ve İskânı*, 397–98.

27. On the communications of 28 October, and 5 and 23 November 1918, see ibid., 399–403.

28. Ibid., 402. For a more detailed work on the returnees, see İbrahim Ethem Atnur, "Tehcirden Dönen Rum ve Ermenilerin İskânı," master's thesis, Erzurum Üniversity, Erzurum, 1991.

29. *Meclis-i Mebusan Zabıt Ceridesi*, Period 3, Assembly Year 5, Vol. 1, 362.

30. Ibid., 114–16.

31. BOA/DH.ŞFR 96/100, EUM cipher telegram to Edirne, Erzurum, Adana, and other provinces; and the Urfa, İzmit, Bolu, and other provincial district governments, 8 February 1919.

32. Müdürlüğü, *Osmanlı Belgelerinde Ermenilerin Sevk ve İskânı*, 412–17.

33. Ibid., 414, 417.

34. Ibid., p. 481.

35. Ibid., 453–54.

36. BOA/Political Division of the Interior Ministry 53/2, AMMU to the Office of the Prime Minister, 19 March 1919.

37. For example, on 19 August 1919, Interior Ministry rejected governor's request that the goods and possessions of Armenians from Trebizond who were not coming back be used for orphaned Armenian children (Müdürlüğü, *Osmanlı Belgelerinde Ermenilerin Sevk ve İskânı*, 497).

38. *Tercüman-ı Hakikat*, 27 March 1919.
39. General Directorate of Land Settlement Archive [henceforth BCA/TİGMA] 272.11/14.50.12., 28 June 1919, referenced in Tayfun Eroğlu, "Tehcirden Milli Mücadeleye Ermeni Malları (1915–1922)," doctoral thesis, Dokuz Eylül Üniversity, İzmir 2008, 135.
40. For the full text of Ahar Mahallere Nakledilmiş Olan Eşhasın 17 Zilkade 1733 Tarihli Kararname Mucibince Tasfiyeye Tâbi Tutulan Emvali Hakkında Kararname [Regulation on properties of people transported to other places subject to liquidation according to the 17 Zilkade 1733 dated regulation], see Kardeş, *"Tehcir" ve Emval-i Metruke Mevzuatı*, 69–91.
41. Ibid., 79–80.
42. Ibid., 83.
43. Ibid., 86.
44. Ibid., 83–84.
45. Throughout the text, we refer to this regulation as the name of the Sultan in order to distinguish it from the many other laws and regulations.
46. Yusuf Halaçoğlu, *Ermeni Tehciri* (Istanbul: Babıali Kültür Yayıncılığı, 2001), 90.
47. Nihat Erim, *Devletlerarası Hukuku ve Siyasi Tarih Metinleri Cilt 1: Osmanlı İmparatorluğu Andlaşmaları* (Ankara: Türk Tarih Kurumu, 1953), 573.
48. Ibid., 573–74.
49. Ibid.
50. *Tebaiyet-i Osmaniye Kanunnamesi* [Law on Ottoman citizenship], *Düstur*, Series 1, Vol. 1 (Istanbul: Matbaa-Amire, 1289). The relevant articles in English translation are as follows:

    Article 5. People entering foreign citizenship from citizenship of the exalted dominion [i.e. the Ottoman Empire] with permission are, from the date they change citizenship, considered as foreigners and are treated in this manner. However, if he [such a person] enters into foreign citizenship without permission from the Sublime State [the Ottoman state], this new citizenship is considered void and he being considered as with citizenship of the Sublime State as he used to be, in all matters he will be treated in the same manner as citizens of the Sublime State. In any case, the abandonment of a person of his citizenship of the Sublime State will depend upon a certificate to be given as a result of an exalted decree [of the Ottoman state].

    Article 6. If the Sublime State desires, it can cast out from its citizenship a person who without permission from the exalted dominion [the Ottoman Empire] changes his citizenship in a foreign land, or enters into the military service of a foreign state; and the return to the imperial domains of this category of people whose citizenship has been rejected is prohibited.

51. For more on this topic, see Akçam, *A Shameful Act*, 19–47.
52. BOA/DH.HMŞ. 15/58, Nezaret-i Celile-i Dahiliye Sicill-i Nüfus İdare-i Umumiyesi Pasaport Kanunu [Passport law of the General Directorate of the Population Registry of the Interior Ministry].
53. *Düstur*, Series 2, Vol. 7 (Istanbul: Matbaa-i Âmire, 1336), 486–491. The text of Article 3 is as follows:

    Persons described below are forbidden to enter the country even if they are bearers of passports in due form.

First: Those who are from the group of vagabonds;

Secondly: Those who for an indeterminate period are being driven away and expelled from the Ottoman dominions, or those who for a fixed period of time are being driven away and expelled, not having completed the fixed period;

Thirdly: Those who generate the suspicion and doubt that they are participating in preparation and instigation occurring with the aim of disturbing the public order of the state;

Fourthly: Those who emigrate without obtaining official permission from the exalted government in accordance with observed custom and current decisions;

Fifthly: Those whose entrance into the Ottoman dominions is forbidden due to the alteration or annulment of Ottoman citizenship.

54. Ibid.
55. BOA/General Administration of the Interior Ministry 20/21–14/04, Passport Law.
56. BOA/DH.ŞFR 99/44, AMMU cipher telegram to Erzurum province, 4 May 1919.
57. BOA/DH.ŞFR 99/369, AMMU cipher telegram to Trebizond province, 28 May 1919.
58. BOA/DH.ŞFR 104/118, AMMU cipher telegram to Teke provincial district government, 10 November 1919.
59. Müdürlüğü, *Osmanlı Belgelerinde Ermeniler (1915–1920)* (Ankara: Osmanlı Arşivi Daire Başkanlığı Yayını, 1994), 189–91.
60. Ibid.
61. It is learned from a note dated 3 May 1919 from the Sublime Porte's Legal Counsel Office that the Interior Ministry prepared a memorandum on 26 March 1919 and had applied to the British High Commission at the start of April (BOA/Foreign Affairs Ministry Legal Counsel Office of Consultation 130/10, Legal Counsel Office of the Sublime Porte, 3 May 1919).
62. BOA/DH.ŞFR 102/56, AMMU cipher telegram to Kastamonu province and Canik provincial government, 7 August 1919. However, it is understood from the continuing warnings to British and French representatives that the desired result was not obtained by the Ottomans and the Ottomans continued to request that these powers return the Greek people who settled in the environs of Aydın to their prior countries of residence. (BAO/BEO., 4606/345376, 1338 Ra 21 [14 December 1919]).
63. For a detailed work on this topic, see Adnan Sofuoğlu, "Kuvay-ı Milliye Döneminde Kuzey-Batı Anadolu (1919–1921)," doctoral thesis, Erzurum University, Erzurum, 1993.
64. BOA/MV, 215/37, 1337 B 10 [11 April 1919].
65. BOA/DH.ŞFR 101/19–17, AMMU cipher telegram to Canik provincial government, 7 July 1919.
66. BOA/DH.ŞFR 96/369, AMMU cipher telegram to Trebizond province, 28 May 1919.
67. BOA/DH.ŞFR 100/21, AMMU cipher telegram to Trebizond province, 4 June 1919.
    BOA/DH.ŞFR 100/21, AMMU cipher telegram to Trebizond province, 4 June 1919. Here it is useful to recall that Ali Kemal, the interior minister who signed the order, was soon going to be called "Artin Kemal" due to his anti-Ittihadist stance, and subsequently was lynched.
68. BOA/ Record Office Responsible for Foreigners of the Interior Ministry Public Security Directorate 28/13, AMMU cipher memorandum to some provinces and provincial districts, 25 August 1919. The full text in English translation is as follows:

It was informed by the Foreign Ministry that upon the initiative which is taking place in the presence of French and English representatives, the non-acceptance of Greeks who went to Greece in accordance with the exchange principle or fled, along with those who are not people of the coast, and the acceptance of those who so far as yet have not cut their connection with the Ottoman dominions were decided, and that it was promised by the French delegation that instructions would be given to those requiring it on this issue. Consequently it is required not to accept for any reason or pretext Greeks who after the Balkan War and during the World War fleeing to foreign lands cut off their connections, that is, who completely or in part transported members of [their] families who were obliged to stay in their own homes and with their food supplies to the places to which they fled, and in this fashion their enrollment in the population registry was cancelled; and if there are people like them who returned earlier, it is necessary to act in accordance with the decision of the Council of Ministers communicated on 16 April 1919.

69. BCA/TİGMA 272.00.00.11.13.47.12.7., War Ministry communication to Interior Ministry, 28 April 1919.
70. BCA/TİGMA 272.00.00.11.13.47.12.5., Harp Esnasında Hudud-ı Hâkânî Haricine Çıkıp El-yevm Dâhile Alınabilecek Osmanlı Ermenilerinin Suret-i Kabulleri Hakkında Talimatnamedir [Regulation on the method of acceptance of Ottoman Armenians who during the war went outside the imperial borders during the war and at present are going to be accepted inside].
71. Ibid.
72. BOA/DH.ŞFR 99/44, AMMU cipher telegram to Erzurum province, 4 May 1918.
73. *Düstur*, Series 3, Vol. 1 (Istanbul: Milliyet Matbaası, 1929), 92–94.The full name of the decree is Memaliki Osmaniye Dahilinde Seyrü Seyahat Edenlerin Seyahat Varakası Almaları Mecburi Olduğu Hakkında Kararname [Decree on those traveling in the Ottoman domains being required to obtain travel documents].
74. Ibid.
75. *Düstur*, Series 3, Vol. 2, 185. The full name of the decree is Seyrü Seyahat TalimatnamesininTadili Hakkında Kararname [Decree on the modification of the travel regulation]. In fact, other changes were made in decrees of 7 October 1920, 17 November, and 12 December 1920, and 22 March and 1 May 1921, which cannot be discussed here.
76. BCA/030–10–00–00–19–109–3-3, Chief of General Staff to the Illustrious Presidency of the Council of Ministers, 11 March 1339 [1923].
77. BCA/030–10–00–00–99–639–6-2, Chief of General Staff to the Illustrious Presidency of the Council of Ministers, 15 March 1339 [1923], with a note that "it is extremely urgent."
78. BCA/030–10–00–00–99–639–6-1, Chief of General Staff to the Illustrious President of the Council of Ministers, Rauf Beyefendi, 16 March 1339 [1923].
79. These congresses, which met in Erzurum in July 1919 and Sivas in September 1919, are considered important milestones in the Turkish national liberation movement. The representatives of various resistance organizations, which were established against the Greek army's invasion, or, in their own terminology, against the "Armenian danger" in the East, came together and made a series of declarations. In Sivas, the Anatolia, and Rumelia Defense of Rights Association, an executive committee was established; it selected Mustafa Kemal as its president. These initiatives were the beginning of the establishment of a government in Ankara.
80. Bekir Sıtkı Baykal, *Heyet-i Temsiliye Kararları* (Ankara: Türk Tarih Kurumu, 1974), x–xi.
81. Mahmut Goloğlu, *Erzurum Kongresi* (Ankara: Nüve Matbaası, 1968), 189.

82. Mahmut Goloğlu, *Sivas Kongresi* (Ankara: Başnur Matbaası, 1969), 219, 221.
83. Tayyib Gökbilgin, *Milli Mücadele Başlarken, II, Sivas Kongresinden Büyük Millet Meclisinin Açılmasına (4 Eylül 1919–23 Nisan 1920)* (Ankara: Türk Tarih Kurumu, 1965), 100–101
84. Ibid., 191–92.
85. For two examples, see BOA/DH.ŞFR 651/35 and BOA/DH.ŞFR 655/64.
86. BCA/TİGMA 030.18.01.01/01.04.10. The authors thank Sait Çetinoğlu for calling attention to this document.
87. BCA/TİGMA 030.18.01/01.4.40.1.
88. Müdürlüğü, *Milli Emlak Muamelelerine Müteallik Mevzuat*, 156.
89. Ibid., 158.
90. On the expulsion and fleeing of Armenians to Syria after 1920, see Vahe Tachjian, "The Expulsion of non-Turkish Ethnic and Religious Groups from Turkey to Syria during the 1920s and early 1930s," in *Online Encyclopedia of Mass Violence*, ed. Jacques Semelin, http://www.massviolence.org/IMG/article_PDF/The-expulsion-of-non-Turkish-ethnic-and-religious-groups.pdf. As a result of deportation and annihilation, practically no Armenian population was left in the eastern regions. Consequently, population movements during clashes with Armenians were extremely limited and cannot be compared with the western regions.
91. Gilbert Jaeger, "On the History of the International Protection of Refugees," *International Review of the Red Cross* 83, no. 843 (September 2001):727–37. For more information on this topic, see the bibliography at the following site: http://www.nobelprize.org/nobel_prizes/peace/laureates/1938/nansen-history.html.
92. Harry J. Psomiades, *Fridtjof Nansen and Greek Refugee Crisis 1922–1924* (Bloomingdale, IL: Asia Minor and Pontos Hellenic Research Center, 2011), 41.
93. Müdürlüğü, *Osmanlı Belgelerinde Ermeniler (1915–1920)*, 230. The report did not state how many of these were Armenians or Greeks.
94. *Memleket* newspaper, 12 March 1919.
95. Müdürlüğü, *Osmanlı Belgelerinde Ermeniler (1915–1920)*, 246.
96. *Ati* newspaper, 3 February 1920.
97. *TBMM Gizli Celse Zabıtları*, Period 1, Assembly Year 3, Vol. 3, 769.

CHAPTER 3

THE TURKISH REPUBLIC
PRIOR TO LAUSANNE

On 16 March 1920 Istanbul was occupied and the sultan officially closed the parliament on 11 April.[1] The parliament, which began its work in Ankara on 23 April 1920, established a 'temporary council of ministers'[2] on 25 April and decreed that all decisions taken by the government in Istanbul after 16 March were invalid. At the same time, according to this decree, all laws and regulations issued before 16 March remained valid. The meaning of this for confiscated Armenian properties was that the Ankara government accepted all the decrees of the Istanbul government taken prior to 16 March concerning abandoned properties, including the Vahdettin Regulation of 12 January 1920.[3]

The First Laws and Regulations of the Turkish Grand National Assembly

The assembly issued many laws and regulations until 6 August 1924, the date at which the Treaty of Lausanne entered into validity. In order not to allow any legal lacunae, these laws and regulations were extremely detailed and prepared in a rigorous fashion. The words used by Finance Minister Hasan Fehmi Bey, while discussing the new Abandoned Properties Law on 15 April 1923, are very telling from this point of view. Referring to the Liquidation Law of 20 April 1922, he said that this law was made with the goal of "assurance of the rights of missing people, working meticulously in legal theory." The minister stated that "it has been two or three years that we here have attempted to pay careful attention to the most delicate and subtle points of our legal principles in the Abandoned Properties Law [of 20 April 1922]."[4]

The first laws or regulations that were issued did not directly concern Armenian properties seized during the deportations. Rather, they dealt with problems connected with a new war that in 1919 began to take on greater dimensions and was still continuing. As we mentioned previously, large forcible population movements took place in this period, with 1,200,000 Greeks and over 100,000 Armenians and Jews being compelled to leave Turkey.[5] The fate of the properties left behind by these people, both during the war and immediately after it, formed a question as important as that of the Armenian properties seized in 1915. The first laws and regulations that appeared in the Republican period therefore dealt primarily with the issues of this second wave of migration, which started after 1919.[6] They would have a direct influence on the legal aspects of Armenian abandoned properties seized in 1915.

The first regulation on this topic was issued on 12 March 1922. Numbered 1483, this regulation was concerned wit whether powers of attorney sent from abroad by people considered lost should be honored.[7] It stated that for people with "causes such as Greek and Pontic aspirations [for an independent state]," after the 1918 Mudros Armistice, "their relationship [with Turkey] is cut off, and fleeing to Greece, Istanbul, or other countries, they join our enemies."[8] The Grand National Assembly considered such people to have betrayed the government. Some of these people, Greeks from the Trebizond, Samsun, Ordu, and Giresun areas, sent certified powers of attorney from Istanbul notaries and attempted to administer their properties. The Ankara government declared these powers of attorney invalid through a decree of its council of ministers and decided that powers of attorney that were sent, or were going to be sent, by people who had revolted would not be accepted by courts or other government offices.

One year later, in Regulation Number 2559 of 28 June 1923, this decree was broadened to include all non-Muslims found abroad. According to this regulation, an Armenian compatriot named Kevork Boyacıyan, who was in Romania, sent a certified power of attorney obtained from the Swedish embassy to Adana. The Abandoned Properties Commission in Adana claimed that according to the 12 March 1922 regulation this should not be accepted and applied to the Finance Ministry.

The Finance Ministry was of the opinion that as the 12 March 1922 regulation concerned only the Greeks of Trebizond, Samsun, Ordu, and Giresun, it should not be applicable to Kevork Boyacıyan. However, for a final decision, the issue was discussed "in a 26/6/1339 [26 July, 1923] meeting of the Council of Ministers," which decided that the 12 March 1922 regulation was unconditionally valid for all people considered lost.[9] Henceforth, it was no longer possible to regain abandoned properties through powers of attorney.

The 20 April 1922 Abandoned Properties Law

The 20 April 1922 law was the first Abandoned Properties Law to be issued by the Grand National Assembly.[10] Although it is known as an Abandoned Properties Law, it should not be confused with the 26 September 1915 Liquidation Law. It basically deals with the abandoned properties of people who fled and were missing after 1919, which is clearly stated. According to its fifth article, the law was "on the movable and immovable property and the agricultural products of people about whom it was determined legally that they were in difficult circumstances due to war or political reasons and fled to other places or were lost."[11]. It said that movable goods abandoned and left without owners who fled or were missing would be sold at auction according to the procedure laid out by the government, while immovable properties and agricultural products would again be administered by the government, and their revenues, rent, and other incomes, after subtracting expenses, would be placed in treasury accounts in escrow. If any of the property owners returned, the immovable properties belonging to them, as well as the sums of money placed in trust in treasury accounts, would be given back to them.

According to the third article of the law, those who seized abandoned, ownerless properties and agricultural products would be required to surrender these things to the government within one week after the date of issue of the law. Legal procedures would be initiated against those who did not comply. With the fourth article, if an individual reported those who secretly kept abandoned properties, he/she would be rewarded one-tenth of the value of said properties. Another important regulation was that the transactions would be accepted and considered valid if the property owner gave power of attorney even without setting expiration deadlines.

As can be understood from these articles, the 20 April 1922 law did not contradict the 12 January 1920 regulation issued in Vahdettin's period, and it stated that properties would be returned to their owners.

In this sense, this law can be seen as an adaptation of the earlier regulation to new conditions.

The Regulations of November to December 1922

As we saw above, the Council of Ministers on 29 October and 14 December 1922 gave permission to non-Muslims, in particular to Greeks, to freely leave the country. Two separate regulations were issued concerning the method of management of the properties that these people would leave behind. First, a regulation issued on 12 November 1922, together with the 29 October regulation, made "the decision that harm is not seen in the transmission of immovable properties to others and the transfer and sale of movable properties [both belonging to those given permission to leave the country]." That is, these people could transfer or sell their properties as they wished.[12] However, later, on 14 December 1922, the practice of free transfer and sale was temporarily halted.[13] It is significant that this regulation was issued on the same day that all non-Muslims were freely allowed to leave the country.

This sudden change in the regulations is due to a very logical reason. Turkey, having won the war against Greece, was thinking of demanding "significant money as war reparations and compensation for destruction and repair from Greece." However, it was also known that "due to Greece's known financial circumstances," it would not be able to provide "the assurance of a full cash indemnity." Therefore, it was planned to seize these properties left behind by Greeks as the equivalent of this indemnity. If this was to be realized, it was expected that two purposes would be simultaneously served: "in this way, the collection of reparations will be facilitated, and the financial connection of Greeks to Anatolia will be found to be cut off."[14]

This proposal originally made by the chief of the general staff later was placed on the agenda of the cabinet by the presidency of the Council of Ministers. In taking such a decision, it was desired that "it be ordered that the wealth and real estate belonging to Greek nationals, and to emigrating Rums [Ottoman Greeks] and Armenians quickly be determined by local governments."[15]

Regulations Relevant to Istanbul

Another issue raised due to the war was connected to Istanbul. On 29 March 1923, the Regulation on Abandoned Properties of People Who

Fled from Istanbul and Are Missing, intended only for Istanbul, was issued.[16] According to the first of its six articles, "Istanbul is one of the occupied cities," and consequently, the provisions of the fifth article of the 20 April 1922 law we summarized above would be carried out "about movable and immovable properties abandoned by fleeing and missing people."[17] The related article determined that the government was going to sell movable property at auction according to accepted procedures and administer the immovable property, placing the revenues they produced, after deducting expenditures, in accounts of local treasury directorates registered in trust for the original owners.

If these people were to return, both their immovable properties and the sums placed in the local treasury directorate accounts would be given back to them. The second article of the regulation dealt with this issue and declared that procedures would be followed according to the provisions of the 20 April 1922 law

> on the abandoned properties of people fleeing or disappearing due to political circumstances or the compulsion of war . . . in the event that they [the properties] are not subject to any claim of rights." If anyone had any claims to these properties, "being satisfied only with recording and identifying the properties, the conclusion of the judgment would be awaited. In the case that there are among the belongings in discussion those which quickly spoil, these will be immediately sold and their value kept in trust in the name of their owners.[18]

According to the fourth article of the 29 March 1923 regulation, properties left by those traveling with travel documents or passports (or both) would not be considered abandoned. This provision is extremely important because in the forthcoming month it would be invalidated by another law (15 April 1923), which meant that the properties of those who left the country by legal means would also be deemed abandoned. Serious confusion was created because the 29 March regulation was intended only for Istanbul and its environs, while the 15 April law was for the whole country.

There are further reasons for confusion and complication. The 20 April 1922 Abandoned Properties Law, which was the basis for a specific regulation for Istanbul (the 29 March 1923 regulation), was annulled by the aforementioned law of 15 April 1923 which also became known as the Liquidation Law. This law was nothing else but the replacement of the Unionist 26 September 1915 law. The reason for this, as we shall discuss further below, was that a new attempt had begun on 14 September 1922 to fundamentally solve the abandoned properties question. The intended target was the Lausanne peace negotiations, as it was desired to avoid difficulties concerning the Armenians' seized properties there. For this reason, it was necessary to revalidate the 26 September law and the 8 November regulation, which together we have called genocidal legislation. This was what took place on 14 September 1922 and 15 April 1923. The most important feature of the 15 April 1923 Liquidation Law was this key point: *no matter how people left their residents/places*, the properties they left would be considered abandoned properties.

To annul the 20 April 1922 Abandoned Properties Law, which formed the basis of the special 29 March 1923 regulation for Istanbul, a new regulation was issued on 29 April 1923, which made the necessary changes to the 29 March 1923 regulation.[19] The first article of this new regulation is extremely important. It stated that the properties of those who left the province of Istanbul prior to 4 November 1922 in any manner and, after that date, those who left without permission from the government, would be subject to liquidation. The properties of those who departed after 4 November 1922 with the permission of the government would not be evaluated in the framework of this law.

The reason for this change is simple. Since the 15 April 1923 law and its most important principle (that the properties of *those who left their places of residence, in whatever manner,* would be seized), entered into force beginning on that date (15 April 1923), it could not be applicable to earlier periods. However, on 4 November 1922 Istanbul came under Turkish sovereignty, and after this date there were people who left the city. Through this change the properties of those who left Istanbul after 4 November 1922, without the permission of the government, could also be seized.

There was only one purpose to all these arrangements. It was to annul the 20 April 1922 Abandoned Properties Law and the regulations which take this law as its basis. It was issued to solve the problems of the Turkish War of Independence. Henceforth, abandoned properties issues after 1919 would also be resolved based on the 26 September 1915 law and 8 November 1915 regulation, which were issued as part of the Armenian Genocide of 1915. Now we can look more closely at this process of returning to the laws made during the Genocide.

The 14 September 1922 Abrogation
of the Property Regulation

The Grand National Assembly of Turkey began to amalgamate procedures connected to abandoned properties created in the period of the
Armenian Genocide, and those in the 1919–22 period, starting on 14
September 1922. In a session on that date, the 12 January 1920 regulation, that we named the Vahdettin Regulation, was annulled. It was
done through an extremely short, one-sentence decree: "The regulation dated 12 January 1920 on the properties subject to liquidation of
people transported to other places is abrogated."[20] Through this decree,
which in practice came to be called the Abrogation of the Property Regulation, the 26 September 1915 law and the 8 November 1915 regulation again came into force and the Republic's process of constructing
laws on the basis of the Ittihadists' genocide laws began.

As seven years had passed since the initial promulgation of these
laws, it was necessary to make some adjustments. The first change was
made on 31 October 1922, with the alteration of some articles of the 8
November 1915 regulation and the removal of others.[21] These changes
concerned the Liquidation Commissions. The commissions henceforth
under the chairmanship of a local treasury official appointed by the
highest-ranking civil servant of the region, would consist of one person
each from the administrative and municipal councils and, if it existed
locally, the chamber of commerce.[22] The new regulation added a fourth
article to the 8 November 1915 rules. According to this new article,
the movable and immovable properties of people who went to foreign
or occupied lands for travel, either before or after the World War, *in
whatever manner* and still had not returned, would be administered by
the government until the return of those people.[23]

In addition to this change, the scope of application of the 1915 law
was broadened. It would include the property of those who left the
country in a new wave of migration after 1918. Another change was
an increase in the wages of the commission members.[24] A new law in
place of the 26 September 1915 law was not issued until 15 April 1923.

Why Was There a Return to the Ittihadist Laws of the Genocide?

The answer to this important question was given during the parliamentary discussions of the abrogation of the Vahdettin Regulation. The aim was clear: the war had been won; there was a good probability that the abandoned properties issue would appear on the agenda of the forthcoming peace negotiations and Turkey could be asked to return the properties to their owners. Yet Turkey could not even tolerate the existence of Armenians inside the country, let alone give back their confiscated properties. The state considered the abandoned properties as an important source of revenue. However, there was an obligation to give back these properties to their owners according to the Vahdettin Regulation, which was still valid. Consequently, it was necessary to abrogate this regulation prior to the commencement of the Lausanne negotiations.

Since the parliamentary discussions on this subject were secret, Finance Minister Fehmi Bey explained all these points in a very open and direct fashion. While the regulation remained in force, the return of all goods and properties that passed into Muslim hands to their original owners would be unavoidable. The Western states would employ pressure on this topic at the approaching Lausanne Peace Conference. In the words of the minister, "I think that if the minorities while this topic is being discussed say we do not want anything else if you carry out once again the provisions which you accepted on this issue and up until today implemented, we will have no answer to give in response."[25] The most thought-provoking point of the minister was that "the treasury [is going to be] obliged to pay the cost of the entire financial and moral responsibility." He said that "the implementation of this regulation is one-tenth of the existing provisions of the law," meaning, in other words, that 90 percent of goods and properties still had not been returned. "However," he continued, "while this regulation exists as law, naturally it should be implemented, [and] they [foreign powers] will pressure us to carry out its provisions. For this reason, the abrogation of the regulation is necessary as soon as possible."[26]

The discussions of the parliamentarians revealed why it was necessary to eliminate this law and, in the contrary case, what would await Turkey. Hakkı Sami Bey, the deputy from Sinop, said, "When we were forming the Assembly here . . . we were unable to find . . . time to deal with such regulations."[27] Trebizond deputy Hasan Bey said, "Peace is near. It is necessary before the problems of peace begin to clear away such things . . . [and] it is necessary to make this regulation decompose from its roots."[28] The words of these two deputies reflected the feelings of all the other deputies who also spoke then.

There is another important reason for the desire to get rid of the Vahdettin Regulation. The finance minister expressed it openly in the secret session devoted to the plunder of Izmir. Abandoned properties were being looted, and the only way to save them from looting was to place them at the disposition of the state.

The Plunder of Izmir and the Independence Tribunals

The looting of abandoned properties was not limited to Armenian properties seized during the Armenian Genocide from 1915 to 1917; perhaps their plunder was in large part completed. In addition to them, the goods and properties belonging to Christians who left the country in the 1919 to 1922 period had been plundered or were being plundered. This plunder took on such great dimensions that the topic was brought to the Assembly and became the cause of serious arguments. At the 25 November 1922 session, a group of deputies who travelled through the Izmir region after the capture of this city proposed the establishment of Independence Tribunals (special courts initially set up to prosecute those opposing the Turkish National Movement) in order to halt plundering in the cities regained from the Greek army.[29]

The topic occupied the agenda of the assembly for a long time. The government proposed establishing temporary criminal courts in place of the Independence Tribunals and protracted discussions took place concerning various options. Some deputies, finding the dimensions of the continuing plunder to be too great and the "strength and power"[30] of normal criminal courts to solve this situation insufficient, defended the necessity of founding Independence Tribunals with special authority in order to "overpower the disgrace of the abandoned properties.[31]" In the end, the government's proposal of criminal courts was rejected, and on 6 December 1922 it was decided to establish three Independence Tribunals to investigate the plunder and lawlessness emerging in the regions freed from occupation and war.[32] However, despite all the legal preparations, due to the dimensions of the looting and the fact that nearly all segments of the population were involved, these courts were never established properly and so never operated.[33]

From the examination of the parliamentary discussions, it becomes clear that everybody was aware of the plunder and its dimensions.

Erzerum deputy Salih Efendi summarized the issue by saying, "Sir, let us not waste our time. Everything was plundered and the matter concluded."[34] Finance Minister Hasan Fehmi Bey's statements, in a long speech in the 27 November 1922 session of the assembly, intended to answer the questions being raised and inform the parliament "about the abandoned properties in liberated lands" that were important for demonstrating the dimensions of the plunder.[35]

Having traveled through the area himself, the minister summarized the situation by saying, "Wretchedness in the liberated lands, plunder and abuse in the liberated lands."[36] The assembly discussions, which began in a public session, were changed to a closed door discussion because of claims that some military officers and parliamentary deputies participated in the looting.[37] The minister in the open session expressed his observations that "some shrewd people . . . entered open houses and settled." He summarized the steps that he took as a representative of the government concerning the abandoned properties as follows: "Immediately dividing the country [Izmir area] into nine zones, directly at each zone . . . I stationed an inspector . . . at each zone, a member of the municipal council, the administrative council of the city, and, as necessary, an abandoned properties official were placed. . . . Immediately an account book was kept of the houses spontaneously being occupied."[38]

Despite all these steps, the minister said that looting occurred even at the hands of some of the appointed officials and "several of these [were sent to] the courthouse for being caught in the act outright." He confessed that "there were people, men from all classes of people being arrested in the act of crime." The words of the minister were enriched with examples of looting he personally witnessed, and when he was relating the plundering of figs by villagers in the province of Aydın he was cut off by shouts of *helal olsun* (take it with God's blessing).[39]

Among those who spoke in response to the minister, there were those who openly supported plundering, saying, "After not going overseas— of those who are of this nation, let whoever steals, steal—let it fall in the pocket of this nation; it still belongs to the treasury. Let us not hold grudges. Only do not go too far." The deputy of the assembly said, "Let what the people, the soldiers stole continuously be God's blessing." The same deputy found "the misappropriation conducted by the Abandoned Properties Commissions" to be inappropriate.[40]

The minister's remarks concerning abandoned properties made it clear that "the iron shutters of sealed stores [were] broken, the wall of the building [was] perforated . . . which was accepted as a warehouse for abandoned properties."[41] The dimensions of the plunder were so great that returning the properties or their equivalent values to their true owners, or the payment of damages by the government, was not possible. The deputy from Trebizond, Ali Şükrü Bey, described the situation during the 4 December session with a Turkish saying: "The man taking his horse passed Üsküdar." In other words, it is too late now: "There is no possibility of [the plundered goods] being gotten back."[42]

In this session, the minister Hasan Fehmi Bey openly explained why the 12 January 1920 Regulation was annulled. However great the dimensions of the plunder may have been due to the absence of a fully functioning state mechanism, a very significant quantity of abandoned goods still remained. The state wanted to prevent it from being plundered so that it itself could make use of it directly. The comparison the minister made between the present situation and the 1915–17 Armenian deportations and plundering of goods was very interesting. The minister said, "Gentlemen, a deportation was conducted previously. Administrative machinery was in place especially for all of Anatolia locally. What was the amount of money recorded in the accounts of the local treasury directorates compared with the amount of money lost as a result of the deportation? It was one hundred compared to ten thousand."[43] Hasan Fehmi Bey thought that even if "the possibility of managing centime by centime" did not exist because of plundering, the abandoned properties constituted an extremely important source of revenue for the treasury and budget shortfalls could be remedied by means of it. The minister had hopes that with, "excluding the burning part [of the city], the movable portion of abandoned properties" in Izmir alone, "our deficits can be met from the start of the national fighting until the end of this year."[44]

If the movable properties could close the budget deficit it is not hard to imagine what the state could gain if the immovable properties were also included. It is useful to quote Kütahya deputy Ragıp Bey's words in order to understand the wealth obtained in Izmir: "Honorable friends, if the size of the army entering Izmir . . . was several times larger, and all of the people of Izmir participated, [and] if the looting lasted two months, the abandoned properties in Izmir would not be exhausted. You can estimate the quantity of these abandoned properties from this. In other words, if a looting procession of one hundred thousand people continued for one month, it still could not be exhausted."[45]

Hasan Fehmi Bey continued, saying that "the wealth buried in places where there was fire, and the safes being taken out from beneath debris, have not arrived yet." He pointed out that the calculations he was making did not include immovable properties. He defined the use of the latter as "a very great matter, a very fundamental issue," and said that they were in the process of preparing a law about it. Immovable properties could also be used in the settlement of Muslim refugees.[46]

Deputy of Karahisar-ı Sahib (today's Afyon) Mehmet Şükrü Bey summarized the policy the government wished to follow in this manner: "As [the minister] today described in a tacit manner, it is my understanding that, in the face of the news of misappropriations that reach us in waves, what happened has happened [i.e., nothing can be done]; after this at least so that the things that the government has been able to take under its control and protection are not misappropriated and so that officials do not become rich, the necessary steps must be taken." The minister responded to this by saying, "The maximum of all types of precautions which are going to prevent misappropriation has been taken."[47] The state henceforth was itself ready to seize the abandoned properties.

It can be seen, as a result of all these reasons which we have touched upon, why the annulment of the 12 January 1920 Regulation was seen as "a very inevitable and pressing issue."[48]

Return to the Ittihadist Mentality: The 15 April Law and 29 April Regulation of 1923

The 26 September 1915 law and 8 November 1915 regulation entered validity again, together with the 14 September 1922 Abrogation of the Property Regulation, though some changes were necessary to adapt to new conditions. These changes, which were delayed for many reasons, were first made through the 15 April 1923 Liquidation Law.[49] This law, with nine articles in all, took as its basis the 26 September 1915 law but formulated various modifications to it. Its seventh article annulled the 20 April 1922 Abandoned Properties Law. Articles 2, 4, 7, and 8 of the 26 September 1915 law were changed, while the ninth article was removed and a new article added.

The sixth article is perhaps the most important of the newly added ones. This broadened the field of application of the law, including in it those who fled or disappeared after 1919. Henceforth, the 26 September 1915 law and the 15 April 1923 law with its changes would be applied together, "to movable and immovable properties, debts and assets abandoned by those disappearing in any way whatsoever, or leaving a place, or fleeing to foreign and occupied lands, or Istanbul or connected places."[50]

With this change, people who it was designated would be covered by the law, as defined in the first and sixth articles, would be identified as those who are *"fugitives, lost,* or *fled* to other places"[51] [italics are ours]. This would form the basis of all civil lawsuits in the Republican era, and it would be primarily Armenians who were referred to by this definition.

The 15 April law's first article is essentially equivalent to the second article of the 26 September 1915 law with some changes, which has extraordinary importance. It annulled the provision existing in the 1915 law, which would return to the original owners the money remaining after the liquidation of their properties. It calculated that people who had already fled and disappeared would not return. In its stead, based on the kind of movable and immovable property, records would be made in the Pious Foundations Ministry or Finance Ministry, and "the sum that will remain after liquidation from the values at which the properties would be appraised [would be registered as] revenue in trust *in the name of* the aforementioned owners" [italics are ours]. In any lawsuits that might arise concerning the properties, the Treasury would be the adversary.[52]

The important point is that, after this date, in official texts concerning abandoned properties the identifications 26 September 1915 and 15 April 1923 would be used together. Consolidation with the Ittihadist regime was complete.

The last step to be taken was, naturally, the issuance of a regulation concerning the application of this law. This was the regulation of 29 April 1923 number 2455, which took the place of the 8 November 1915 regulation.[53] It was almost the same as the 8 November 1915 regulation and, like the latter, consisted of twenty-five articles. The extended scope of the law was repeated in the first article, which used the expression "people being transported or who in any manner whatsoever by going from the place at which they are located to another place disappear, or are leaving a place."[54]

The distinction between *heyet* (committee) and *komisyon* (commission) was identically maintained, and the duties of both were separately detailed. According to the regulation: the day after this regulation was officially communicated, in every county in which the aforementioned people were to be found, a committee would be formed by that locality's highest-ranking civil servant under the chairmanship of that locality's highest-ranking treasury official with one member each from the tax, title deed registry, population registry administrations, and local police, and, if it existed locally, a foundations administration. The first five articles described in detail what work the committees were to do.[55]

The second part of the regulation, again like the 8 November regulation, concerned the commissions to be formed and their duties, making a few small changes. The activities of the commissions basically remained the same. The power to seize all the money, goods, and other properties of departed people was given. The commissions would conclude all the transactions concerning the assets and liabilities of these people. The provision existing in the 8 November 1915 regulation that "the values of properties the owners of which are not known are going to be registered in the name of the village or neighborhood in which the articles are located and later will be sent by the government to the place where the people of the aforementioned village or neighborhood were settled," was changed since it had no meaning any longer. With the new arrangement, the prices of these properties would be registered as revenue in accounts of the local treasury directorate.[56]

A Brief Evaluation

Throughout the Republican era, abandoned property transactions were carried out according to the 15 and 29 April 1923 law and regulation. Here, again, the dominant logic of the Ittihadist era was maintained. Only the provision that the sum remaining after the liquidation of properties would be returned to the original owners was eliminated. Henceforth, it was considered that those people who fled and disappeared would no longer return. The state issued a detailed list of properties belonging to disappeared people and prepared detailed record books about them. After concluding the necessary transactions concerning eliminating debts and assets, it registered them in the treasuries of the Finance Ministry and Pious Foundations Ministry. Like other immovable properties belonging to the Finance Ministry or Pious Foundations Ministry, these would be managed by means of administrative councils.

The most important point here is that all of these transactions are being conducted in the names of the disappeared people. For this reason, the question of what would happen to these properties if the disappeared people once more appeared is an important one. As a matter of fact, in the Lausanne Treaty the provision was accepted that if these lost people appeared their properties, or the equivalent values of the latter, would be returned to them and appropriate arrangements were made accordingly in Turkish domestic law. This is the chief tension, which we mentioned above, that exists in the legal system. The state did not advance the claim that the rights of the disappeared people over their properties were completely lost, but instead continued to keep them registered as the owners of the latter. For this reason, the potential exists in the law for the right of the original owners to demand their properties or equivalent values back. This situation will appear more clearly after the Lausanne Treaty takes effect.

Abandoned Properties and National Tax Obligations (Tekalif-i Milliye)

Before closely examining the great changes the Treaty of Lausanne brought about in the practices concerning abandoned properties, it is worth mentioning an important detail of the Tekâlif-i Milliye national tax obligations orders. This topic is important for demonstrating the Nationalist movement's viewpoint concerning the Armenians and Greeks and the properties that they left behind. The National Tax Obligations Orders were issued by command of Mustafa Kemal, head of the Grand National Assembly and commander in chief of the Turkish Nationalist army, in order to finance the War of Independence against Greece. The abandoned properties were also seen as an important source of financing for the war, and Mustafa Kemal attempted to take advantage of them.

The sixth of the ten orders of the National Tax Obligations Orders directly concerned abandoned properties, stating, in particular, how they must be seized. The points of this order, which consisted of five articles, are as follows: Article 1 stated that "the abandoned properties existing in various places that are goods or foodstuff will be impounded by the National Tax Obligations Commissions, their quantity will be determined and their value estimated, [and] a record in *kuruş*'s [piastre] will be given to the local treasury directorate."[57] The second article ordered that the National Tax Obligations Commissions keep "an orderly record book with three copies" on the abandoned properties that were taken in this fashion.[58] The fourth article declared that those who attempted during the impoundment of abandoned properties to carry out abuses and usurp properties for themselves would be accused of the crime of betrayal of the homeland.[59]

Properties taken according to the National Tax Obligations orders were akin to taking on a debt or loan, and the government of the

Grand National Assembly, in a law issued on 12 April 1923, decided to pay that debt. Finance Minister Hasan Fehmi stated that the value of the National Tax Obligations was 6,361,634 liras, of which 75 percent had not been repaid.[60] One year later the topic again appeared on the agenda during budget discussions. The government presented the draft of a law to repay all treasury debts from the period of 1 July 1908 to 31 December 1923. The question of whether the Armenians and Greeks should also be repaid came up during the discussion of this bill. Some deputies were concerned that the article of the law was too obscure and that Muslims would be mistreated.

The head of the related parliament commission and the former finance minister, Hasan Fehmi Bey, spoke to dissipate this worry. He explained that "the intent of the article is not substantially to provide compensation for the National Tax Obligations and War Tax receipts of the Greeks and Armenians who were deported and lost."[61] Any attempt to pay them would be impossible to realize. In the words of the minister, "Prior to the world war Muslims did not engage in commerce . . . Consequently, the major part of the National Tax Obligations were taken from them [Greeks and Armenians]; the receipts are in their hands." If an attempt were made to pay them, it would cost millions. "Today, in my estimation, just in the interior of Anatolia, there is probably not less than four or five hundred thousand liras in the hands of non-Muslims. Up until today not a single one of these [debts] has been given [repaid] or has been settled." Consequently it was necessary to arrange the article in such a way that Christians could not take advantage of their right to be repaid.[62]

The minister spoke very candidly since the discussion was during a closed session. He said, "A remedy has been thought of so that the Greeks [and] Armenians do not benefit from the worth of these National Tax Obligations official receipts. However, we [Turks] were not able to say this openly as Greek and Armenian. Various forms and formula were written. Investigations were conducted on various manners. Finally we found this least objectionable or unobjectionable method."[63]

What is significant is that they took the Abandoned Properties Laws in 1915 as a model for the solution they sought. Finance Minister Hasan Fehmi said, "Remember, please, that at one time an abandoned properties law was legislated. It said that the government would liquidate the properties of those who fled. I ask you, friends. . . . Which government official liquidated even one Muslim's properties? The intent [of this law] is to disguise these two elements [Greeks and Armenians] . . . Their properties were subject to liquidation." After the minister promised, in the secret session of the assembly of that period, that the finance minister was going to "assure that with this article, the law is not going to include those Muslims who are fleeing and disappearing," he declared that this law was issued "in general against the world." This was what was being done at the moment.[64]

A separate procedure also took place that confirmed that the expressions used in the assembly were intended to mean Armenians and Greeks. The treasury minister sent to the provincial financial administrators a secret order in which he said this article "only pertained to Greeks and Armenians." If an Armenian or a Greek applied to them, the *defterdar*s (provincial financial administrators) were to declare, "We are investigating; we are conducting an inquiry," and thus delay until the period of the law's applicability passed. In the word of Konya deputy Refik Bey, "We met with the minister of the treasury too. After promising that we would issue a secret communication, we accepted this article."[65]

Refik Bey was the person who desired the topic "to be discussed in a secret session;" in his speech he concluded that "the intention was realized."[66] In fact, the attitude of the Republican regime concerning the Greeks and Armenians and their properties was so clear that no commentary is necessary about it. No payment was going to be made to Christian compatriots with official state documents as receipts in their hands, and their loans would not be repaid. The only sorrow of the assembly's deputies was that the Jews were not included in this law. This topic, though, was left to the authority of the government to manage.

An additional point became clear through the discussions. It was feared that with the signing of the Lausanne Treaty, and opening a door for the Armenians, some of them might wish to come back and claim their properties. Mustafa Abdülhalik (Renda),[67] who played an important role in the Armenian Genocide, was interior minister and summarized the views of the state on this in only one sentence: "We will cause difficulties as much as possible for those who do not belong to us [our nation]."[68]

There is one truth that all the changes made to the laws and regulations show. Turkey knew what was expected of it at Lausanne, and made the necessary preparations so that it was ready. İsmet İnönü, the chief of the Turkish delegation at Lausanne and second president of Turkey, openly spoke of this point in the foreword that he wrote for the minutes of the Lausanne proceedings published by Seha Meray in 1969. He summarized the entire Lausanne negotiations: "It was expected that great opposition would arise at the conference because of the minorities, with the habits that arise from history. The issue of the minorities was actually solved before going to the conference. For this reason, it was not possible to pressure Turkey."[69] Now we can look more closely at the Lausanne negotiations.

Notes

1. Zeki Sarıhan, *Kurtuluş Savaşı Günlüğü, Erzurum Kongresinden TBMM'ye*, Vol. 2 (Ankara: Öğretmen Dünyası Yayınları, 1984), 419.
2. TBMM, *TBMM Zabıt Ceridesi*, Period 1, Assembly Year 1, Vol. 1 (Ankara: TBMM Matbaası, 1940), 37, 58, 72, 203.
3. The law considering all decrees taken after 16 March was accepted after lengthy discussions on 17 June 1336 [1920] (TBMM, *TBMM Zabıt Ceridesi*, Period 1, Assembly Year 1, Vol. 2, 132).
4. TBMM, *TBMM Zabıt Ceridesi*, Period 1, Assembly Year 3, Vol. 29, 161.
5. Murat Koraltürk, *Ekonominin Türkleştirilmesi* (Istanbul: İletişim Yayınları, 2011), 56.
6. The Grand National Assembly of Turkey, which began work in 1920, held a lot of discussions and listened to many proposals on the subject of properties left behind by those fleeing due to war. For more detailed information on this subject, see Eroğlu, "Tehcirden Milli Mücadeleye Ermeni Malları (1915–1922)," 170–78.
7. Kardeş, *"Tehcir" ve Emval-i Metruke Mevzuatı*, 125–26. The full name of the regulation is Hali Gaybubette Olan Anasırı Gayrimüslimenin Göndereceği Vekâletnamelerin Kabul Edilmemesi Hakkında Kararname [Regulation on the nonacceptance of the powers of attorney sent by non-Muslim elements who are absent].
8. Ibid.
9. Ibid., 129–30.
10. Ibid., 95–98.
11. Ibid., 98.
12. Müdürlüğü, *Milli Emlak Muamelelerine Müteallik Mevzuat*, 158.
13. Ibid.
14. BCA/30.10.218.472.11.2, Chief of the General Staff to the Presidency of the Council of Ministers 27 September 1922.
15. BCA/30.10.218.406.6.1.2, Hüseyin Rıfat in the name of the President of the Council of Ministers to the Presidency of the Council of Ministers, 28 September 1922.
16. Kardeş, *"Tehcir" ve Emval-i Metruke Mevzuatı*, 153. The full name of the law was Bilâd-ı Meşguleden Olan İstanbul'dan Firar ve Tagayyüb Eden Eşhâsın Emvâl-i Metrukesi Hakkında Talimatname [Regulation on abandoned properties of people who fled and disappeared from Istanbul, which is one of the occupied cities].
17. Ibid.
18. Ibid.
19. Ibid., 128. The full name of the regulation is İstanbul'dan Firar veyahut Tagayyüp Etmiş Olan Eşhasın Menkul ve Gayr-ı menkul Malları Hakkında Yapılacak Muameleye Dair Kararname [Regulation on the procedure to be carried out concerning movable and immovable goods of people who fled or disappeared from Istanbul].
20. Kardeş, *"Tehcir" ve Emval-i Metruke Mevzuatı*, 122. The full name of the decree is Ahar Mahallere Nakledilmiş Eşhasın Tasfiyeye Tâbi Emvali Hakkında Mevcut Kararnamenin Reddine Dair Heyet-i Umumiye Kararı [Decree of the general

assembly on the abrogation of the existing regulation on assets subject to liquidation of people who were transported to other places].

21. Ibid., 126. The full name of this regulation is Mahall-i Ahara Nakledilen Eşhasın Emval-i Metrukesi Hakkında 17 Zilkade 1333 [26 Eylül 1915] Tarihli Kanun-u Muvakkatin Suver-i İcraiyesine Mütedair 26 Teşrinievvel 1331 [8 Kasım 1915] Tarihli Nizamnamenin Bazı Mevaddını Muaddil Kararname [Regulation modifying some articles of the regulation dated 26 Teşrinievvel 1331 [8 Kasım 1915] concerning manners of execution of the temporary law dated 17 Zilkade 1333 [26 Eylül 1915] on abandoned properties of people who were transported to other places].
22. Ibid., 127.
23. Ibid., 127–28.
24. Ibid., 127.
25. *TBMM Gizli Celse Zabıtları*, Period 1, Assembly Year 3, Vol. 3, 769.
26. Ibid., 769.
27. Ibid., 776.
28. Ibid., 773.
29. TBMM, *TBMM Zabıt Ceridesi*, Period 1, Assembly Year 3, Vol. 25 (Ankara: TBMM Matbaası, 1960), 65. The article connected with the legislative proposal is the following: "[P]rohibiting the boundless lawlessness resulting from the abandoned properties, the immediate sending of Independence Tribunals to the liberated province in order to assure the preservation of the rights of the Treasury, and punish those who were involved in treachery to the homeland during the period of occupation together with those afflicted by this moral plague."
30. Ibid., 65.
31. Ibid., 65.
32. Ibid., 167–80, 187–204.
33. Ergün Aybars, *İstiklâl Mahkemeleri* (Ankara: Bilgi Yayınevi, 1975), 185–88.
34. TBMM, *T. B. M. M. Zabıt Ceridesi*, Period 1, Assembly Year 3, Vol. 25 (Ankara: TBMM Matbaası, 1960), 69.
35. Ibid., 69.
36. Ibid., 97.
37. The discussions that took placed in the closed session indicate that some deputies and officers entered empty homes and settled there, while First Army Commander Nurettin Pasha used bombs to explode safes in some banks and usurp the money they contained (*TBMM Gizli Celse Zabıtları*, Period 1, Assembly Year 3, Vol. 3, 1134).
38. TBMM, *T. B. M. M. Zabıt Ceridesi*, Period 1, Assembly Year 3, Vol. 25, 99–102.
39. Ibid.
40. Ibid. 142.
41. Ibid., 147.
42. Ibid., 195.
43. *TBMM Gizli Celse Zabıtları*, Period 1, Assembly Year 3, Vol. 3, 1140.
44. Ibid., 1131.
45. Ibid., 1137.
46. Ibid., 1131.
47. Ibid., 1133.
48. Ibid., 769.
49. Müdürlüğü, *Milli Emlak Muamelelerine Müteallik Mevzuat*, 159–161; in addition, see Kardeş, *"Tehcir" ve Emval-i Metruke Mevzuatı*, 100–104. The full name of the law is Ahar Mahallere Nakledilen Eşhasın Emval ve Düyun ve Matlubât-ı Metrukesi Hakkındaki 17 Zilkade 1333 [26 Eylül 1915] ve 13 Eylül 1331 [26 Eylül

1915] Tarihli Kanun-ı Muvakkatin Bazı Mevaddı ile 20 Nisan 1338 [20 Nisan 1922] Tarihli Emvâl-i Metruke Kanununu Muaddil Kanun [Law modifying the 20 April 1338 dated abandoned properties law and several articles of the 17 Zilkade 1333 and 26 September 1331 dated temporary law on the possessions and debts and abandoned debts of people transported to other places].

50. Kardeş, "Tehcir" ve Emval-i Metruke Mevzuatı, 103. For full text see. Kardeş, "Tehcir" ve Emval-I Metruke Mevzuatı, 100–04.

51. Ibid., 103.

52. Ibid., 101.

53. Ibid., 154–164. Its full name was 13 Eylül 1331 Tarihli Kanun-ı Muvakkat ile İşbu Kanunun Bazı Mevaddını Muaddil 15 Nisan 1339 Tarihli Kanunun Suver-i Tatbikiyesini Mübeyyin Talimatname [Regulation that explains the manners of application of the 15 April 1339 law modifying the 26 September 1915 dated temporary law and some articles of this law].

54. Ibid., 154–55.

55. Ibid., 154–56.

56. Ibid., 163.

57. Serpil Sürmeli, Milli Mücadele'de Tekâlif-i Milliye Emirleri (Ankara: AKDTYK Atatürk Araştırma Merkezi, 1998), 68–69.

58. Ibid., 69.

59. Ibid.

60. Nevzat Onaran, Emvâl-i Metrûke Olayı, Osmanlı'da ve Cumhuriyette Ermeni Mallarının Türkleştirilmesi (Istanbul: Belge Yayınları, 2010), 186–92.

61. TBMM Gizli Celse Zabıtları, Period 2, Assembly Year 2, Vol. 4, 429.

62. Ibid., 429.

63. Ibid., 429.

64. Ibid., 429.

65. Ibid., 430.

66. Ibid., 430.

67. On Renda's role during the Armenian Genocide, see Vartkes Yeghiayan, Malta Belgeleri: Türk Savaş Suçluları Hakkında İngiltere Dışişleri Bakanlığı Belgeleri (Istanbul: Belge Yayınları, 2007), 266–81.

68. TBMM Gizli Celse Zabıtları, Period 2, Assembly Year 2, Vol. 4, 430–31.

69. Seha L. Meray, Lozan Barış Konferansı, Tutanaklar-Belgeler, Vol. 1 (Istanbul: Yapı Kredi Yayınları, Istanbul, 1993), xi.

CHAPTER 4

THE TREATY OF LAUSANNE
A TURNING POINT

T he Treaty of Lausanne[1] must be accepted as a partial turning point
for the abandoned properties issue, and indeed, as shall be discussed
further below, the Constitutional Court of Turkey in a 1963 decision
noted it as such.

The importance of this treaty is through it Turkey promised to
return, to Armenians who continued to live within its boundar-
ies, their impounded properties. Laws and regulations issued later
treated the date the treaty came into force, 6 August 1924, as a
milestone. The issue of the properties of Armenians residing abroad
remained open to interpretation, despite the fact that the various
articles of the treaty, including those pertaining to nationality, were
very clear. As we will discuss below, although various articles did
propound the principle of giving these individuals either the properties or their equivalent values, by interpreting these articles in a
different manner Turkey did not make such restitution. Moreover,
it thwarted the return of Armenians to Turkey to obtain their properties. It was as if Turkey was erecting fortifications everywhere to
prevent Armenians from entering the country.

The Abandoned Properties Question
in the Negotiations and Treaty

Directly or indirectly, four different segments can be identified in the Lausanne Treaty as relevant to the abandoned properties question. In the order of the articles of the treaty themselves, first are the provisions of Articles 30 and 36 connected to citizenship in Part I Political Clauses, Section II "Nationality"; second, the provisions of Articles 37 to 45 in Part I, Section III "Protection of Minorities"; third, the provisions of Articles 65–72 of Part III Economic Clauses, Section I "Property, Rights and Interests." According to Articles 65–72, it was decided to form a Mixed Arbitral Tribunal. The duties and manner of operation of this tribunal were defined in Articles 92–98 of Part III, Section V "Mixed Arbitral Tribunal." The fourth and final segment relevant to abandoned properties is the appendix titled Notice and Protocol on the Declaration of Amnesty.

It can be seen from reading the minutes of the Lausanne Treaty that aside from several occasions at the Minorities Subcommittee where the issue came up somewhat indirectly, there was practically no direct discussion of the Abandoned Properties Laws. However, as can be understood from the list we prepared above and the discussions summarized below, the topic actually was touched on throughout the treaty. Like a ghost, it was everywhere and it remained on the agenda of the negotiations until their very last day.

For this reason it is necessary to correct a very widespread and dominant error on this topic. In Turkey, the issues of non-Muslims generally are identified as minority questions, and it is asserted that this topic was basically covered in Articles 37–45 of the Treaty of Lausanne, in Part I, Section III. However, this viewpoint is deficient and wrong. It would be more correct to approach the issue as one of Christian compatriots inherited from the Ottomans. If their citizenship was not removed through a special decision of the Council of Ministers, Christians who were Ottoman citizens according to the 1869 Ottoman Citizenship Law would have continued to remain citizens of the Republic of Turkey until 1964. For this reason the issue of non-Muslims, and Christians in particular, is not the so-called minority question of the Republic of Turkey, but rather is a basic issue connected to its foundation.

Mass and Individual Repatriations
and the Armenian Homeland

It is possible to sum up the negotiations conducted at Lausanne that are connected to this study under four major headings. First, liberty of language, religion, and education for minorities continuing to live in Turkey. Second, a general amnesty for crimes committed after 1 November 1914. Third, uniting families torn apart after 1 November 1914, and the return of their properties to those who were deprived of them. And, fourth, Liberty of migration and domestic travel at the discretion of the minorities.[2]

The most important of these issues was the return of the Christians (Armenians, Greeks, Syrian Orthodox, and Chaldeans) who had left Turkey. Three types of return were possible. First, the creation of an Armenian homeland to be located somewhere in Turkey, and settlement there (a similar process would take place for Syrian Orthodox and Chaldeans); second, a mass repatriation on condition that it would be in a dispersed fashion with no concentrations of population in any particular location; third, even if mass repatriation were to be prohibited, the return of individuals.

In fact, Turkey's policy concerning Christians in general, and Armenians in particular, was very clear prior to Lausanne. The policy was that any Christians outside of the borders of the Turkish state, that were being newly created, were not permitted to enter, and if possible it also expelled those who remained inside Turkey's borders.

İsmet İnönü went to Lausanne with a fourteen-article directive. The first and ninth articles of the directive were immediately relevant for this study: 1. *Eastern border*: there can be no question of an Armenian Homeland; if there is, the negotiations will be cut off. . . . 9. *Minorities*: the basis is exchange.[3] On the Armenian homeland issue in particular, Turkey "is adamant to the point of willing to take the risk of war . . . If the Armenian Homeland is desired . . . The negotiations will immediately be halted."[4] Thus, the proposal of such a demand would be considered as a threat to snatch land away from Turkey and break the unity of the country, and would lead to an end to negotiations.

Several examples can be given. During the general session of 31 December 1922, İsmet Pasha said, "Turkey is obliged to consider the separation of land which is part of the country in order to found an Armenian Homeland as a new attempt at dividing Turkey . . . Turkey . . . Does not have a handsbreath of land which can be separated from the mother country."[5] During the discussion in the subcommission on the topic of the general amnesty, the Turkish representative committee declared, "In an open and clear fashion to all questions directed to it, whether on the topic of . . . Armenians or Assyrian-Chaldeans . . . That it considered these not to be discussible."[6] Consequently, the

Turkish committee left the negotiating session at which it was desired to discuss such issues.[7]

Turkey refused the demand for an Armenian homeland, but the questions of whether Armenians could have the right to return en masse and settle in a dispersed fashion, or to return as individuals, continued to be discussed until the last days of the Lausanne negotiations. Turkey's position on this topic was clear. Prime Minister Rauf Bey gave the committee explicit instructions on 17 December 1922. He said, "I submit that we cannot agree to the return of Armenian refugees who left our lands, creating many incidents."[8]

The mass return of the Armenians was resisted by Turkey until the very end of the negotiations. It was discussed mostly in the context of the general amnesty. Since Turkey did not want the return of the Armenians, it attempted to keep this issue out of the general amnesty negotiations.

The Allies objected that the refusal to allow repatriation was contrary to the meaning and spirit of the general amnesty as well as contrary to the rights of the minorities.[9] In the words of the Italian delegate, not giving permission for repatriation meant to condemn "thousands of people who remained forced to leave Turkey without passports because they were unable to carry out several procedures to perpetual exile and the confiscation of their properties. . . . [Moreover,] these people left their homes for political reasons; and the general amnesty, before anyone else, must be applied to them."[10] During the negotiations, İsmet Pasha declared he was "astonished at the Allies' attempts to discuss, again, a question which was definitively solved during the last ten years. . . . To accept the desire of the Allies is going to mean again to give permission for the coming of immigrants and the creation of new difficulties."[11]

The most heated discussion of the topic took place at the 4 June 1923 session. Turkey insistently repeated its desire to treat the question of the return of the Armenians domestically, "keeping it outside of international discussions and only within the authority of the Turkish government."[12] On the other hand, both French and British representatives wanted guarantees that Turkey would not oppose the return of the Armenians. Turkey, however, was extremely determined. In İsmet Pasha's words, "The Turkish government . . . [is not going to be subject to] any new ruling."[13] At a certain point, the British representative declared, "Thousands of Armenians have been dispersed to neighboring countries. It is necessary to know whether permission will be granted for them to return to their homes." İsmet Pasha responded that "no obligation will be accepted on this topic."[14]

Turkey's main argument was that of national security concerns. According to the Turkish representative committee, it was impossible to even discuss the return of Armenians, who had caused great harm to Turkey. They participated in revolts and rebellions during the world war and afterwards, as well as in activities behind the war lines. İsmet Pasha said, "The desire for permission to be given for the return of one hundred thousand Armenians casts the question into something completely different; in this form, the problem in question directly concerns the security of the state." Turkey's "acceptance of an obligation which is going to limit its freedom to act concerning the defense of its security" is not possible. For this reason, the Turkish committee "does not wish to study the question of the mass return to Turkey of people who left Turkey."[15]

The result of Turkey's unbending stance was the closure of the topic without reaching any result, or, more exactly, the exclusion of the question of the mass repatriation of Armenians from the scope of the general amnesty. The issue concluded with the complaint of the British representative that Turkey's position destroyed "the hope of Armenians to return to their homes," and the lament of the French representative saying, "With very great sorrow I was stupefied by the stance of the Turkish Representative Committee."[16]

After having such success in preventing the Armenian homeland or mass repatriation of Armenians, Turkey encountered difficulties in attempting to prohibit the individual return of Armenians. During negotiations on this topic the Turkish side first said that, according to Turkish law, anybody obtaining foreign citizenship was required to leave Turkey, so that "according to Turkish law, those who lost Turkish nationality could no longer enter the country of Turkey." However, after objections were made, Turkey had to take a step backward and accept "the necessity of the consideration of former Turkish citizens [in other countries] as in the situation of other foreigners and this topic being connected to the question of a more general nature of the regime to be applied to foreigners."[17]

Turkey, forced to accept in principle repatriation on an individual basis, wished to reserve for itself the right to determine to whom it would give the right of entry. During the 4 June 1923 session discussed above, Rıza Nur declared, "Coming to the people left out of the agreement [on population exchange], the Turkish government, like any government, reserves the right to take security measures against revolutionaries, conspirators, and in general bad elements, in addition to elements which cause disturbances. Naturally, those who keep to themselves and are innocent, together with those who do not stir up trouble, remain outside the scope of this notice."[18] In the same session, İsmet İnönü repeated the principle that "if a few Armenians were to get up and come to Turkey, they would not be prosecuted. . . . People who do not stir up trouble will be able to freely return to Turkey."[19]

İnönü reported the situation the same day, 4 June, to Ankara finding that the British representative Horace Rumbold interpreted the discussion to mean "no obstacle remained to the return of the Armenians." And İnönü correctly perceived that the Allies "won't insist [any further]" on the issue of the repatriation of the Armenians. According to İsmet Pasha, "If this issue is not provoked anew in another connection, the question of the return of the Armenian refugees . . . [must be considered] closed." He stated that "the return of quiet compatriots who are not of the elements of disturbance, revolution and conspiracy is considered normal," while "no promise for return in a mass fashion" was given.[20]

The topic again came up during the 17 July 1923 session in connection with the general amnesty issue, and the Allies insisted that the Armenians should be permitted to return. İsmet Pasha closed the topic by saying, "The Turkish Representative Committee expressed its view in earlier meetings concerning refugee Armenians. The Turkish Representative Committee is of the opinion that a return anew to this topic cannot provide any benefit." The Armenians' "return to Turkey, is dependent on the permission of the Turkish government, and this permission only can be given to those who keep to themselves and in the past did not have bad behavior."[21]

İsmet Pasha reported the situation to Ankara the same day by telegraph, writing, "The . . . committee of the conference concluded its last meeting and all matters were closed . . . They made a total and final attack on the question of the return of the Armenian refugees. We said in a clear manner that we cannot make a commitment for the return of the Armenian refugees. The argument ended in this way."[22]

The argument may have ended, but the issue was not solved. İsmet Pasha summed up the matter in his memoirs years later as "those who went and left the country can come. Everyone can come. But we could not accept harmful people who in every way violated the security of the country with some bad movements like revolutionaries, insurgents, [and] conspirators." He said that "the government must give permission . . ." and "the government had to determine" who will come.[23] The practice of the government, however, was the exact opposite of this. Turkey pronounced all Armenians, without exception, to be "harmful people" and did not permit them to enter the country. This situation after Lausanne was going to lead to serious diplomatic crises between countries.

A Plan to Expel the Armenian Population

According to the directive prepared while Turkey was getting ready for the Lausanne Treaty negotiations, Turkey planned to expel the Armenians remaining within its borders by means of a population exchange.[24] As soon as İsmet Pasha arrived in Lausanne, he began to work on the topic of what was called the exchange of minorities. He met with American and British representatives. They asked with whom he would exchange the Armenians and how. When reporting his first impressions of the negotiations, İsmet İnönü said, "In my opinion, it is not possible to propound the expulsion of the Armenians outside the country against the world," and proposed that the discussion of population exchange be limited only to Greeks. He also made an important request: "I categorically request that at this time new deportations and exiles not be conducted from Anatolia."[25]

The answer given on 28 November 1922 declared that a definite decision had been made on the issue. It stated, "The Council of Ministers intends and has decided on the exchange of the Armenians in Turkey with Turks in Armenia, and that the Turkish Orthodox stay in the country, on the condition that they do not claim a privileged right, sir."[26] On 4 December 1922 the same decision was repeated: "The point of view of the Council of Ministers concerning local Armenians and Orthodox Greeks was communicated in a telegram dated 28 November. Our opinion is for the exchange of local Armenians with Turks in Armenia, and that the Turkish Orthodox stay in the country on condition that they do not claim a privileged right."[27]

Ankara's firm stance left İsmet Pasha in a difficult position. In a telegram he sent on 6 December, he wrote about the disadvantages to negotiations with the governments of Russia and Armenia. To negotiate with Armenians meant "to make the eastern borders and the Moscow treaty a topic of discussion with them," while to negotiate with Russians would lead to "their participation in the Straits and other issues." According to the pasha, "neither could be done and therefore there was no interlocutor to make the exchange of the Armenians a topic of discussion." For this reason, İsmet Pasha said, "I do not see anything else that can be done for the minorities besides the exchange of the Greeks and the others staying in the country."[28]

Prime Minister Rauf Bey answered, "The opinion concerning the exchange of the Armenians with the Turks in Turkey is the decision of the Council of Ministers. . . . Today again [after] discussing [this] in the meeting of the Council of Ministers, I will immediately present the result of the discussion." He later reported, "I discussed again the exchange of the Armenians at the Council of Ministers. As a result, acting according to the proposal of your excellence was approved, sir."[29] İsmet Pasha's advice was accepted and the exchange of the Armenians was abandoned.

The Question of the Belongings That Were Left Behind

After seeing the question of the return of Christians, in particular the Armenians, partially solved, what was Turkey going to do concerning confiscated properties? On this issue, Turkey wanted to act on the principle of "non-intervention of anybody from the outside." At the 31 December 1922 session of the First Commission in Lausanne, İsmet Pasha summarized the basis of this policy as follows. "Ensuring the freedom of movement of the minorities and guaranteeing their ownership of movable and immovable properties . . . in compliance with the line of behavior adopted by the Turkish government are topics that Turkish laws have regulated and will continue to regulate in a fashion to give complete satisfaction."[30]

Turkey's goal was not to have to sign any international binding provision concerning abandoned properties. However, this was extremely difficult in connection with the question of nationality and reparations since a large portion of the surviving Armenians lived outside of Turkey, and Turkey did not give permission for mass repatriation. Armenians living within the borders of signatory states came under the protection of those states, which began to demand the Armenians' rights. This soon became a serious issue between Turkey and the other signatory states.[31]

The position Turkey took at Lausanne on abandoned properties was extremely inconsistent. On the one hand, it was forced to accept the principle of returning these properties to their owners due to the principles evident in the arrangements concerning property, rights, and interests, and on nationality or citizenship. On the other hand, Turkey used all means possible to prevent the return of Armenians living outside of Turkey and the repossession of their properties. This internal contradiction became evident during negotiations and Turkey was accused of preventing the return of the Armenians and the Istanbul Greeks, as well as of confiscating their properties.

For example, during the 19 May 1923 meeting of the First Committee, the English diplomat Sir Horace Rumbold said, "As I learned from many sources, the Turkish authorities already are prohibiting the return of Armenians and Istanbul Greeks who had recently left their native country." This led to the confiscation of the properties of these people, which could not be accepted. Rumbold continued, "In this situation, I would like to direct these questions to His Excellence İsmet Pasha. Is it true that Turkey has not given permission for the return of people who are members of minorities and are not included in the scope of the population exchange? Is it true that the Turkish authorities intend to liquidate the real estate of these people without their permission and under conditions which clearly do not permit the defense of their rights?"[32]

İsmet Pasha was stupefied by Rumbold's questions. He "was unable to immediately answer the question directed at him," and promised to ask his government about this topic.[33] Indeed, he telegraphed his government that day and asked it for clarification. He repeated Rumbold's questions and openly voiced his concern: "I fear that the question of the return of the Armenian refugees will be stirred up in connection with the general amnesty." The pasha was aware of the situation and consequently, knowing the debate, attempted to stay away from the topic of the Armenians and focus "the discussion completely on those who left Istanbul . . . without the necessary documents and passport." However this topic also was not pleasant from Turkey's point of view. The pasha, noting that "the liquidation of the properties of the people of Istanbul [who were not subject to the population exchange with Greece] and the prevention of their return" would place Turkey in a position of acting contrary to the treaty, said "I do not see the possibility of refusing" this claim.[34]

The reply—or, more precisely, the lack of a reply—to the questions that arrived from Ankara was very interesting. The questions were considered "of the nature of interference in our internal affairs," and it was advised that the "atrocities" carried out by Great Britain in Egypt, India, Ireland, Iraq, and Palestine, along with the "oppressions and attacks" carried out by Greece in Thrace and the islands, be raised for discussion. "Since if some concessions were made in response to such interventions, the attempts and proceedings which are very detrimental for our state would never cease, its rejection with the deserved intensity and decisiveness and the dismissal of the questioners" was instructed.[35]

İsmet Pasha approached the issue in a more coolheaded fashion. In a telegram of 4 June 1923, he stressed that it was necessary to make a distinction between those who fled from Istanbul and those who fled from Anatolia, and that in particular the return of those who left Istanbul will be "imperative sooner or later." According to the pasha, there was no doubt that "we will absolutely be required to reimburse the transactions that we conducted in the past concerning their wealth and real estate."[36]

During the negotiations, the revalidation of the 26 September 1915 Liquidation Law by the 15 April 1923 law was an important point of criticism. In fact, even before the proclamation of this law, for example in December 1922, questions were asked about the Ittihadist abandoned properties (liquidation) laws and information was requested as to "whether the laws are still valid."[37]

İsmet Pasha conveyed the protest to Ankara on 22 June, and received the following response on 26 June: "The point of view of our government on the Abandoned Properties Law which the Grand National Assembly of Turkey drew up and placed into practice is only directed toward the protection of the properties and rights of citizens, and concerning the protection of the abandoned properties of those who are fleeing or lost. The amount of their values are registered in their own accounts [at the relevant ministry]; and in this respect, whatever is necessary to do for the preservation of their rights is being assured."[38]

Turkey was not able to say that it confiscated the properties of Armenians and was not going to return them to their owners. Instead, it presented what it did as protection of the properties of its citizens, registering them in the names of its citizens so that no harm would come to the properties. This is farcical, since Turkey at the same time was doing all it could to prevent these citizens returning and demanding their belongings.

On the other hand, Turkey was not telling the complete truth, since the provision of the law was clear: the properties of those who had fled or were lost were neither being protected, nor were going to be registered—just the opposite, they would be sold off. This was the real basis of the complaints and protests of the Allied powers. İsmet Pasha, on 14 July 1923, asked Ankara whether it was true that the properties would be sold: "Is it certain that the immovable properties of those who are lost or runaways are also going to be sold in the 15 April 1923 Abandoned Properties Law? If not, keeping them in the charge of their owners, is the value of their rent going to be preserved in treasury accounts in their names?" The pasha asked that "this information which is essential for responding to the notes known to you immediately" be sent.[39] Right away, the next day, an answer was sent to the telegram: "In accordance with the special law, the values of the properties of those who flee or are lost are being registered as revenue in their own names, sir."[40]

Putting aside whether this response was communicated to the Allies, there is an important aspect to this response. Turkey again and again was accepting that the "fleeing" Armenians were the true owners of their properties and that the revenues obtained from the latter would be registered in their name in the treasury.

The Amnesty: Draft Proposal and Final Form

There is one last question that came out during the negotiations: Was the uniting of families torn apart during the deportations and massacres to continue along with the return of these people's properties? Commencing after the 1918 Armistice, the question of uniting divided families—in particular assembling little children torn away forcibly from their families and girls and women held in Muslim houses—became an issue as important as the repatriation of the deportees. The Allied powers, the Ottoman government, and the Armenian Patriarchate of Constantinople, in three parallel channels, organized the collection of Armenian women and children from Muslim homes and even attempted to form joint commissions as provided in the Treaty of Sèvres to solve problems that were evident.[41]

During the negotiations for the Treaty of Lausanne, the Allied powers wished to continue these efforts. The third article of the Draft Proposal on the Protection of Minorities, prepared on 15 December 1922, concerned this issue: "The Turkish government, in order to achieve the return to their families or communities of people who were lost or separated from their families from 1 August 1914 until the present, whatever their numbers or religions may be, and return properties to people who were left deprived of them in a lawless manner, confirms that it accepts the results of efforts made from 30 October 1918 until the present. Turkey is going to provide all conveniences so that these efforts are not interrupted."[42]

During the discussions on this topic, the British representative said, "I did not want to return more than necessary to problems belonging to the past," but he stressed that during the war years, many injustices were carried out, such as the splitting up of families or the seizure of properties through the Abandoned Properties Law. After the armistice, some efforts were made to get rid of these injustices. He said that commissions were founded and, as the result of the work conducted, many children and women were united with their families, and a great deal of property was returned to its owners. He declared that these efforts outside of Istanbul were not very successful "due to local conditions." Two things were intended by the article that was being proposed: "To consider what has been done up until now valid, and to not allow an attempt to make its completion impossible due to unfavorable conditions." The British representative asked that this work be completed under the protection of the League of Nations.[43]

Turkey declared that it "definitely is not going to accept the third article which concerns the past."[44] The Turkish Committee "thinks like the other representative committees on the issue of not reopening the debates of the past," and all these questions "remained in the past; whereas the conference must struggle with the future."[45] During the negotiations, Turkey made a counter-proposal and "informed that it intended not to protest the procedures which took place between 30 October 1918 and 20 November 1922." It would even not obstruct "the procedures under discussion from being reviewed, upon the requests of interested parties," and would accept that "requests for rights concerning properties . . . be concluded by an arbitration commission to be established."[46]

In the end, the issue was formulated in the way Turkey desired with a minor change of dates in the sixth article of the amnesty bill: "The Turkish government, sharing the desire for a general peace felt by all states, with the goal of bringing back together families scattered by war and reuniting legitimate holders of rights with their properties, announces that under the protection of the Allies it intends not to object to procedures conducted between 20 October 1918 and 20 November 1922." Moreover, it said "requests for rights concerning people and properties will be studied by a commission composed of one representative each from the Red Crescent and the Red Cross."[47]

Could this article be interpreted to mean that Turkey did not accept returning abandoned properties to their owners after 20 November 1922? Actually, in some works, this article is interpreted in the sense that the abandoned properties issue only appeared on the agenda in Lausanne within the framework of the discussion on amnesty and that Turkey refused to discuss this topic—which is false.[48] As shall be demonstrated, the abandoned properties question was directly or indirectly on the agenda during negotiations concerning many other issues. One result of the understandings reached concerning these issues was that after Lausanne, Turkey was going to accept the return of the confiscated abandoned properties to the Armenians. This procedure, however, would remain limited only to those Armenians actually in Turkey. It would exclude all the Armenians living outside of Turkey. As a matter of fact, this is a summary of the entire fight Turkey waged at Lausanne.

It can be said that the greatest deficiency of the negotiations in Lausanne about the repatriation of the Christians and the return of their properties, was the lack of an entity to defend the desires and wishes of the Armenians. The Armenians had no representation and, for this reason, after a short period of time they were left in the lurch. There is a reminiscence related by İsmet İnönü in his memoirs that can be taken as a very striking summary of the negotiations:

> At the conference, for a period of time I began to have to have serious doubts as to whether the English wanted to make peace or not due to the propaganda, attacks and so forth conducted as a result of the Armenian cause and the Greek cause. There was a very constructive and sensible diplomat in the English committee. I called him . . . I said to him that the issue of the minorities . . . had awakened a serious suspicion in me . . . I was not sure as to whether the English for this reason . . . intended to subject the conference to an interruption . . . he advised [me] to see as natural violent displays and a great racket on the issue of the minorities. I asked how should I see this as natural; I asked how are you saying this to me? He gave the following answer: İsmet Pasha! For years we said many things, we promised many things. We entered into many commitments throughout the world. Now while putting an end to them, why do you find carrying out this much ceremony strange?[19]

The Lausanne Regulations: The Question of Nationality

The question of the return of the confiscated properties of the Armenians was directly connected to the articles concerning nationality. A number of new states were formed on the territory of the Ottoman Empire after its collapse, which made the resolution of the nationality or citizenship question imperative. The question in essence was quite simple: according to the 1869 Citizenship Law would people who were Ottoman citizens and found themselves on the other side of the border when new states were created on Ottoman territory compulsory citizens of the new states? Would there be a choice for them?

The answer to these questions was given in Articles 30–36 of the Lausanne Peace Treaty under the heading of Nationality. According to Article 30, "Turkish subjects habitually resident in territory which in accordance with the provisions of the present Treaty is detached from Turkey will become ipso facto, in the conditions laid down by the local law, nationals of the State to which such territory is transferred."[50] Article 31 confirmed that such individuals would automatically lose their citizenship of the Republic of Turkey, but allowed them the right to make a choice: "Persons over eighteen years of age, losing their Turkish nationality and obtaining ipso facto a new nationality under Article 30, shall be entitled within a period of two years from the coming into force of the present Treaty to opt for Turkish nationality."[51]

These arrangements concerning nationality also directly pertained to goods and properties, and this matter was clarified in Article 33:

> Persons who have exercised the right to opt in accordance with the provisions of Articles 31 and 32 must, within the succeeding twelve months, transfer their place of residence to the State for which they have opted.
> They will be entitled to retain their immovable property in the territory of the other State where they had their place of residence before exercising their right to opt. They may carry with them their movable property of every description. No export or import duties may be imposed upon them in connection with the removal of such property.[52]

The provisions of Lausanne are extremely clear. If someone claimed to possess Ottoman nationality and was living in the states outside of Turkey's borders did not apply for that nationality within a period of two years, they would automatically lose it. However, even if they lost nationality, their ownership of immovable properties within Turkey's borders would be preserved.

Turkey clearly trampled on these fundamental principles of Lausanne, that pertain to the Armenians, and it continues to trample on them today. First, it did not permit the return of hundreds of thousands of refugees who had been forced to leave their homes due to war conditions. All efforts, which were made after 1920 by the League of Nations by means of the High Commissioner of Refugees Fridtjof Nansen, or at Lausanne, came to naught. These people were not only cut off from their homes and homeland, but they also lost the right to possess their belongings.

The first form of Turkey's violation of Lausanne was not annulling the Ottoman citizenship of Armenians living in many different countries and who used to be Ottoman citizens. Second, it did not recognize the property rights of Armenians who remained outside of Turkey and who according to the treaty "will be free to own the immovable properties which they possessed." Instead it confiscated these properties according to the Abandoned Properties Laws.

The first issue, that those considered Ottoman nationals according to the 1869 Citizenship Law continued to be considered Turkish nationals, was resolved through laws in 1927 and 1928. According to the first law of 23 May 1927, "The council of ministers permitted the annulment of the Turkish citizenship of an Ottoman citizen who did not participate in the National Struggle during the period of the independence wars, remained outside of Turkey, and from 24 July 1923 until the promulgation of this law did not return to Turkey."[53]

One year later, in May 1928, the first citizenship law of the Republican period was promulgated. The first article of this law stated, "Children born of a Turkish father and mother who are born in Turkey or in foreign countries are Turkish citizens."[54] According to it, the children born to Armenians who were Ottoman citizens outside of their country would also be considered citizens of the Republic of Turkey. Articles from 7 to 10 of the law, concerning "Denaturalization and Annulment of Citizenship," decreed that leaving or annulling citizenship could only take place by a decision of the Council of Ministers. That meant that if Ottoman Armenians and their children did not obtain a special decision of the Council of Ministers, they would continue to remain Turkish citizens. A guide to citizenship issued in 1939 by the Turkish Interior Ministry further specified this point as follows: "Denaturalization is contingent on obtaining special permission. Even if a citizen obtained a different citizenship without obtaining permission, this ruling does not express anything. He will still be treated as a Turkish citizen."[55]

Ottoman Armenians and their children lost their Turkish citizenship en masse automatically in 1964. A temporary supplemental article concerning "lost people," which was added to Citizenship Law Number 403 of that year, ruled that Armenians (without actually stating this name) would automatically lose their citizenship.[56] Thus, if Ottoman Armenians had not been specifically removed from Turkish citizenship through a ruling of the Council of Ministers, they would have continued to be Turkish citizens until 1964.

The question requiring an answer is the following: Why did Turkey continue to consider Armenians as citizens until 1964 despite Lausanne's clear provisions? The answer is simple and directly concerns the Abandoned Properties Laws. By doing this, not only did Turkey preserve its right to seize the properties of the Armenians, but it also gained many other advantages. First, the Abandoned Properties Laws could be applied only to citizens of the Republic of Turkey. Second, if Turkey denaturalized the concerned individuals, the new states from which these people would obtain citizenship would be obliged to accept the right of protection for these individuals. Third, Turkey could only prevent these individuals from entering the country on the condition that they were its own citizens. It must be remembered that according to the sixth article of the 1869 Citizenship Law, an individual who without permission accepts the citizenship of another country, can be removed from Ottoman citizenship *if the state wants* and subsequently can be prohibited from entering the country.[57]

At Lausanne, especially during negotiations with the United States, one of Turkey's greatest fears was that the Armenians living in the United States could come to Turkey as citizens of another country. Consequently, for example in the telegram sent by Prime Minister Rauf Bey to İsmet İnönü on 28 July 1923, Rauf informed that it was "an absolute necessity" to "absolutely avoid conditions that would make possible the return of Armenians to our country with any citizenship."[58]

There is one more important detail here that must not be overlooked. The 1927 law was not a comprehensive citizenship law but only a law consisting of one article. It only made an arrangement concerning denaturalization. A real citizenship law appeared only one year later. Moreover, though it dealt with a topic connected with citizenship, it came as a legislative bill to the Assembly through the Foreign Affairs Committee. In other words, the source of the bill was the Foreign Affairs Ministry. Thus, in the official report of the committee, it was openly stated that "the proposal of the minister of foreign affairs [was] discussed and disputed with peace and interest."[59]

Why did the Foreign Affairs Ministry propose such a bill? The reason is quite simple. Negotiations concerning reparations would commence at the start of 1927 with the United States. A separate Lausanne Treaty was signed on 6 August 1923 with the United States, which was not a party to the Lausanne negotiations. However, opposition led to a delay in its ratification by the U.S. Senate and, finally, on 18 January 1927, the U.S. Senate rejected the treaty. After this the two sides, on

17 February 1927, sent reciprocal notes of good intention and established diplomatic relations.[60]

One of the biggest problems during the negotiations for reparations was the issue of paying for the losses suffered by Armenians who were American citizens during the war—that is, restituting the value of their confiscated properties. According to the provisions of the part of the Lausanne Treaty, titled "Property, Rights and Interests," Turkey was required to reimburse the loss of rights of American citizens during the war. There was only one way not to pay reparations to Armenians who were American citizens and continue to control their properties and belongings in Turkey: reject the American claim that these people were American citizens and instead insist that they were still Turkish citizens.

For this reason, the Turkish Foreign Affairs Ministry's rapid dispatch of the one-article law of 23 May 1927 to the Assembly, immediately after establishing diplomatic relations on 17 February, was due to extremely "rational" causes. Turkey did not wish to return the properties of Armenians who were killed during the war or who had remained abroad. It should be added that this question did not pertain only to Armenians who had settled in the United States, but also concerned Armenians in Lebanon and Syria under French mandate.

In summary, Turkey did not only violate the clear provisions of the Treaty of Lausanne, but also the Turkish legal system and one of its foundations, the Citizenship Law, was organized in accordance with this violation. This is one of the reasons for the central argument of this book namely that the so-called Armenian issue thus cannot be viewed only as a minority question; in fact, the Abandoned Properties Laws form one of the cornerstones of the Republic of Turkey.

The Lausanne Regulations: Property, Rights, and Interests, or, The Issue of Compensation

The Abandoned Properties Laws and the issue of the return of the properties left behind by Armenians are directly connected to the provisions of Articles 65–72, in the section "Property, Rights and Interests." No matter how much Turkey insists that these articles settled the war damages of citizens of relevant states according to the principle of reciprocity between the signatory states of Lausanne and Turkey, and consequently are not connected to the Abandoned Properties Laws, which form a topic for Turkish domestic law, this is not true. There is a very simple reason behind our claim: in 1915 and the following period, a majority of the Armenians whose properties had been confiscated, ended up outside of Turkey's borders and became citizens of the new states within whose borders they now lived. Thus, these articles at the very least directly concerned the Abandoned Properties Laws in this sense.

Moreover, it appears that the arrangements made in Turkish domestic law after the Treaty of Lausanne—and in particular the rule that abandoned properties will be given back to people who are with their properties—were formulated according to the principle accepted in the third paragraph of Article 65, or at least were in harmony with this paragraph.

The first paragraph of Article 65 of the Treaty arranged reparations for damages of individuals who were citizens of the Allied powers. It declared, "Property, rights and interests which still exist and can be identified in territories remaining Turkish at the date of the coming into force of the present Treaty, and which belong to persons who on the 29th October, 1914, were Allied nationals, shall be immediately restored to the owners in their existing state."[61]

The second paragraph formulated the principle of reciprocity: "Property, rights and interests which still exist and can be identified in territories subject to the sovereignty or protectorate of the Allied Powers on the 29th October, 1914, or in territories detached from the Ottoman Empire after the Balkan wars and subject to-day to the sovereignty of any such Power, and which belong to Turkish nationals, shall be immediately restored to the owners in their existing state."[62]

The third paragraph is of vital importance:

> All property, rights and interests situated in territory detached from the Ottoman Empire under the present Treaty, which, after having been *subjected by the Ottoman Government to an exceptional war measure*, are now in the hands of the Contracting Power exercising authority over the said territory, and *which can be identified*, shall be restored to their legitimate owners, in their existing state. The same provision shall apply to immovable property which may have been liquidated by the Contracting Power exercising authority over the said territory. All other claims between individuals shall be submitted to the competent local courts. [italics are ours].[63]

Here, the question of whether the expression "subjected by the Ottoman Government to an exceptional war measure" includes the Abandoned Properties Laws is extremely important. It is not possible to suggest that this expression excludes these laws, because the Ottoman government itself presented and defended these laws as an "exceptional war measure." Moreover, the mixed arbitral tribunals established through Articles 65 to 72 in order to solve questions of reparations for damages made similar determinations. For example, the British-Turkish Mixed Arbitral Tribunal considered the Abandoned Properties Law as an "exceptional war measure" and decided that it was necessary for reparations to be paid for the confiscated properties of some Armenians who were British subjects.[64] In other words, the treatment of the Abandoned Properties Laws, in the framework of Article 65 of the Lausanne Treaty, appears to be an international legal norm.

Of course, the expression "exceptional war measure" would also cover other laws and regulations with no connection to the Abandoned Properties Laws, such as the 20 March 1916 Law on Lands and Buildings Which Are Going to Be Confiscated during the [War] Mobilization.[65]

Article 66 decreed that if property had been liquidated, reparation would be made in the form of payment of its value: "When at the date of the signature of the present Treaty the property, rights and interests, the restitution of which is provided for in Article 65 have been liquidated by the authorities of one of the High Contracting Parties, that Party shall be discharged from the obligation to restore the said property, rights and interests by payment of the proceeds of the liquidation to the owner."[66] Articles 65 and 66 also instructed the establishment of a mixed arbitral tribunal to solve any questions that might arise.

Articles 92–98 of Part III, Section V, specified how the mixed arbitral tribunal would be founded, its conditions of work, and its life span. According to these articles, these tribunals would be established within a period of three months after the treaty entered into force with each of the Allied states. Each tribunal would be composed of three people (Article 92). The center of the tribunals would be Istanbul. If their work could not be completed within a period of two years, they could be transferred to another place (Article 93). Decisions would be made by a majority and would be binding (Article 94). Applications could be made for a period of six months after the tribunals had been established; after this, no applications would be accepted. However, for "distance and compelling causes," "special permission seen as a justified exception" might be considered (Article 95).[67]

Gündüz Aktan, an influential former Turkish diplomat and one of the theorists behind the Turkish state's denialist policy concerning the Armenian Genocide, also argued that the arrangements made by Articles 65–72 of the Lausanne Treaty pertained to the Abandoned Properties Laws and that, through these articles, the return to the Armenians of their confiscated properties had been accepted. He wrote, "The most interesting provisions indirectly connected to the Armenians are the provisions of Articles 65–72 in the economic section. The connection of economic rulings with the Armenians cannot immediately be understood. . . . Among the economic provisions is a section named 'Property, Rights, [and] Interests.' In this section, all the rights and interests of those subject to deportation are protected."[68]

According to Aktan, the return of the Armenians' properties was guaranteed at Lausanne and the most important aspect of this matter was the statute of limitations. Aktan, referring to the parts of the articles formulating the work of the mixed arbitral tribunals, which concern time deadlines, wrote, "In this framework, for example when an Armenian has applied to the Turkish public administration, he must receive a positive response within a period of six months; if not, it is accepted that he may apply to the mixed civil tribunal during the following year." Aktan continued, "Within a period of eighteen months in all from the date of signing of the Lausanne Peace Treaty, the process of resolving disputes concerning property was concluded; if it were necessary, bringing the issue before a court was required. Disagreement would be unequivocally decided through the decision of this hybrid court. In this fashion, as a result of the periods of limitation, at present no field of application has remained for these provisions."[69]

Gündüz Aktan's basic thesis that, at Lausanne, the Armenians' rights originating from the deportations and the confiscation of their properties were guaranteed is correct. However, he is mistaken on the subject of the statute of limitations and the fields of jurisdiction of the courts for two reasons. First, the establishment of the mixed arbitral tribunals and the completion of their work did not take place as decided at Lausanne. For example, the determination of the rules of operation of the British-Turkish Mixed Arbitral Tribunal was only concluded in December 1925. Its first session, however, did not take place until 22 February 1927. The conclusion of the work of the tribunal did not occur within three years, as foreseen in the Lausanne Treaty, but instead occurred five years later, toward the end of 1932. The tribunal was not even able to look at many files that it already possessed, which remained a topic for negotiations between Turkey and Great Britain as late as 1944. During the year that the work of the British-Turkish tribunal was concluding, that of the tribunals formed with France and Greece was still continuing.[70] The second and more important issue, is that Article 95 of the treaty contained provisions qualifying the statute of limitations through "special permission seen as a justified exception."[71]

Another very important matter on which Gündüz Aktan was mistaken concerned the field of competency of these mixed arbitral tribunals. He was not correct that these tribunals were the designated authority to which all Armenians could apply. The tribunals were basically founded in order to solve issues of reparations between subjects of Allied countries and Turkey. Consequently, problems between Armenians who were Turkish citizens and Turkey were not within the jurisdiction of these tribunals. The reason was that, according to the Lausanne Treaty, at least theoretically, the repatriation of Turkish citizens and the restitution of their goods by Turkey were required. Turkey obstructed this repatriation and did not allow these people to enter the country. Even if these people were to have succeeded in applying to the mixed arbitral tribunals, their applications would be considered as invalid due to noncompetence.

Even when an Armenian was a citizen of any of the signatory countries to the treaty and thus in a position to apply, Turkey would obstruct this. Turkey used two different arguments here. First, if the individuals in question had assumed foreign citizenship prior to 1914—and in this sense fit the criteria of the Lausanne Treaty—they had done so without informing the Ottoman government and, consequently, would still be considered Turkish citizens by Turkish law. Thus any payment of reparations was rejected. Second, that some applicants accepted foreign citizenship after 1914 meant that for this very reason it was not possible for their rights to be defended by other countries.

For all these reasons, the problem of citizenship was one of the issues with which the mixed arbitral tribunals were most engaged. Several examples can be given showing that Turkey was not going to recognize the Armenians' status as citizens of Allied countries and would attempt to prevent the mixed arbitral tribunals from issuing verdicts on this topic. In essence, a competent authority could not be found to raise the problems of the Armenians who remained outside of Turkey and, for this reason, the problems remained unsolved. The Armenians had been abandoned.

A Brief Evaluation of Lausanne

The Lausanne Treaty provisions are extremely clear. In particular, they guaranteed that restitution would be made for the confiscated properties of the Armenians, particularly in the "Nationality" and "Property, Rights and Interests" sections. However, Turkey did not carry out these provisions. It gave back the properties only of Armenians who remained within Turkey's borders or who succeeded in entering Turkey unnoticed, while it attempted to confiscate the properties of

Armenians living outside of Turkey. On this topic there are five issues that are somehow interrelated and worth briefly discussing.

First, through domestic legislation changes were made to the Lausanne Treaty, such as those made by the 5 February 1925 and 13 June 1926 regulations, in connection with the Abandoned Properties Laws.[72] In these alterations, the date of validity of the Treaty of Lausanne is considered as a historic turning point. Changes made in domestic law from the date of validity of the Lausanne Treaty must be considered as directly related to the provisions in the "Nationality" and "Property, Rights and Interests" sections.

Second, the Lausanne Treaty, and in particular Articles 65 and 66, was interpreted by Turkey to mean that if the person whose property was confiscated was at the location of his property at the time that the Treaty went into effect, the property would be returned to its owner. If the person was not in Turkey, he would be considered lost and fleeing, so that the properties of such people would be regulated according to the Liquidation Laws of 26 September 1915 and 15 April 1923. Consequently, people who left Turkey prior to the Lausanne Treaty would not be able to get back their properties in any manner. Turkey blocked this possibility.

Third, because Turkey interpreted the Treaty of Lausanne as saying "only if the person is with his property (i.e., in Turkey) would it be given to him," Armenians who wanted to return to Turkey prior to or after the date of validity of the Treaty in order to be with their properties, would not be able to enter Turkey. In order to prevent Armenians abroad from coming to the country to claim their properties, their entry would be prohibited and those who did manage to enter would be identified and forcibly expelled. Moreover, a regulation (no. 2559) issued several weeks before the signing of the treaty, on 28 June 1923, prevented individuals abroad from claiming their properties via proxy statements.

Fourth, Turkey interpreted the articles in the section "Property, Rights and Interests" as concerning reciprocal reparations of the damages of citizens of the Allied states who were in Turkey and of Turkish citizens in other countries.[73] Therefore, Turkey claimed that these articles did not pertain to Armenians found abroad. During bilateral negotiations on reparations, Turkey objected to the desire of signatory countries to defend the rights of Armenians who now were their own citizens, with the justification that they were Ottoman citizens during the years of the war. Turkey said that only if Armenians had accepted foreign nationality prior to 1914, in accordance with the 1869 Citizenship Law by obtaining permission from the Ottoman state, could providing them reparations be acceptable.

It is necessary here to add as a note that the Abandoned Properties Laws already required that people who had adopted foreign citizenship prior to 1914 not be deported and their properties not be confiscated. However, in practice this was almost never complied with. Even if Armenians were citizens of foreign countries, they were deported and their properties were confiscated. There are several examples of this. Here is just one from a telegram dated 8 July 1915, stating that American citizens were being deported from Elazığ. The government asked that "if there really are people with American citizenship among those who are being deported, communicating their numbers and the reasons for their deportations" be carried out. If they really were American citizens, "their being set aside from deportation" was desired.[74] The Ottoman government, relying in general on the 1869 Citizenship Law, recognized the foreign citizenship of such individuals. There were only rare cases in which confiscated properties were returned through the intervention of foreign states.[75]

The fifth and final point concerns the situation of individuals who, "while not citizens of the Allied states, [are under] the de facto protection of these states." Turkey proposed that the signatory states were unable to defend the rights of these people who were not their citizens. However, this circumstance is a clear violation of the provisions of the Lausanne Treaty. The reason for this is that, in the third section of the treaty which deals with economic rights, Article 64 defined Allied citizens, and clearly stated that they would include individuals "who while not citizens of Allied states, benefited from the de facto protection of these states . . . they [were] treated by the Ottoman authorities as if they were Allied citizens."[76]

While the matter appears quite complicated, it is in fact very simple. Turkey, contrary to a principle of the Lausanne Treaty, determined not to return the properties of Armenians who ended up outside of the country. For this reason, these Armenians were prevented from returning to Turkey and, on the rare occasions that some succeeded in returning, they would be forcibly expelled. This situation is a type of economic plundering, or, as the Turkish finance minister explained during discussions in the Grand National Assembly, a desire to close all deficits by confiscating Armenian and Greek properties.[77] It can be argued that the policies followed by Talat Pasha in 1916, aiming at "completely eliminating the [Armenian] existence," continued in the Republican period.[78] Indeed, Turkey, in the period following Lausanne, began to practice a systematic policy of expelling Armenians who remained on its territories.

Notes

1. The minutes of the Lausanne Conference and texts of the agreements signed at Lausanne are printed in *Conférence de Lausanne sur les affaires du Proche-Orient (1922–1923)*. *Recueil des actes de la conférence* (Paris: Imprimerie Nationale, 1923). The records of the first phase of the conference, not including the minutes of the subcommittees, are printed by the British Government in Great Britain, Parliamentary Papers, Cmd. 1814, *Turkey No. 1 (1923): Lausanne Conference on Near Eastern Affairs, 1922–1923: Records of Proceedings and Draft Terms of Peace* (London: His Majesty's Stationery Office, 1923) (http://archive.org/details/recordsofproceed00confuoft). For quotations from the actual Treaty of Lausanne, the English version of the text was used; that text was published in Lawrence Martin, compiler, *The Treaties of Peace 1919–1923*, Vol. 2 *Containing the Treaties of Neuilly and Sèvres, the Treaties between the United States and Germany, Austria and Hungary Respectively, and the Treaty of Lausanne, the Convention Respecting the Regime of the Straits and Other Instruments Signed at Lausanne* (New York: Carnegie Endowment for International Peace, 1924). The Treaty is also available online at http://wwi.lib.byu.edu/index.php/Treaty_of_Lausanne, in the World War I Document Archive, ed. Richard Hacken, 2010, Brigham Young University Library, Utah; subsequent references to the Treaty of Lausanne will be to that website.
2. The topic was summed up in a ten-article protocol under the heading Summary of Issues Discussed at the Subcommission on the Topic of the Protection of Minorities (Meray, *Lozan Barış Konferansı*, Vol. 2, 157).
3. Bilal N. Şimşir, *Lozan Telgrafları I (1922–1923)* (Ankara: Türk Tarih Kurumu, 1990), xiv.
4. Ibid.
5. Meray, Lozan Barış Konferansı, Vol. 1, 212.
6. Ibid., 314.
7. The Turkish committee participated in the entire meeting except for the period when the French delegate was going to speak, at which time it left the session. On the minutes of 6 January 1923, number 16, see ibid., Vol. 6, 271–81.
8. Şimşir, Lozan Telgrafları I (1922–1923), 232.
9. Cemil Bilsel, *Lozan, İkinci Kitap* (Istanbul: Ahmet İhsan Matbaası, 1933), 291.
10. Meray, *Lozan Barış Konferansı*, Vol. 6, 123.
11. Ibid., Vol. 1, 307.
12. Ibid., Vol. 6, 158.
13. Ibid., 159.
14. Ibid., 161.
15. Ibid.
16. Ibid.
17. For some arguments made on the topic, see ibid., Vol. 3, 88–89, 186, 189–90.
18. Ibid., Vol. 6, 157.
19. Ibid., 158, 161.
20. Şimşir, *Lozan Telgrafları II* (Şubat–Ağustos 1923), 396.
21. Meray, *Lozan Barış Konferansı*, Vol. 6, 192.
22. Şimşir, *Lozan Telgrafları II* (Şubat–Ağustos 1923), 581.
23. İsmet İnönü, *Hatıralar, 2. Kitap* (Ankara: Bilgi Yayınevi, 1987), 139.
24. Şimşir, *Lozan Telgrafları I* (1922–1923), xiv.
25. Ibid., 124.
26. Ibid., 143.
27. Ibid., 162–63.
28. Ibid., 172.

29. Ibid., 174–76.
30. Meray, *Lozan Barış Konferansı*, Vol. 1, 211–12.
31. On this topic it is necessary to distinguish between two groups of Armenians. The first were Armenians who became citizens of signatory states prior to 1914, such as the United States. The second were Armenians who became citizens of France or Great Britain or came under their protection through their mandatory regimes in places such as Iraq, Syria, Lebanon, or Jordan.
32. Meray, *Lozan Barış Konferansı*, Vol. 6, 120–22.
33. Ibid., 22.
34. Şimşir, *Lozan Telgrafları II* (Şubat-Ağustos 1923), 324.
35. Ibid., 337.
36. Ibid., 396.
37. On Venizelos asking this question during the meetings of the Minorities Subcommission, see Meray, *Lozan Barış Konferansı*, Vol. 2, 205.
38. Şimşir, *Lozan Telgrafları II* (Şubat-Ağustos 1923), 473–74, 494.
39. Ibid., 570.
40. Ibid., 575.
41. For more information on Armenian children and women who converted religions and were dispersed among Muslim families, see Akçam, *İnsan Hakları ve Ermeni Sorunu*, 430–45; İbrahim Ethem Atnur, *Türkiye'de Ermeni Kadınları ve Çocukları Meselesi (1915–1923)* (Ankara: Babil Yayıncılık, 2005), pp. 113–235. On the Armenian-Greek Section created within the framework of the British High Commission, see Vartkes Yeghiayan, ed., *British Reports on Ethnic Cleansing in Anatolia, 1919–1922: The Armenian-Greek Section* (Glendale, CA: Center for Armenian Remembrance, 2007).
42. Meray, *Lozan Barış Konferansı*, Vol. 2, 161.
43. Ibid., 183–84.
44. Ibid., 184.
45. Ibid., 161, 204.
46. Ibid., 238, 254.
47. Ibid., Vol. 8, 93. The commission discussed here should not be confused with the Mixed Arbitral Tribunal, the formation of which was discussed in the section Property, Rights and Interests.
48. Here are two examples: Uğur Ümit Üngör ve Mehmet Polatel, *Confiscation and Destruction: The Young Turk Seizure of Armenian Property* (London and New York: Continuum International Publishing, 2011), 54; and Eroğlu, "Tehcirden Milli Mücadeleye Ermeni Malları (1915–1922)," 181–82.
49. İnönü, *Hatıralar*, 93.
50. Treaty of Lausanne, as accessed at http://wwi.lib.byu.edu/index.php/Treaty_of_Lausanne.
51. Ibid. The right of people to choose their citizenship did not only exist between Turkey and other states. Article 32 confirmed this right to exist between all separating states.
52. Ibid.
53. *Resmi Ceride*, No. 598, 31 May 1927. The full name of the law was Şerâit-i Muayyineyi Hâiz Olmayan Osmanlı Tebaasının Türk Vatandaşlığından Iskatı Hakkında Kanun [Law on annulment of Turkish citizenship of an Ottoman citizen who does not possess determining conditions].
54. *Resmi Gazete*, No. 904, 4 June 1928. The 1869 Ottoman Citizenship Law was annulled by the fifteenth article of this law.
55. İlhan Unat, *Türk Vatandaşlık Kanunu* (Ankara: S.B.F. Yayınları, 1966), 139.
56. *Resmi Gazete*, No. 11638, 22 February 1964.

57. See the section in chapter 2 titled "The Articles of Law Used to Prevent Their Return."

58. Şimşir, *Lozan Telgrafları II* (Şubat-Ağustos 1923), 615.

59. *TBMM Zabıt Ceridesi*, Period 2, Assembly Year 4, Vol. 1, 16 May 1927 (Ankara: TBMM Basımevi), 169.

60. Fahir Armaoğlu, *Belgelerle Türk-Amerikan Münasebetleri* (Ankara: Türk Tarih Kurumu, 1991), 111.

61. Treaty of Lausanne, as accessed at http://wwi.lib.byu.edu/index.php/Treaty_of_Lausanne.

62. Ibid.

63. Ibid.

64. W. H. Hill, "The Anglo-Turkish Mixed Arbitral Tribunal," *Juridical Review* 47, no. 3 (1935): 247.

65. *Takvim-i Vekayi* No. 2481, 15 March 1916.

66. Treaty of Lausanne, as accessed at http://wwi.lib.byu.edu/index.php/Treaty_of_Lausanne.

67. Ibid.

68. Gündüz Aktan, "Ermeni Sorununun Tarihsel Boyutu: Lozan Barış Antlaşması ve Ermeni Sorunu," Avrasya Stratejik Araştırmalar Merkezi Ermeni Araştırmaları Enstitüsü, http://www.eraren.org/bilgibankasi/tr/index1_1_2.htm.

69. Ibid.

70. Hill, "The Anglo-Turkish Mixed Arbitral Tribunal," 241, 243.

71. Ibid., 243.

72. The full name of the 5 February regulation is Lozan Muahedenamesinin Kabul Edildiği Tarihten Sonra Gitmiş Olanların Gayr-ı menkullerine Müdahale Edilmemesi Hakkında Kararname [Regulation on not interfering with immovable properties of those who left after the date of acceptance of the Lausanne Treaty]. The full name of the 13 June 1926 regulation is 13 Eylül 1331 [26 September 1915] Tarihli Kanun ile Bu Kanunun Bazı Maddelerini Muaddil 15 Nisan 1339 [15 April 1923] Tarihli Kanunun, Lozan Ahidnamesine Nazaran Suret-i Tatbikini Temin Maksadıyla Tanzim Edilmiş Olan Talimatnamenin Kabulüne Dair Kararname [Regulation on the acceptance of the regulation which was drawn up with the goal of assuring the method of application according to the Lausanne Treaty of the 26 September 1915 dated law and the 15 April 1923 dated law which modifies some articles of this law].

73. For example, for İsmet İnönü's report to Istanbul on the negotiations on the founding of the mixed arbitral tribunals and their powers, see Şimşir, *Lozan Telgrafları II* (Şubat-Ağustos 1923), 375–76.

74. BOA/DH.ŞFR 54/356, EUM cipher telegram to Mamuretülaziz province, 8 July 1915.

75. For example, there are the efforts of the American consul in Aleppo Jackson on behalf of Moses and Nerc(s)es Demirdjian, who in 1903 became American citizens but whose properties were seized in 1915. As a result of a note sent by the United States, their properties were retrieved. See BOA/HR.SYS 2875/5/7, "Correspondence on the Proceedings of the Abandoned Properties Commission and the Properties in Antep of individuals named Moses and Nerc(s)es Demirdjian, American Citizens and Living in New York."

76. Meray, *Lozan Barış Konferansı*, Vol. 8, 22–23.

77. *TBMM Gizli Celse Zabıtları*, Period 1, Assembly Year 3, Vol. 3, 1131.

78. BOA, DH.ŞFR. 68/215, Directorate of Public Security of the Interior Ministry cipher telegram to Fourth Army Commander Cemal Pasha, 7 October 1916.

CHAPTER 5

AFTER LAUSANNE

THE ARMENIANS REMAINING
OUTSIDE OF TURKEY

The signature of the Treaty of Lausanne can be accepted as the official birth of a new diaspora created by the Armenian Genocide. Starting on this date, the Genocide and the issue of the properties of the Armenians confiscated during the period 1915–22 must be addressed on two different levels, inside and outside Turkey. It is also useful to divide Armenians living outside of Turkey into two groups—Soviet Armenians, comprising those in the state of Armenia, and Armenians living in Western countries. The issues of the return of properties and reparations manifested distinct differences dependent on the country in which Armenians were living.

For Soviet Armenians and the Armenian state, these two issues were discussed only in an extremely limited fashion in the Treaties of Gyumri, Moscow, and Kars in connection with any Armenians still living within Turkey's borders. Questions of 1915 were not at all on the agenda, because the territories covered in these treaties were under Russian control until 1918 and were not locations of deportation and confiscation. Problems concerning Armenians living in Western countries varied according to their legal status in these countries.

Efforts were made to resolve the issues related to Armenian properties through bilateral treaties between Turkey and the country concerned, or through the mixed arbitral tribunals established according to the Treaty of Lausanne.

Two general observations can be made about reparations and the return of properties for Armenians living outside of Turkey. First, there was no administrative or legal institution directly representing the Armenians. Thus, they never had any opportunity to directly negotiate with Turkey at an institutional level. All the concerned powers (Turkey and the West) desired to settle their problems in an unrepresentative fashion and without accepting them as interlocutors.

Second, this lack of a representative institution created another extremely important question. The question of reparations for Armenians living in Western countries in particular was discussed only as the issue of paying the value of the properties, which belonged to the Armenians who had survived and taken refuge in these countries. The Armenians applied to the governments of the countries in which they now lived, to the mixed arbitral tribunals created in accordance with the Treaty of Lausanne, or to the League of Nations, asking for reparations for their losses in the manner decided at Lausanne. However, the issue of the confiscated properties of the Armenians did not concern only the Armenians surviving the Genocide: there were more than 1 million Armenians annihilated after 1915 and, as a result of the lack of a representative institution, the confiscated wealth of these annihilated individuals was never placed on the agenda for negotiations.

A report prepared by the Armenian delegation during the Paris peace negotiations was an exception on this topic. The report presented a list of Armenian losses and requested from the Peace Conference a "decision to demand reparations for the losses incurred by the Armenian people from deportation, massacre, plundering, usurpation and destruction." The Armenian committee was in favor of punishing the Turks for the crimes they had committed and reparations were one form of this punishment. "Taking into consideration the difficult conditions of the Armenians, payment of reparations as soon as possible" was necessary. According to the committee, "the quickest and most suitable way would be for the Allied states to hold in pledge the revenues of the properties of the Turkish state and foundations in order to provide for the damages of the Armenians."[1]

As can be understood from these lines, the Armenian delegation's approach to the reparations issue was to consider it as a collective problem concerning the Armenian nation and its solution was sought on this basis. However, the Armenian committee was not even given permission to participate in the Paris negotiations as an official party. As a result, reparations for the damages the Armenians suffered as a group remain a problem to this day.

Here, we provide several examples concerning how the issue was treated during the period following the Lausanne Treaty in the bilateral negotiations conducted between countries, at least from the point of view of the surviving Armenians, and how it remained unresolved.

The Treaties of Alexandrapol (Gyumri), Kars, and Moscow

The first example concerning the problems of Armenians outside of Turkey is the Caucasus. There are three relevant treaties: the Turkey-Armenia Peace Treaty, signed in Gyumri on 2 December 1920; the Turkey–Soviet Russia Friendship and Brotherhood Treaty; signed on 16 March 1921 in Moscow; and the Friendship Treaty between Turkey and Armenia, Azerbaijan, and Georgia, signed in Kars on 13 October 1921. It must be noted here that these treaties have no connection to the Abandoned Properties Laws. As a large part of the region was under Russia's control during the war years, neither deportations nor Abandoned Properties Laws were applied occurred there. The treaties were intended to deal with issues arising from the redrawing of borders, but because they were the first treaties related to Armenians, they deserve to be discussed.

The Armenian government signing the 2 December 1920 Alexandrapol (Gyumri) Treaty was overthrown and, because at this time Armenia entered under Bolshevik control, it was not ratified and did not become effective. This extremely short eighteen-article treaty has only one formulation indirectly connected with this book's topic. In the sixth article, the parties stated, "Permission is granted for refugees, outside of those who during the great war joined enemy armies and used arms against their own states, or participated in wholesale massacres in occupied territories, to return to their homes within the old borders." The parties also guaranteed that those returning to their territories would be "benefiting from all of the rights enjoyed by minorities in the most civilized countries, in a reciprocal fashion." The seventh article stated that the return of the refugees to their homes must take place within a period of one year.[2]

These points were repeated in a slightly expanded fashion in the Treaties of Moscow and Kars. According to Article 12 of the Moscow

Treaty of 16 March 1921, "anyone of the people of lands [which used to be under Russian control prior to 1918, but entered Turkish sovereignty] who so desires may freely leave Turkey and will be able to take his goods, properties, and money with him."[3] The same point was repeated in Article 13 of the 13 October 1921 Treaty of Kars. Moreover, Article 15 of this treaty proclaimed "a full general amnesty for the benefit of citizens of the other party for crimes committed on the Caucasian front due to war."[4]

After these treaties, protocols were signed between Turkey and the Russian Soviet Federative Socialist Republic, and laws and regulations were issued concerning how the people on either side of the border could cross to the other side and what their rights would be. The first of these protocols that we have been able to identify is a regulation dated 13 February 1923.[5] The regulation determined the rights of Molokans, a Christian sect living within Turkey's borders, to sell their properties. The second regulation was dated 21 February 1926 and gave permission for Armenians who wished to go to Russia from Kars, Ardahan, and Artvin to sell their immovable properties.[6]

Later, on 31 May 1926, a protocol was signed in Moscow concerning Articles 12 and 13 of the Moscow and Kars Treaties. This protocol was accepted on 9 June 1926 in the form of a law. According to the protocol, those people on either side of the border who so desired, could cross to the other side within the period of one year and preserve all their rights. On 12 June 1932, a regulation was published accepting transactions of transfer or sale of immovable properties in the provincial districts of Batum, Kars, and Ardahan; that were sold from outside to citizens of the Republic of Turkey with notary deeds, due to the lack of land registry documents; and which belonged to Armenians who left their country within the designated period of one year after the entry into validity of the 9 June 1926 protocol.[7]

These treaties and protocols were limited to the regions of Kars, Ardahan, and Artvin, and were not connected to 1915 and its problems. Due to changes in the border, they merely made arrangements for people who were permitted to cross the border if they wanted. Those who went to the other side, had the liberty to sell their properties.[8]

Turkey-France: A Pair of Treaties

At Lausanne, while the issue of the mass repatriation of the Armenians was being discussed, it was really the Armenians of Syria and

Lebanon that were specifically thought of, as this was one of the most feared issues for Turkey. One of the questions Turkey was most asked during the negotiations, was whether it would take back the Armenians who had escaped to these countries.[9] Turkey, however, forcefully opposing the repatriation of the Armenians, was seizing the properties these people had left behind through the Abandoned Properties Laws. This situation created a problem between Turkey and France, which had established a mandate government for Syria and Lebanon. The French argued that Turkey's actions were contrary to the Treaty of Ankara, which had been signed on 20 October 1921.

According to the fifth article of this treaty, a complete amnesty was going to be proclaimed by the signatory parties. The sixth article accepted that Turkey, "on the same basis as that established by the conversations on this subject between the *Entente* powers, their enemies and certain of their Allies," was going to confirm "the rights of minorities solemnly recognised in the [Turkish] National Covenant." The most important part of the treaty immediately relevant is Article 13, which recognizes the rights of the people on both sides of the border to protect their property and pass freely over the border. The article states that for "the inhabitants, whether settled or semi-nomadic who enjoy rights of pasturage or who own property on one or other side of the line fixed in article 8 shall continue to exercise their rights as in the past." These people "shall be able, for this purpose, freely and without payment of any duty of customs or of pasturage or any other tax, to transport from one side to the other of the line their cattle together with their young, their implements, their tools, their seeds and their agricultural produce."[10]

The French believed that Turkey was not complying with the principles of the treaty. This issue also appeared on the agenda at Lausanne. İsmet İnönü summarized their complaints as follows: "General Pelle . . . bringing up the issue of the Armenians going to Syria complained that the general amnesty existing in the Ankara Treaty was not being carried out and he said that in accordance with the Abandoned Properties Laws belongings and real estate were confiscated in various manners in absentia and in this way they [the Armenians] were deprived of everything." The Turkish government, in its answer to these criticisms, denied these accusations and claimed that rather, it was the French who had acted contrary to their promises.[11]

The properties left by the Syrian and Lebanese Armenians in Turkey continued to constitute a problem for Turkey and France after Lausanne. In essence, as we have noted, the Treaty of Lausanne's provisions, whether concerning "Nationality or Property, Rights, and Interests," were extremely clear. Accordingly, Armenians who won the right to be citizens of Syria and Lebanon after the date the treaty went into effect, on 6 August 1924, still maintained rights to their properties in Turkey.[12] It was necessary to either restore to them their properties or pay them their equivalent values.

The Turkish government struggled with this issue prior to the date of validity of the Lausanne Treaty, as well. Turkish newspapers dated 24 July 1924 reported, "Since the Lausanne Treaty is not valid yet, Syrians [were] still retaining Turkish nationality," and real estate was confiscated from "those Syrian people who possess property in Turkey, according to the Abandoned Properties Laws."[13] However, only a very short time remained before the Lausanne Treaty would go into effect. The Ministry of the Treasury, taking this into consideration, asked the office of the prime minister what should be done. Through these ministerial exchanges of letters, we learn that the viewpoint of the Foreign Affairs Ministry was that the Syrians should still be considered Turkish citizens. The ministry believed that even though it might be legal to seize their properties in accordance with the Abandoned Properties Laws, "the treaty will soon be in effect, and thinking of the probability that the real estate in Syria of Turkish citizens could be harmed, the postponement of the application of the procedure" was desired.[14]

According to the newspaper, "The Council of Ministers, examining the matter from both points of view, decided not to consider the properties of the Syrians as abandoned properties, on condition that the Syrians reciprocally act in the same manner."[15] This cleared the way for the transfer of these properties. However, the important aspect of this is who was being considered Syrian. Logically, the Armenians who survived the 1915 deportations and were still living in Syria would enter into this category. However, Turkey did everything possible to prevent the Syrian Armenians from being able to benefit from these rights. The treaties signed with France were worded to exclude the Armenians of Syria and Lebanon.

The first treaty concerning this issue was signed on 30 May 1926.[16] It included only an arrangement concerning "people living and present in Turkey" during the signing of the agreement who were over eighteen years old, and "among the people of territory separated from the Ottoman Empire and under the authority of the French Republic." These people "within a period of six months beginning from the date of effectiveness of the agreement, have the right to choose the citizenship of those countries [in which they now live]. . . . Those who make use of the right of choice must transfer their places of residence outside of Turkey during the following twelve months." These people in Turkey "will be free to preserve their immovable properties . . . and can take with them all types of movable properties."[17] As can be seen, since this treaty included only Syrians and Lebanese living in Turkey in 1926, those who were at that time in Syria were excluded. Articles 9 and 10, formulated in the same fashion as Article 13 of the Ankara Treaty, clarified the right to freedom of movement of the people living on both sides of the border. According to these articles, those people would get a border document that would allow them to cross the border and be valid for a range of not more than five kilometers from this border.[18] France and Turkey would continue to struggle in the forthcoming years with the question of the rights of the people living on both sides of the border to free movement and property rights.[19]

New negotiations took place concerning the properties left behind in Turkey by the Armenians of Syria and Lebanon in connection with the agreement of 30 May 1926, after which many new regulations were issued. The first one was dated 4 May 1927. It decided upon the return of the immovable properties of Syrians living in Turkey, which were seized by the government in accordance with the laws of 26 September 1915 and 15 April 1923.[20] However, the regulation used the words "those Syrian in origin who chose Syrian citizenship" is clear that this expression was chosen in order to exclude the Armenians whose properties were confiscated according to the liquidation laws from the regulation.

The most important step concerning Armenian properties was taken through the treaty of 27 October 1932.[21] The treaty regulated real estate belonging to Turks in Syria and Syrians in Turkey, in light of the articles in the "Nationality" section of the Treaty of Lausanne. This was specified in the official name of the treaty, "Law on the Agreement Concluded in Ankara with the French Government on Real Estate Belonging to Syrians in Turkey and Real Estate Belonging to Turks in Syria," which was accepted on 9 January 1933. Reading this title one would automatically think that it includes Armenians who had become citizens of Syria and Lebanon. However, a careful reading of the treaty shows that the Syrian Armenians were excluded.

In fact, the appearance of the 1932 treaty was not directly connected to Armenian properties. Turkey was confiscating the properties of the Orthodox Syrians, who were Greek in origin. The majority of these Orthodox Syrians had immigrated to Lebanon, where they had a great influence on political life. By pressuring France they succeeded in bringing this issue to the forefront. Turkey did not wish to discuss this topic, so France began to confiscate the properties of Turks in Syria. Turkey was thus forced to negotiate on this issue. In this situation, Armenian properties also became a part of the negotiations, even though Turkey did not want this at all.[22] Turkey's goal was to lift the restrictions placed on the properties of Turks in Syria. This was done through the first article of the treaty.[23]

The fourth and fifth articles of this treaty are extremely important. The fourth article refers to the 30 May 1926 treaty and, in accordance with the contents of this treaty, removes all constrictions on immovable property in Turkey of people who left the Ottoman Empire for lands under French administration and became French citizens. These people could regain their properties and the value of the rents obtained from them after this treaty went into effect. Armenians were clearly excluded in this article, since for the 1926 treaty to be remembered meant that it concerned the Syrians in Turkey in 1926.

The fifth article of the treaty identified in detail those who could benefit from this right. It intentionally utilized extremely complex language. According to the article,

> a) "*Turkish citizens of all origins*" who have been living in Syria and Lebanon as of 29 October 1914 and chose the citizenship of these countries in accordance with Article 30 of the Treaty of Lausanne; b) those living at least one year in Syria or Lebanon since the date of validity of the Treaty of Lausanne, with *either themselves or their father born in these countries* (Syria or Lebanon), and who *obtained citizenship on territory which separated from the Ottoman Empire and is under French control according to Article 30 of the Treaty of Lausanne*; and c) people who took advantage of the choices presented in Articles 32 and 34 of the Treaty of Lausanne could benefit from this right. [Italics are ours].

All measures restricting the rights of these people to freely dispose of their properties were removed from the date of validity of this treaty. Moreover, if the individuals identified in this treaty after the Lausanne Treaty had any confiscated properties, these properties or their equivalent values would be given back to them.[24]

This treaty truly was very ambiguous as to whether it covered the Armenians of Syria and Lebanon, and at first reading, it is not possible to determine this. However, after reading it very carefully many times, it can be understood that this treaty excluded these Armenians. Naturally, the signatory parties could not openly admit this. However, reading its criteria carefully, it becomes clear that it does not include the Armenians who, from 1915 to 1923, were deported or forced to flee to Syria and Lebanon. For example, at first glance in the second part of Article 5 the phrase *"those who obtained citizenship according to Article 30 of the Treaty of Lausanne in a territory which separated from the Ottoman Empire and is under French control* [italics are ours]" can comfortably be claimed to include the Armenians.[25] However, this phrase is connected to the restriction of being born in Syria. It might also be thought that the references to Articles 32 and 34 of the Lausanne Treaty, which are found in the third part of Article 5, correspond to the situation of the Armenians. Once again, however, reading the relevant articles shows that they in fact clearly exclude the Syrian Armenians.[26]

Why was such a complicated and difficult language chosen? The essence of the matter is that the Lausanne Treaty categorically protected the property of a citizen of any of the states that emerged on Ottoman territory, no matter in which of the other states this property was located. In this understanding, the property of the Armenians in Syria was guaranteed by Lausanne. Knowing this, Turkey and France understood that they could not openly use language denying the rights of Armenians arising from Lausanne.

When the negotiations began in 1927, in order to exclude the Armenians, the Turkish side directly declared that they were against using Lausanne as a basis. French Ambassador Chambrun, informing Paris of this, asked that the Turkish demands be taken into consideration since acceding to Armenian requests would have a fatal influence on Turkish-French relations, which were only recently improving.[27] By the end of 1929, France was convinced. In an official document written in October 1929, the Turkish side openly confessed that "the question of Armenian claims, for reasons of expediency, must be kept out of the debate."[28] One year later, the French foreign affairs minister stated that France's responsibility toward native Syrians was greater than toward the Armenians. According to him, France had already fulfilled its duty to aid Armenians coming to Syria.[29]

In the end, a treaty was signed by both parties that only appeared to include the Armenians of Syria and Lebanon. While to state and claim that the Armenians were not Syrians would be factually incorrect, the name of the treaty made it appear as though they were included, while effectively excluding them through the use of masterful diplomatic language. In practice, Turkey already did not recognize the rights of the Armenians in Syria. According to this treaty, only the Armenians of Aleppo and Antakya would be able to claim rights to their properties.

Articles 7, 8, and 11 of the treaty were also important. According to Article 7, if the properties in question had been "sequestered, transferred or liquidated," the equivalent value of the property would be paid.[30] Article 8 determined the period of time for all procedures. It stated that the identification of the values of the properties would be conducted within one year and that all liquidation transactions must be completed within eighteen months. Article 11 repeated that the individuals discussed in Articles 1–5 of this treaty would receive either their properties back or their equivalent values; this article especially stressed that these individuals could legally seek their rights if problems arose during this process. The article further decreed that the aforementioned individuals had two years in which they could apply.[31]

But Turkey did not see all these acrobatics as sufficient. In the signing protocol for the acceptance of the treaty, Foreign Affairs Minister Tevfik Rüştü Aras of Turkey added a restriction to the first paragraph of Article 11: "It will be accepted on condition that it is carried out by them in their country solely in a manner consistent with existing laws and rules." Moreover, Aras, referring to a decision rendered by a Turkish court of appeal, "considers it a duty to declare" that Turkish courts are not going to accept cases being initiated "concerning the return of movable property left by its owners while they were still Turkish citizens."[32] In other words, if a Syrian Armenian attempted to use the provisions of this treaty in his own favor and asked for his property, this supplementary protocol would stop him.

This issue continued to be a problem for France and Turkey. Thus, the Foreign Affairs Minister Aras—aware that the supplementary protocol left this matter insoluble—sent a letter to the French foreign affairs minister written on 27 October 1932 and informed him of "the Turkish government being in agreement on . . . the matter to undertake negotiations."[33]

Laws issued on 7 April 1934, 4 July 1934, 15 April 1935, 30 March 1936, and 31 July 1936 continually extended the periods for application on issues concerning immovable properties.[34] However, the issue remains unresolved to this day.[35] A little while after these laws, one more "Property Treaty in Ankara on the day of 27 October 1937" was going to be readied on the immovable property of Turkish citizens in Syria and Syrian citizens in Turkey, "but the implementation of the treaty dragged on and on, and to this day, a positive outcome could not not be attained."[36] A study prepared in 1992 stated that the properties of Syrian citizens in Turkey were still under the control of the state treasury.[37]

A large number of Syrian and Lebanese Armenians, in later years, migrated to the United States and became American citizens. In this fashion, the treaties signed between France and Turkey were binding for Armenians who became American citizens, and the issue became a problem for Turkish-American relations too. The United States asked Turkey to annul the Turkish citizenship of all the Syrian and Lebanese Armenians, but Turkey, fearing that these people as citizens of foreign countries would demand their properties, refused this proposal. Negotiations were conducted on this issue until around 1945, but failed to reach any conclusion.[38]

The 25 October 1934 Turkey–United States Compensation Treaty

The United States was not a party to the Treaty of Lausanne. It only participated as an observer and did not sign the treaty. However, the reason the United States did not sign was not only due to its status as an observer. Other reasons are revealed in a report sent by the Department of State to the American committee at Lausanne on 18 January 1923. This report summarized American interests in seven points, which included the investments of the American missionaries in Turkey, issues of reparations for American citizens, rights of protection of minorities, the arrangement of reciprocal citizenship rights, and capitulations.[39] Every one of these issues concerned Armenians directly and the United States calculated that it would obtain some concessions on them.

Unofficial discussions among the Turkish and American delegates began in November 1922, and official meetings began in June 1923. At the end of the negotiations, a separate Treaty of Lausanne known as the General Treaty was signed on 6 August 1923.[40] The problem of reparations for Armenians who had become American citizens almost brought the negotiations to a deadlock. As the two parties adopted very different positions, the issue could not be solved and it was decided to have it discussed in a bilateral commission, which would be created after the ratification of the treaty by the legislatures of the two countries.

The United States, by bringing up its missionary schools in Turkey and other similar assets, attempted in the Lausanne negotiations to obtain various special concessions not granted to other countries. The Turkish government, however, was against any special deal. It instructed the Turkish committee running the negotiations at Lausanne "on not giving to the Americans more than was given to the others."

One of the most important aspects of these instructions was the question of repatriation of the Armenians, on which the Turkish committee was reminded in particular not to enter into "an engagement which would cause the return of the Armenians to our country."[41] The U.S. ambassador to Switzerland, Joseph C. Grew, who was conducting the negotiations on behalf of the United States, reported the general principle that was agreed upon on 22 July: "The United States will get whatever was given to the Allies, nothing more."[42]

One of Turkey's fears was that the United States might demand reparations for Armenians who had become American citizens. Prime Minister Rauf Bey, in a telegram sent to İsmet İnönü dated 28 July 1923, openly expressed this concern: "Our anxieties on this matter . . . the Americans demanding from us the damages of many Armenians as their citizens."[43] It was necessary to prevent this. The instructions given specified that it was absolutely necessary to avoid pledges that are "going to make possible the return of Armenians to our country under any citizenship."[44]

The negotiations reached a stumbling block due to the issue of the Armenians' reparations. In a telegram he sent to Ankara on 21 July, İsmet İnönü summarized the situation as follows: "I met with the American delegate Grew . . . they are being insistent on the issue of naturalization. We want the inclusion explicitly in the agreement of our opposition to our former citizens coming [back] after leaving our country and obtaining American citizenship. They are evading this. This point is vital for us."[45]

In truth, the question of the citizenship of Armenians who had become U.S. citizens constituted a problem between the United States and the Ottoman Empire from the second half of the nineteenth century. Armenians who went to the United States and became citizens there would return to the Ottoman Empire and want to take advantage of the rights secured by the capitulations for American citizens. The United States considered it a requirement of its own citizenship law to defend the rights of people who had become its citizens in the countries to which they later went. Turkey, however, argued that the 1869 Citizenship Law did not recognize Armenians' U.S. citizenship—in many cases because they obtained it without obtaining Ottoman permission—and so atill considered these individuals Ottoman citizens. This situation had created serious legal and diplomatic problems between the two countries.[46]

The dimensions of the issue actually extended beyond the Armenians to include all Ottoman citizens who went to the United States from the Ottoman Empire. In a study carried out in 1931, the number of all Ottoman citizens who had gone to the United States was given as 376,468. From 1900 to 1924, of these people, 70,000 returned to the Ottoman Empire and it was assumed that they would be able to benefit from the privileges of the capitulations as American citizens.[47]

If Turkey were to recognize the American citizenship of these people, who went to the United States at various times, it would be obliged to pay considerable reparations. For this reason, it did not accept the American citizenship of Armenians who went to the United States before 1914, and rejected paying them reparations. In order to do so, Turkey developed an interesting legal category called "original and non-original Americans." Turkey declared that it was ready to pay the damages of American citizens in the category of "original Americans." The goal was to exclude the Ottoman Armenians. However, it was not possible for the United States to accept such a distinction. Thus, on the day of the signing, İsmet Pasha reported to Ankara that he was informed that it was not possible to accept the separation "into two of American citizens as original and non-original."[48]

Since each side insisted on its position, no understanding could be reached on the payment of damages suffered during the war by American citizens and the issue was not mentioned in the treaty that was to be signed. Instead, reciprocal letters were issued on restitution and it was decided that negotiations would begin on the subject at the latest within twenty days of the signature of the treaty.[49]

The twenty days were greatly extended, but finally on 24 December 1923, a partial solution was reached. The parties decided on the creation of a mixed commission to evaluate the demands for reparations. The mixed commission was going to meet in Istanbul within six months of the ratification by both sides of the 6 August 1923 treaty, in order to study the requests for reparations and issue decisive verdicts.[50]

The ratification of the Treaty of Lausanne in the American Senate encountered such stiff opposition that it was continually postponed. Finally on 18 January 1927, it was rejected in a vote.[51] After this, diplomatic relations were established between the two parties through a reciprocal exchange of notes on 17 February 1927. In these notes, it was decided that the problems of citizenship and reparations that remained unresolved between the parties, together with issues of commerce and reciprocal right of residence, would be solved and that within six months after the treaty entered force a commission would meet.[52]

The first step was taken on 1 October 1929, when a trade agreement was signed. This was followed by an agreement arranging the reciprocal settlement and residency rights of citizens, which entered into force on 15 February 1933. It was already necessary within six months after this date for the commission to discuss reparations to be created, and so the commission held its first meeting on 15 August 1933.[53]

An American jurist named Fred K. Nielsen chaired the American committee and prepared a detailed report in 1937 about the activities and outcomes of the commission. We learn from his report that the last application to the commission for reparations took place on 15 February 1934.[54] The American Department of State accepted about 2,630 requests for reparations, which were for a sum of approximately US$55 million.[55] Assuming that Turkey would not be able to pay such a large amount, the United States asked for a total of only US$5 million. During the negotiations, whether American Armenians would be included in this restitution was an important issue in terms of the total sum to be paid as reparations. In one American diplomat's words, Nielsen "had come over to jam the claims of 2,000 Ottomans down the Ambassador's throat." The head of the commission asked Nielsen to find a solution to this problem.[56]

The Turkish side, with the intent of finding out the answers to matters like who the applicants were and what their citizenship statuses were, asked detailed questions about the nature of the demands for reparations. They again reminded the American authorities that, according to the 1869 Ottoman Citizenship Law, the American citizenship of the Ottoman Armenians could not be accepted.[57]

At the first session of 5 August 1933, the United States presented three separate lists consisting respectively of 96, 280, and 1,504 names of people. The third list of 1,504 people was solely composed of former Ottoman citizens' demands for reparations. Turkey was extremely insistent that these people were all still its own citizens and did not want to pay any reparations at all.[58] Negotiations and discussions on this topic took nearly one year. Ultimately, Nielsen found the solution to be separating the dossiers belonging to former Ottoman citizens, estimated to be 1,900 in all by the Department of State, whose citizenships were the subject of debate between the United States and Turkey. The requests of these people for reparations were taken off the agenda of the negotiations.[59]

On 13 July 1934 a long directive sent to Nielsen gave full authority to exclude the reparations of people whose citizenships were topics of dispute from the total amount of reparations.[60] In a note given on 14 August, Nielsen officially informed the Turkish authorities that these people's demands had been removed from the total sum of money requested. With the removal of about 1,900 applications, the negotiations continued on the approximately 600 remaining dossiers.[61] Nielsen had complied with the demand of the Turkish side.

During the negotiations, there were other demands for reparations, which Turkey also wished to exclude. Nielsen considered them as five separate items. First were the reparations for damages from the Izmir fire[62]—the Great Fire of Smyrna—and its aftermath. Turkey refused to accept any responsibility on this topic. In the end, all applications in connection with it were rejected.[63] Second were damages that resulted from people being driven from one region to another. This category was debated in terms of whether removal took place due to war, and it ended up being excluded. Third were demands for reparations for some properties left in Turkey. Here, Turkey's most important objection was that it was not clear as to whether the immovable properties claimed to have been left behind had been confiscated by the Turkish authorities. The American committee wanted to examine individually the demands in this category, but basically recognized the Turkish protests as justified. Fourth were damages that occurred outside of Turkey's borders and fifth were the demands for reparations of American citizens of Ottoman origins who became the citizens of a third country. This last category comprised the demands of Ottoman Greeks who had become citizens of Greece, demands that Turkey wished to resolve through bilateral negotiations with Greece.[64]

In the end, a great deal of bargaining took place on the total amount to be paid and the parties settled on the amount of US$1.3 million.[65] "The Treaty Involving the Solution of Reciprocal Demands for Reparations" was signed on 25 October 1934. According to the first article of the treaty, the Turkish government would pay the U.S. government US$1.3 million, interest-free. The payment, beginning on 1 June 1936, consisted of US$100,000 annually in thirteen installments. According to the second article, the Turkish government would be released from all debts discussed in the 24 December 1923 protocol.[66] This article was extremely important because, while excluding all requests of Armenians who were U.S. citizens, it was accepted as solving all problems between Turkey and the United States related to reparations.

How the reparations being paid should be distributed among American citizens constituted another problem. The question that comes to mind is that no matter how much the Armenians were excluded, the reparations, as articulated in the note of 24 December 1923, were carried out with the goal of satisfying all damages between the two countries. So would it not be possible for the United States to pay the

Armenians from this money as well? After all, the payment was not based on individual items, but was conducted in a lump-sum fashion.

Whether this was possible legally is a different issue, but there is already a detailed list available on how this money was distributed. Fred K. Nielsen, representing the United States in the reparations commission by the authority he received from the U.S. Senate, opened an office in Washington in March 1935 and conducted the distribution of the money, which he received. Nielsen, in the final report published in 1937, stated that only thirty-three applications received positive responses. The largest payments were made to the missionary organization called the American Board of Commissioners for Foreign Missions and to two other establishments.[67]

Nielsen, after releasing a list of the payments that were necessary to make, determined that there was a surplus of US$400,661.91 and reported the situation. The United States decided to reduce the amount to be received from Turkey by this sum. Accordingly, Nielsen reported to Turkey that the final payment would not be in 1948, as had been decided, but in 1944. The American diplomat conveying this decision to Turkish ambassador Münir Ertegün recounted that tears of joy spilled forth from the latter's eyes.[68]

The decisions taken by Nielsen were protested by the Allied Turkish-American War Claims Association, which represented two hundred American citizens of Ottoman origin, for not taking their members' claims in consideration, upon which the U.S. Department of State was forced to issue an explanation in response. This statement said that it would not have been possible to have any treaty at all if the United States had remained insistent on the demands for reparations of all American citizens who were of Ottoman origin. Moreover, using the money from Turkey to pay reparations to people excluded from the treaty could not morally be defended.[69] This statement is very important from two points of view. First, the demands of the Ottoman Armenians were not taken into account in the treaty on reparations; second, the U.S. Department of State officially recognized its natural consequence—that no Armenian was paid reparations.

An Interim Note on Turkey-United States Compensation Treaty

In the state of California, a judge in a 2007 interim decision given in a lawsuit on reparations initiated by a group of American citizens of

Armenian origin against Deutsche Bank in 2006 rejected the request for reparations, giving as justification the 25 October 1934 treaty between the United States and Turkey.[70] The judge's main claim was that even if this treaty had not taken into account the demands of the American Armenians, all demands concerning reparations between Turkey and the United States were solved in the end. Consequently, an American citizen could not open a case again for reparations concerning the war years.

The court verdict engendered much joy in circles defending the official Turkish state theses. Turkey pointed to the 1934 agreement and the court decision as reasons why the reparations issue connected to the Armenian Genocide was basically finished, claiming that "the Armenians cannot demand reparations."[71]

The issue for the United States and Turkey has two different dimensions. First, could the 1934 treaty be used as an argument against demands for reparations being made today? Can it be said, as the judge of the California court claimed, that even if the demands of the American Armenians were not taken into consideration, since the treaty ultimately solved all issues of reparations between Turkey and the United States, it is impossible to initiate a new lawsuit on this question?

While we write these lines, the verdict still had not been finalized. However, even if it were final, it must be accepted that the situation is extremely strange legally since the United States would be considering the reparations treaty to be valid for citizens who clearly had been excluded from its authority. This would be equivalent to accepting Turkey's proposal at Lausanne to distinguish between "original and non-original citizens." The question is whether the American legal system would accept such an interpretation, which proposes discrimination against its own citizens. From a moral standpoint, to say to one group of your citizens that "at that time we rejected your demands and we did not pay reparations for your damages, so now too we will not do it," remains a very difficult argument to defend legally.

There is also a Turkish dimension to the issue. Did the 1934 treaty really completely solve the issue of Armenians' reparations? If it really did, as is claimed by the Turkish Historical Society, this can be accepted as an indirect acknowledgment of the need to pay reparations to the Armenians, which then must be considered a new state of affairs concerning the official Turkish theses. After all, as of today, Turkey has not accepted such a right of the Armenians. If the argument is that the 1934 treaty resolved all reparations issues, this would mean that the Armenians have the right to reparations. Yet as these payments had already been made by means of this same treaty, the issue was effectively closed.

However, if the Armenians' demand for reparations is generally accepted, it is impossible to claim that the 1934 treaty solved this issue, since the treaty concerned only the United States. Actually, it only concerned the 1,900–2,000 American Armenians who responded to the treaty and applied for reparations. The number of Armenians deported and killed during the Genocide exceeds 1 million. In this case, according to the logic of the Turkish Historical Society, the problem of reparations for the Armenians not covered by the 1934 treaty still faces Turkey today.

There is also another important dimension to the issue. It is not possible to interpret the 1934 treaty as having provided for reparations to the American Armenians from the point of view of the Turkish legal system. The Turkish side took a very tough position on this during the negotiations and, as a result, the issue did not even appear on the agenda. It is not possible to consider a matter, which did not enter the agenda, to exist. Turkey knew that if it made even the slightest concession on this matter during the negotiations with the United States, this would serve as an example for other countries. Consequently, the question of reparations for the losses suffered by Armenians was categorically rejected and was unremittingly kept out of international negotiations.

We know that Turkey was extremely attentive to this issue from regulation number 2559, issued on 28 June 1923. Readers may recall that Turkey, through this regulation, prevented Armenians abroad from demanding their properties by means of powers of attorney. In other words, putting aside the question of whether the issue was the subject of international negotiations, Armenians were even denied the possibility as individuals of using proxies in Turkey to seek their rights. It is for this reason that none of the dozens of laws and regulations issued during the Republican period, especially in the 1920s and 1930s, contain any statements concerning special arrangements made for Armenians living in any country abroad.

The International Commission and Mixed Arbitral Tribunals

The restitution of the confiscated properties of Armenians was discussed in three other major international platforms. One of them was the Inter-Allied Commission for the Assessment of Damages Suffered in Turkey, established by a protocol signed by the Allies in Paris on 23 November 1923 and known as the Paris Commission.[72] Another was the Mixed Arbitral Tribunals whose establishment was discussed in Articles 65 and 66 of the Treaty of Lausanne. The third one was the League of Nations. Armenians directly applied to the General Secretariat of the League of Nations to seek their rights in accordance with the provisions of the articles protecting minorities in the Treaty of Lausanne.

According to Article 58 of the Lausanne Treaty, which constituted the basis of the Paris Commission, Turkey and the other signatory states, excluding Greece, between 1 August 1914 and the date of entry into force of the Treaty of Lausanne, were going to "reciprocally renounce all pecuniary claims for the loss and damage suffered respectively by Turkey and the said Powers and by their nationals (including juridical persons) . . . as the result of acts of war or measures of requisition, sequestration, disposal or confiscation."[73]

This article introduced two important restrictions. First, this renunciation would not impair the economic provisions in Section III, especially those pertaining to property, rights, and interests. Second, Turkey renounced in favor of the Allied states (except Greece) any right to gold transferred by Germany and Austria under Article 259 of the Treaty of Versailles with Germany, and Article 210 of the Treaty of Saint-Germain with Austria.

This gold, estimated at a total value of £5 million sterling at that time, would be used to pay for the war reparations owed by Turkey to the citizens of Great Britain, Italy, France, Romania, and Japan.[74] The 23 November 1923 protocol mentioned above was signed for this purpose. The creation of a commission within one month of the entry into force of the Lausanne Treaty was decided upon.[75] The commission would be comprised of British, French, and Italian representatives. A period of one year would be allowed for all applications. The sixth article of the protocol would determine which damages would be compensated for. It is very important that forcible requisition, along with sequestration or confiscation, were considered losses experienced as a result of the Izmir fire.[76]

The commission began its work in 1925 and concluded on 15 March 1930,[77] all in all receiving and investigating approximately 15,600 applications.[78] In the course of their work, the members of the commission, in order to study applications in situ visited Istanbul, sent a subcommission to Palestine and established permanent subcommissions in

Izmir and Istanbul.[79] Ultimately, US$25,628,595.53 in reparations were paid to Armenian citizens of France, Great Britain, Italy, Romania, and Japan.[80]

The main task of the commission was to make restitution for the losses of citizens of the Allied states. Among these citizens were individuals of Ottoman origin (chiefly Greeks and Armenians) who also applied to the commission for compensation for losses they endured during the war. However, the commission asked them to demonstrate that they had obtained their new citizenship prior to 1914. Reparations were not only for confiscated property and wealth, but also could be for the murder of family members of these individuals. Ultimately, the commission allocated a specific amount of money for murdered spouses, for each murdered child, and provided compensation to applicants of Ottoman origin too.[81] There were people of Armenian origin among the recipients of payments. It is significant that the Paris commission made payments to French, British, and Italian citizens of Armenian origin.[82]

The Mixed Arbitral Tribunals whose, establishment was foreseen in the "Property, Rights and Interests" section of the Treaty of Lausanne, composed another international forum in which the question of the restitution of confiscated Armenian properties could be discussed. Their work conditions and period of time were defined in Articles 92–98 of the treaty. The formation of such tribunals was mentioned in many treaties signed after World War I.[83] The dates of establishment of these tribunals and their periods of operation differed greatly. For example, the preparation of the sixty-three-article protocol specifying the conditions of work for the British-Turkish Mixed Arbitral Tribunal was delayed to a great extent due to long arguments. Consensus was finally reached and the Tribunal was estrablished on 29 December 1925, and its first session took place on 22 February 1927. On 16 May 1933, in a response to a question in the British parliament, it was declared that both the Paris Commission and the British-Turkish Mixed Tribunal had finished their labors and had been disbanded by that date.[84]

In fact, the information given about the British-Turkish Mixed Tribunal was not completely correct. The tribunal had not been able to complete its work and had not been able to examine a great many dossiers. Negotiations attempted to solve this problem. In the end, the parties on 23 March 1944 through the exchange of a reciprocal letter reached an understanding. Turkey agreed to pay 107,100 Turkish liras without interest in ten installments in order to close all these remaining cases. The letter given by the Turkish government stated that the payment of this sum "is going to exempt the Turkish government from the obligations born [from the decisions] . . . of the Turkish-English Mixed Arbitral Tribunal of the English government and its citizens." In its responding note, the British embassy repeated that this agreement, which was previously oral in nature, was by its government.[85]

The decisions of the Mixed Arbitral Tribunals themselves are the subject of a separate study. What is important from the point of view of this study is that the tribunals, the Abandoned Properties Law—and based on this the confiscation of Armenian properties—and the burning of Smyrna are evaluated in the framework of Article 65 of the Lausanne Treaty. Moreover, the fact that some applications of Armenians from relevant countries were accepted and others were rejected is interesting. Here, the contents of each dossier played an important role.

The question of citizenship, which we have frequently discussed throughout this work, is the topic that caused the most work for the tribunals and affected their verdicts. Turkey argued that the Mixed Arbitral Tribunals were only competent to deal with issues between Turkey and citizens of the relevant countries (e.g. Great Britain, France, and Italy), claiming that Armenians of Ottoman origin could not be dealt with in this context. There are some important differences in the decisions taken by the tribunals in regard to this question.

For example, in a case involving eighty Cypriots the British-Turkish Mixed Tribunal ruled that it was not possible to consider the latter British citizens. This is because on 5 November 1914 Cyprus was made a British territory (through annexation), while the tribunal dealt only with issues of reparations for people who were citizens of Allied countries as of 29 October 1914. However, this did not mean that Cypriots would be deprived of reparations. The tribunal was of the opinion that the Cypriots were included in the definition of "Allied nationals," specified in Article 64 of the Treaty of Lausanne. According to this definition, persons "without having the nationality of one of the Allied Powers, in consequence of the protection which they in fact enjoyed at the hands of these Powers," can be considered as "Allied nationals." Cyprus had been under British protection since 4 June 1878.[86]

On the other hand, in the case of a British citizen of Ottoman origin named Agopian the same tribunal accepted Turkey's contention that this individual was a Turkish citizen. According to the tribunal, if a person who had been naturalized as a British citizen had not been removed by Turkey from Turkish citizenship, he could still be considered a Turkish citizen.[87] Thus, with Agopian a Turkish citizen, his case could not be heard by the tribunal.

The French-Turkish Mixed Arbitral Tribunal took a completely contrary position concerning citizenship and did not accept Turkey's argument. In the case of a French citizen named Apostolides in 1928, Turkey proposed its classic argument, maintaining that Apostolides' French citizenship was invalid because he had obtained it without permission from the Turkish authorities. According to Turkey, Apostolides was still a Turkish citizen so the tribunal was not empowered to look at his case. The tribunal, however, declaring that it was indeed authorized to examine this case, decided against Turkey. It acted in its verdict on the principle that the authority of the state whose citizenship was abandoned was not sufficient; all other states had to also recognize the citizenship status.[88] A similar decision was issued in a case between the United States and Egypt, in which the tribunal rejected Egypt's argument which took the 1869 Ottoman Citizenship Law as its basis, just as Turkey had done.[89]

It is also useful to mention the decision reached by the Turkish-Greek Mixed Arbitral Tribunal concerning the Izmir conflagration. The issue, which was also discussed in a secret session of the Grand National Assembly of Turkey, concerned stolen jewels. They had been kept in a bank safe and were forcibly opened. In this suit, initiated by Baron de Nordenskjoeld and Ahmed Rechid Kyriacopoulus, Turkey was found guilty and had to pay reparations.[90]

One of the authorities to which Armenians had applied while seeking their rights was the League of Nations itself. The best known example is the application made by M. Essayan, secretary of the Athens Armenian Refugees Committee, in both his own name and that of other Armenians. Essayan's appeal to Secretary General Eric Drummond of the League asking for the Armenian refugees' "return to the Turkish Republic, the removal of the embargo on bank accounts in Izmir, and the return of properties in Anatolia" had no result. The League of Nations, finding Turkey's procedural objection in its 20 October 1925 response justified, was not going to do anything concerning the application. It wrote that Essayan, the citizen of one state (Greece), did not have the right to apply to the League on an issue concerning a different state (Turkey).[91] The attempts of Armenians to repatriate, and to demand their properties back, were going to disappear in the corridors of the League.

The final outcome of the question of the confiscated properties of the Armenians scattered outside of Turkey after Lausanne, who composed the great majority of Armenians that survived the Genocide,[92] was that Turkey did not pay any compensation or return the properties. There were two determinative causes that led to this result. First, in order not to satisfy the rights of Armenians originating in international treaties, Turkey saw nothing objectionable in violating treaties that it had itself had signed, and it obstructed the attempts of Armenians as individuals to enter Turkey to obtain their properties. Second, as the negotiations and treaties made between the United States and France discussed above clearly showed, the Armenians' fundamental problem was the lack of an organization to represent them. As a result of this absence of a representative authority, any state, while negotiating with Turkey, saw Armenian demands as an obstacle to its own relationship with Turkey, and so saw no disadvantage to leaving them off the agenda. Consequently, the Armenian demands continue unanswered to the present day.

Notes

1. For the full text, see *Zhamanag*, 19 and 20 March 1335 [1919]. The authors greatly thank Şuşan Özoğlu for translating this from Armenian.
2. İsmail Soysal, *Tarihçeleri ve Açıklamaları ile Birlikte Türkiye'nin Siyasal Antlaşmaları, 1. Cilt (1920–1945)* (Ankara: Türk Tarih Kurumu, 2000), 20–21.
3. Ibid., 35.
4. Ibid., 44–45.
5. Müdürlüğü, *Milli Emlak Muamelelerine Müteallik Mevzuat*, 618.
6. Ibid., 619.
7. Ibid., 617–19. The full name of the regulation is Kars ve Moskova Muahedelerinden Sonra Memleketi Terk Eden Ermenilerin Tebaamıza Satmış Oldukları Elviyeyi Selâse'deki Gayrimenkuller Hakkında Kararname [Regulation on immovable Pproperties in the three provincial districts which were sold to our citizens by Armenians leaving the country after the Kars and Moscow Treaties].
8. According to the oral tradition of the people of the area of Ardahan and Hanak, when the Armenians left they were not actually permitted to take anything with them. Perihan Akçam described this situation to her son (the coauthor of this work) several decades ago.
9. For example, in the 4 June 1923 session, the French representative said that "during the last three years . . . about 100,000 Armenians [had] left Turkey," and asked whether "their right to return to Turkey" existed (Meray, *Lozan Barış Konferansı*, Vol. 6, 161).
10. Great Britain, Parliamentary Papers, Cmd. 1556, Turkey No. 2, Despatch from His Majesty's Ambassador at Paris, Enclosing the Franco-Turkish Agreement Signed at Angora on October 20, 1921 (London: His Majesty's Stationery Office, 1921), http://www.hri.org/docs/FT1921/Franco-Turkish_Pact_1921.pdf.
11. Şimşir, *Lozan Telgrafları II* (Şubat-Ağustos 1923), 562–63.
12. Armenians who were Ottoman citizens until the signing of the Lausanne Treaty lost their Turkish citizenship through the August 1924 and January 1925 regulations

issued by France, and became Syrian or Lebanese citizens. As mentioned above, the Turkish government did not automatically denaturalize these Armenians until 1964. On Lebanon, see Nicola Migliorino, *(Re)constructing Armenia in Lebanon and Syria: Ethno-cultural Diversity and the State in the Aftermath of a Refugee Crisis* (New York, Oxford: Berghahn Books, Oxford, 2008), 55; on Syria, see Uri Davis, "Citizenship Legislation in the Syrian Arab Republic," *Arab Studies Quarterly* 28, 1996, 35.

13. Ibid.
14. Ibid.
15. *Tevhid-i Efkâr*, 24 July 1924. Also see *Cumhuriyet*, 22 July 1924.
16. Soysal, *Tarihçeleri ve Açıklamaları ile Birlikte Türkiye'nin Siyasal Antlaşmaları, 1. Cilt (1920–1945)*, 293–311.
17. Ibid., 294.
18. Ibid., 296.
19. In protocols completed on 29 June 1929 and 17 March 1930, this topic was discussed in greater detail and the range from the border on both sides was extended to ten kilometers (Müdürlüğü, *Milli Emlak Muamelelerine Müteallik Mevzuat*, 322–24).
20. Ibid., 321. The full name of the regulation that was numbered 5130 is "Aslı Suriyeli olup Suriye tabiiyetini ahkâmı ahdiye mucibince ihtiyar etmiş olanlara ait emvali gayrimenkuleden hükûmet yedinde mevcut olanların iadesi hakkında kararname [Regulation on the restitution of immovable properties in the hands of the government belonging to those Syrian in origin who chose Syrian citizenship according to the treaty provisions]."
21. Ibid., 325–30.
22. Vahe Tashjian, "Recovering Armenian Properties in Turkey through the French Authorities in Syria and Lebanon in the 1920s," a report submitted to an international conference called the Armenian Genocide: From Recognition to Compensation? (Beirut, 23–25 February 2012). The authors thank Vahe Tashjian for sharing this hitherto unpublished work.
23. Müdürlüğü, *Milli Emlak Muamelelerine Müteallik Mevzuat*, 325.
24. Ibid., 326–27.
25. Ibid., 327.
26. Article 32 of Lausanne states the right of a person who settled in a state that had separated from Turkey, but who was not of the majority composing the people of that state, to choose a state in which his own people were the majority. For example, an Arab living in Greece could go to Syria or Lebanon, while a Greek living in Syria or Lebanon could go to Greece. Article 34 concerned the right of individuals who are members of the native population of a territory, which separated from Turkey (e.g., Turks, Greeks, or Arabs) but settled in other countries (e.g. United States, France, Great Britain) to be able to choose the citizenship of the state in which they are part of the native population. Armenians were not included in these categories.
27. Tashjian, "Recovering Armenian Properties in Turkey." Tashjian gave the following source for the ambassador's letter: France, Ministère des Affaires Étrangères [Foreign Affairs Ministry; henceforth MAE], Levant 1918–1940, Turquie, Vol. 260, Letter of Charles de Chambrun, ambassador of France to Turkey at Locquin, deputy, vice president of the Commission of Finances, Chamber of Deputies, 10 July 1929, Constantinople, f° 27.
28. Ibid., France, Ministère des Affaires Étrangères [Foreign Affairs Ministry], Levant 1918–1940, Turquie, Vol. 260, Secrétariat général, bureau diplomatique, "Négociations relatives aux biens syriens et libanais en Turquie: état de la question du 21 octobre 1929" [Negotiations concerning Syrian and Lebanese property in Turkey:

The state of the question on 21 October 1929], 22 October 1929, Beyrouth, f° 231. The original French is as follows : « la question des réclamations arméniennes, pour des raisons d'opportunité, doit être maintenue hors du débat».

29. Ibid., France, Centre des archives diplomatiques de Nantes, Record Group Ankara, No. 129, Foreign Affairs Minister Aristide Briand, Letter No. 281, to Charles de Chambrun, 15 December 1930, 3. The original French quotation follows: "nos obligations sont incontestablement moins impératives à leur égard [des Arméniens] que vis-à-vis des Syriens d'origine. . . . [D]epuis leur arrivée [des Arméniens] en Syrie, nous avons largement rempli vis-à-vis d'eux notre devoir d'assistance."

30. Müdürlüğü, *Milli Emlak Muamelelerine Müteallik Mevzuat*, 328–29

31. Ibid, 328–29.

32. Ibid., 330.

33. Ibid., 332.

34. Ibid., 333–35.

35. One of the reasons for the issue remaining unresolved is the situation of the Greek Orthodox who migrated to Syria. Turkey considered them Greek, and based on Article 13 of the 1932 treaty, claimed that their property questions had been dealt with in the framework of the population exchange with Greece, and refused to give to the properties of the Syrian Greek Orthodox. A special regulation issued in 1935 attempted to work out this issue. Ibid., 335.

36. Soysal, *Tarihçeleri ve Açıklamaları ile Birlikte Türkiye'nin Siyasal Andlaşmaları I. Cilt (1920–1945)*, 292.

37. Fügen Sargın, "Yabancı Gerçek Kişilere Ait Taşınmaz Malların Tasfiyesi," *Türkiye Barosu Dergisi* 1, 1992, 31–32. The topic includes some extremely serious legal details that lie outside of the scope of this work.

38. For more detailed information, see Roger Trask, *The United States Response to Turkish Nationalism and Reform 1914–1918* (Minneapolis: The University of Minnesota Press, 1971), 188–200.

39. United States Department of State, *Papers Relating to the Foreign Relations of the United States, 1923*, Vol. II (Washington, DC: U.S. Government Printing Office, 1939), 1045–46; also see http://digicoll.library.wisc.edu/cgi-bin/FRUS/FRUS-idx?type=goto&id=FRUS.FRUS1923v02&isize=M&submit=Go+to+page&page=1045.

40. For the full English and Turkish texts of the treaty, see Armaoğlu, *Belgelerle Türk-Amerikan Münasebetleri*, 90–109.

41. Şimşir, Lozan Telgrafları II (Şubat-Ağustos 1923), 610–11.

42. Ibid., 611.

43. Ibid., 615.

44. Ibid.

45. Ibid., 589.

46. For detailed information on the different concepts of citizenship of the two countries according to international law, see Leland J. Gordon, "The Turkish American Controversy over Nationality," *The American Journal of International Law* 25, no. 4 (October 1931):658–69.

47. Ibid., 658.

48. Şimşir, Lozan Telgrafları II (Şubat-Ağustos 1923), 629.

49. For the exact texts of these letters, see United States Department of State, *Papers Relating to the Foreign Relations of the United States, 1923*, Vol II, 1143–44.

50. E. Russell Lutz, "Claims against Turkey," *American Journal of International Law* 28, no. 2 (April 1934): 346.

51. The necessary two thirds majority could not be attained to ensure the acceptance of the treaty in the Senate. For more detailed information on the opposition to

Lausanne, see Gregory Aftandilian, *Armenia Vision of a Republic, The Independence Lobby in America 1918–1927* (Boston: Charles River Books, 1980).

52. United States Department of State, *Papers Relating to the Foreign Relations of the United States, 1927*, Vol. III (Washington: U.S. Government Printing Office, 1942), 794–95.

53. Trask, *The United States Response to Turkish Nationalism and Reform*, 198–99.

54. Fred K. Nielsen, *American-Turkish Claims Settlement under the Agreement of December 24, 1923, and Supplemental Agreements Between the United States and Turkey, Opinions and Report* (Washington, DC: U.S. Government Printing Office,1937), 11.

55. By 1932 1,880 people had applied. Later through newspaper announcements an addition 750 new applications were collected. United States Department of State, *Papers Relating to the Foreign Relations of the United States, 1934*, Vol. II (US Government Printing Office, 1934) , 895–97.

56. Trask, *The United States Response to Turkish Nationalism and Reform*, 205.

57. Letter from the Turkish Foreign Affairs Ministry to the American Embassy, 27 June 1933, in United States Department of State, *Papers Relating to the Foreign Relations of the United States, 1934*, Vol. II, 901–2.

58. Ibid., 903–5.

59. Nielsen, *American-Turkish Claims Settlement*, 9–11, 14–15.

60. United States Department of State, *Papers Relating to the Foreign Relations of the United States, 1934*, Vol. II, 917.

61. Ibid., 919–22.

62. The Great Fire of Smyrna was a fire destroyed much of the port city of Smyrna aka İzmir in September 1922.

63. Nielsen, *American-Turkish Claims Settlement*, 24, 323–26. See next note, 24–40

64. Ibid., 24–40.

65. United States Department of State, Papers Relating to the Foreign Relations of the United States, 1934, Vol. II, 933.

66. Ibid., 934. *Resmi Gazete*, No. 2896, 2 January 1935.

67. Nielsen, *American-Turkish Claims Settlement*, 780–84.

68. Trask, *The United States Response to Turkish Nationalism and Reform*, 208.

69. Ibid., 209.

70. For more detailed information on this topic, see Lee Boyd, "Pursuing Stolen Armenian Art (and other Armenian Assets) in U.S. Courts: The Nascent Stage," a paper delivered at the international conference Beyond the Armenian Genocide: The Question of Restitution and Reparation in Comparative Review which took place at Clark University, Worcester, on 27–28 October 2011.

71. Kemal Çiçek, "The 1934–1935 Turkish-American Compensation Agreement and its Implication for today," *Review of Armenian Studies*, no. 23 (2011):93–146. For commentary by Kemal Çiçek'in on this topic, see http://www.dunyabulteni.net/index.ph p?aType=haber&ArticleID=125395.

72. For the full text of the protocol, see "British Empire, France, Italy, Japan and Rumania, Convention concerning the Assessment and Reparation of Losses Suffered in Turkey by Nationals of the Contracting Powers, together with Protocol," signed at Paris, November 23, 1923, *League of Nations Treaty Series*, no. 713 (1924), http://www.worldlii.org/int/other/LNTSer/1924/160.pdf.

73. Treaty of Lausanne, as accessed at http://wwi.lib.byu.edu/index.php/ Treaty_of_Lausanne.

74. The source of this gold, which was placed in a German bank in Berlin, has been the subject of debate. A statement in the name of the Turkish Historical Society claims

that this confiscated gold belonged to Armenians and was transported to Berlin in 1916 by the Ittihadists. Based on this, any reparations to Armenians should be made by the British and French who seized this gold (*Bugün*, 26 June 2012). However, this gold has no connection to the Armenians. The money had been given to the Ottoman state, to the Ottoman Public Debts Administration in particular, by Austria and Germany as credit. This establishment in turn placed the money in a bank in Berlin in 1915. The Ittihadists transported the Armenians' money in 1916, and its fate remains unknown. For more detailed information on this subject, see Hrayr S. Karagueuzian and Yair Auron, *A Perfect Injustice, Genocide Theft of Armenian Wealth* (New Brunswick, NJ: Transaction Publishers, 2009), 99–135.

75. *League of Nations Treaty Series*, no. 713 (1924), http://www.worldlii.org/int/other/LNTSer/1924/160.pdf.
76. Ibid.
77. Errol M. McDogall, *Reparations, 1930–31. Special report upon Armenian claims* (Ottawa: F.A. Acland, Printer to the King, 1931), 3.
78. This figure only concerns applications from Great Britain, France, and Italy. If Japan and Romania were added, a larger number would be reached. The figure of 15,600 was given by the Financial Secretary to the Treasury in the 23 May 1928 session of the British parliament (http://hansard.millbanksystems.com/written_answers/1928/may/23/turkey-british-claims#S5CV0217P0_19280523_CWA_84).
79. Isabel Kaprielian Churchill, *Like Our Mountains, A History of Armenians in Canada* (Montreal: McGill-Queen's University Press, 2005), 208.
80. Lutz, "Claims against Turkey," 348–49.
81. In the decision made concerning the application of Canadian Armenians, for each spouse killed during massacres 100 liras would be paid, while 20 liras would be paid for each child killed (McDogall, *Reparations*, 10).
82. The importance of the isuse is that, as seen above, the Turkish government during negotiations in Lausanne and later bilaterally with the United States, considered that those Ottoman Armenians who became naturalized citizens of other states acted contrary to the Ottoman 1869 Citizenship Law and did not inform the Ottoman government before adopting new citizenships. To what degree these protests of Turkey were taken into consideration by the Paris Commission is the topic of an important but separate study. The commission rejected the demands of Canadian Armenians for reparations. It only wished to pay money in amounts so miniscule as to be comic in cases of killings of family members. For detailed information, see Isabel Kaprielian-Churchill, *Like Our Mountains*, 210–14.
83. Only one or two examples are given here in order to avoid too greatly broadening the extent of this work and entering into detailed technical discussions connected to international law. The decisions of the relevant mixed arbitral tribunals were published in ten volumes: Gilbert Gidel, *Recueil des decisions des Tribunaux Arbitraux Mixtes institus par les Traites de Paix*, 10 vols. (Buffalo, NY): William S. Hein & Co., 2006).
84. http://hansard.millbanksystems.com/commons/1933/may/16/turkey-british-claims#S5CV0278P0_19330516_HOC_151.
85. "Exchange of Notes between His Majesty's Government in the United Kingdom and the Government of the Turkish Republic concerning the Liquidation of Unexecuted Judgments of the Anglo-Turkish Mixed Arbitral Tribunal, Ankara 23 March 1944," Treaty Series, no. 48 (1946) (London: His Majesty's Stationery Office, 1946).
86. Hill, "The Anglo-Turkish Mixed Arbitral Tribunal," 248. In a similar case, the tribunal rejected the application because it was unable to prove the status of a "person placed under protection by Britain" (Arnold D. McNair and Hersch Lauerpacht,

eds., *International Law Reports, AnnualDigest of Public International Law Cases, Years 1927 and 1928*, Vol. 4, Cambridge: Grotius Publications Ltd., 1981, 309–10).

87. Ibid., 248–49.
88. McNair and Lutterpacht, *International Law Reports*, 312–13.
89. Paul Weis, *Nationality and Statelessness in International Law* (Alphen aan den Rijn, the Netherlands: Sijthoff & Noordhoff International Publishers B.V., 1979), 130.
90. McNair and Lutterpacht, *International Law Reports*, 395. The case was initiated based on Article 67 of the Treaty of Lausanne. According to this article, Turkey, Greece, Romania, and the Serb-Croat-Slovene state reciprocally accepted "to facilitate . . . the search on their territory for, and the restitution of, movable property of every kind taken away, seized or sequestrated by their armies or administrations" (Treaty of Lausanne, as accessed at http://wwi.lib.byu.edu/index.php/Treaty_of_ Lausanne). Turkey objected that paper money, coins, and stock certificates were not included in the scope of this article, and did not submit any list to the tribunal. The tribunal in its 26 July 1928 verdict accepted the list and the values submitted by the supplicants, and Turkey was sentenced to pay restitutions accordingly.
91. "League of Nations: Council, Return to Turkish Armenian Refugees in Greece of their Deposits in Foreign Banks at Smyrna and Their Property Left in Asia Minor (the Essayan Petition)," Geneva: n.p., 1925. Also see Mehmet Şükrü Güzel, "Anayasal Düzen, Hukuk, Adalet, Diaspora Ermenilerinin Türkiye Cumhuriyetine Toplu Geri Dönebilmeleri Mücadelesi," http://www.21yyte.org/tr/yazi6103-Diaspora_ Ermenilerin_Turkiye_Cumhuriyetine_Toplu_Geri_Donebilme_Mucadelesi__.html.
92. The number of Armenians surviving the Genocide and the following 1919–22 period is a topic of serious debate. On 16 November 1922, in a report prepared in the context of the discussions over an Armenian homeland, the Armenian Delegation estimated the number of surviving Armenians to be 817,873. Of these, 281,000 were estimated to be living in Turkey (Levon Marashlian, "The Armenian Question from Sèvres to Lausanne: Economic and Morality in American and British Policies, 1920–1923," Vol. 1, doctoral thesis, University of California, Los Angeles, 1992, 490–91).

CHAPTER 6

TURKEY AFTER LAUSANNE
RAISING A VIRTUAL WALL AROUND
ITS BORDERS LIKE A FORTRESS

The Treaty of Lausanne entered into force on 6 August 1924. The most important change the treaty introduced concerning abandoned properties was the requirement to return Armenians' properties to those who managed to remain in Turkey. Consequently, it was necessary to introduce some changes to the Abandoned Properties Laws in order to bring them into accord with the provisions of Lausanne.

Turkey faced a serious problem in bringing its laws into accord with Lausanne. What would happen if Armenians living abroad came back individually and began to demand their properties? This situation was not given a clear solution at Lausanne. Turkey had objected to the mass return of Armenians, and prevented this, but it was forced to accept individual repatriation in principle. Now, in order to prevent these repatriations, it was necessary for Turkey to raise a virtual wall around its borders like a fortress.

As noted above, the government, calculating that certain results would emerge from Lausanne, took some steps prior to the conclusion of this treaty. On 14 September 1922 it cancelled the 8 January 1920 regulation that stipulated the return of properties to the Armenians and put the 26 September 1915 Liquidation Law back into service. Then, on 31 October 1922, the government chronologically extended the authority to confiscate properties regulated by the 8 November 1915 decree to include the 1918–23 period. Accordingly, movable and immovable properties would be administered by the government until the return of individuals who, prior to or after the world war, in any manner whatsoever, went to foreign or occupied territories with the aim of travel and who still had not returned.

This step was later reinforced through a law dated 15 April 1923. Its sixth article in particular clearly stated that the 26 September 1915 law and the changes made to the latter through the 15 April law concerning "movable and immovable properties, debts and amounts receivable which were left by those *in any manner whatsoever lost or leaving a place or fleeing to foreign or occupied territories*, or to Istanbul or its environs" [italics are ours] would be applied.[1]

The government did something else in this period. Without waiting for the provisions of the Treaty of Lausanne, it began to distribute the abandoned properties under its control. For example, through a law issued on 13 March 1924, it began to give "abandoned property and land found in the hand of the government belonging to people not subject to [population] exchange" to those whose properties were destroyed during the war, "on condition that those who are destitute be preferred."[2] Similarly, on 3 April 1924 a regulation was issued facilitating the transfer to the government of the buildings that the government viewed to be necessary.[3]

If the Armenians, taking advantage of the opportunities created by Lausanne, would want to return despite the measures taken and the start of the distribution of properties, what would happen? The only alternative for Turkey, as it did not want to return the properties of these people, would be to obstruct their reentry into the country. It was not possible, however, to completely prohibit their entry due to the Lausanne Treaty. Turkey identified two feasible means. The first was the 1869 Citizenship Law and, in particular, its fifth article; the second was security investigations, which would be carried out on an individual basis. However, as we will show below, these two means did not serve a useful purpose. Instead, they paved the way to diplomatic crises with various countries abroad and to political scandals domestically.

The crisis was not limited to Armenians abroad coming to Turkey. Armenians in Turkey who had been forced to change their places of residence might want to return to their former locations and obtain their properties. It was necessary to prevent Armenians from returning to their former location and obtaining their properties. Consequently, the laws for entry and exit from the country were changed and prohibitions were placed on internal travel. Turkey was transformed into a fortress surrounded by ramparts.

American Armenians Are Not Permitted to Enter Turkey

The first political crisis emerged with the United States. A group of American Armenians, wanting to use their right of entry as individuals to regain their properties, in August 1923 attempted to enter Turkey with American passports but were arrested and sent back. The American high commissioner in Istanbul, Admiral Mark Bristol, in a telegraph to the U.S. State Department wrote the following: "Several naturalized Americans of Ottoman origin who arrived recently from the United States on [the] steamer *Canada*, with their passports properly visaed by Spanish consul, New York City, were refused permission to land, and were [are?] now threatened with deportation." In the ensuing negotiations, the Ottoman authorities informed Bristol that "no more naturalized citizens of Ottoman origin would be permitted to enter Turkey and that orders will be sent Spanish consul in New York to refuse visas to this class of persons." Consequently, Bristol suggested that "no passport be issued to persons of Ottoman origin for return to Turkey," and added, "I will continue opposition in every practicable way possible to this Turkish attitude toward admission of these naturalized Americans."[4]

In another telegram he sent the same day, Bristol reported another decision of the Turkish government: "Adnan Bey informed me . . . that naturalized Americans of Hellenic [non-Ottoman] origin, as well as naturalized Americans of Russian-Armenian origin, will be permitted to enter Turkey freely. He assured me that should naturalized Americans of Ottoman origin arrive [in] Turkey they will not be arrested but will be requested by the police to leave the country, and he further assured me that I would be notified in each case."[5] The decision is an interesting one. The entry of Greeks and Armenians to Turkey was free on condition that they were not of Ottoman origin, while Ottoman Armenians were prohibited entry.

It is useful to remember that this decision was based on the 1869 Ottoman Citizenship Law and the November 1918 Passport Law. The Citizenship Law gave Turkey the possibility of not accepting the

American citizenship of the Armenians. If Turkey wished to do so, it could remove these individuals from Turkish citizenship. It did not do this, however, as this would create the risk of these people entering Turkey as foreign citizens. Meanwhile, according to the third article of the Passport Law, even if refugees who came without permission of the Turkish government or people stripped of their citizenship possessed appropriate passports, they could not enter the country. Moreover, according to Article 23 of the same law, "if [an individual who was still an Ottoman citizen] bearing a foreign passport enters the Ottoman domains, [he may be given a sentence ranging from] six months to two years [in] prison."[6] Turkey, while not denaturalizing American Armenians, kept all these alternatives in reserve. It told America, however, that it would not arrest these people, but would send them back immediately to the United States.

The State Department, responding to Bristol's request not to give passports to Americans of Ottoman origin, stated that the

> Department . . . cannot make the distinction between classes of citizens implied by your suggestion that no passport be issued to persons of Ottoman origin desiring to return to Turkey. The *Revised Statutes of the United States* distinctly provide in section 2000 as follows: "All naturalized citizens of the United States, while in foreign countries, are entitled to, and shall receive from this Government, the same protection of persons and property which is accorded to native-born citizens." . . . The most that can be done is to warn such travelers, when issuing passport to them of present Turkish regulations and of the fact that naturalized American citizens who evade those regulations or conceal their nationality for the purpose of travel in Turkey cannot expect full American protection."[7]

The State Department also made clear that Bristol should not communicate this information to the Turkish authorities. He "should continue to make it clear to them that under American law one citizen has as good a right to protection from this Government as another."[8]

This issue became an obstacle to the ratification of the Treaty of Lausanne by the American Senate. A second note by the State Department, written to Bristol in Istanbul on 29 September 1923, stated that even though it never actually went into effect there was a treaty signed in 1874 on this subject. Moreover, it was said that the 1869 Citizenship Law was a product of special conditions, like the capitulations, and that after the removal of the latter there was no longer a need for such a law. Therefore, Turkey must change its position on this issue.[9]

Another important point that Bristol was asked to tell the Turkish authorities, was that America's position of defending the rights of people who became its citizens did not mean retrospective protection of their rights concerning periods in which they were not yet American citizens. The United States would only protect Armenian rights over properties after the Armenians had become American citizens, and would not cover transactions conducted in the period prior to their citizenship.[10]

The parties during these negotiations, as we discussed above, postponed the reparations issue through the exchange of letters on 23 December 1923 and decided it would be examined by a joint commission to be established after the ratification of the treaty. On 31 December Bristol proposed that a similar stance be adopted concerning the citizenship issue because he observed that "the Turks seem at present unreasonably hostile toward all questions concerning naturalized citizens of Ottoman origin."[11] Bristol believed that there were two reasons for this. First was the propaganda conducted by Armenians and Greeks in the United States against the Turks. The second was the fear that if these two peoples were permitted to return, they would again gain control of the Turkish economy. Consequently, it was not possible in a short period of time to expect any solution of this issue. The Department of State accepted this proposal and the issue was postponed.[12] The significance of this was simple: Armenians who had become American citizens would not be able to go to Turkey and obtain their properties.

The Return of the Armenians:
A Question of the Honor and Pride of the State

It was not only the American Armenians who thought that Lausanne made it possible for them to regain their properties and wanted to go back to Turkey to do so. Other Armenians and Greeks with the financial ability wanted to do the same thing. In addition, some of these Armenians had not adopted other citizenships, meaning that there was no possibility of using the 1869 Citizenship Law against them. The only thing left for Turkey to do was to prevent them from entering the country by citing security concerns. This is exactly what it did.

We were able to find two separate regulations on this issue. The first was a circular of the Interior Ministry dated 18 June 1923. It stated that permission for entry into the country would be granted only to those who requested it from the ministry and who had visas in their passports from Turkish diplomatic representatives or recognized embassies and consulates.[13] The second was the 5 September 1923 decree number 6549 of the General Directorate of Security. The fifth article of this decree stated that "those cooperating with the enemy who flee or emigrate from our country or went with a foreign passport or laissez-passer, [and] Ottoman Greeks subject to population exchange cannot return."[14] However, it was not possible to entirely prevent the types of entry into the country noted by these regulations. Moreover, the latter were propitious for the creation of an environment very suitable for bribery. In fact, this is what ended up being created and in 1924 and 1925 a great uproar started as a result of some great scandals.

Some Armenians who had learned about the significance of 6 August 1924 wanted to enter Turkey and take back their properties. With the Istanbul newspapers pressing the issue, their return to Turkey became one of the most talked-about topics of 1924, and in a short time turned into a scandal. The issue ramified and grew so rapidly that commissions of inquiry were established and secret sessions were devoted to it in the Grand National Assembly. The government, in a 29 May 1924 regulation, described the entry of Armenians into Turkey as a matter concerning the honor and pride of the state.[15] As a result of the investigations, on 21 May Interior Minister Ferit Bey was forced to resign and many high-ranking bureaucrats were removed from office and arrested.[16]

The scandal began with the appearance of some articles in newspapers on 31 March and 1 and 2 April under the caption "Issue of the Return of Rich Armenians to the Country."[17] According to the news, three Armenians entered Istanbul through bribery. The interesting aspect of these discussions of scandal and bribery that enveloped the entire country was that there was no legal obstacle whatsoever to the entry of these people into Turkey. Even the daily newspapers presenting this news as scandal were aware of this: "No one has the right to prevent the entry of people with Turkish citizenship unless their treason has been established and unless an imperative decision preventing their return exists."[18] Commenting on this topic, the governor-general of Istanbul said that as far as the return of non-Muslims was concerned, a security investigation of each person would be conducted and the Interior Ministry would make its decision based on the results.[19] Later similar views would be repeated at the secret sessions of the Grand National Assembly and the internal affairs minister would be acquitted.

When this news appeared in the newspapers, the aforementioned three Armenians (Karnik Sübuhyan, Gümüşgerdanyan, and Benon

Değirmenciyan) were hastily and forcibly expelled from the country.[20] The newspapers justifiably asked why they had been admitted into the country if their expulsion was necessary.[21] The Istanbul police director summarized the situation concisely: "They gave orders; I let [them] in. They gave orders; I expelled [them]."[22]

In a secret session held in the assembly on this topic, the interior minister openly confessed that these expulsions were illegal. He said about the Armenians that "they were expelled abroad by me. Not at all—[they] were not expelled. They themselves requested their going abroad and they agreed. Gentlemen, because the law of personal immunity gave no one this right. The right to expel anyone who has Turkish citizenship, whether Ottoman Greek or Armenian—whoever it may be—has not been given."[23]

Even though the Armenians were expelled pell-mell, the press was not ready to let go of the issue. It wanted to reveal that there were claims of bribery, and to expose those who took the bribes. It even went after Armenians who entered Istanbul with normal passports, hostilely writing against these individuals.[24] Citizens also joined the chorus and began to flood the press with denouncements of individuals suspected of entering without permission. Headlines, such as "Two Fugitives Still in Our City!" and "To the Attention of the Police Directorate and the Liquidation Commission" appeared, and the names and addresses of many Armenian people were published.[25]

Letters sent to the Istanbul press from the provinces make it evident that the problem was not restricted to Istanbul. Armenians in many places in Anatolia wanted to return and get their properties. The newspaper *Tevhid-i Efkâr* published news such as this: "It is learned as days pass that the irregularities of the return of the rich Armenians is not exclusive to Istanbul. On the contrary, this misconduct, like an infectious disease, exists in nearly every corner of our country . . . Many fugitives in an influx return[ed] to their old places."[26]

Despite the efforts of the government to cover up the incident, the press continued to write about it. *Vatan* believed that if a thorough investigation were to be conducted, then a large gang would be discovered.[27] The issue stirred up the Republican People's Party, which had heated arguments in its Assembly group meetings. As a result of the intensity of the criticisms, a vote of confidence concerning the interior minister was held. With eighty-three votes, the minister won back the deputies' confidence. However, some deputies were so angry that they walked out before the vote.[28]

Nonetheless, the topic progressed from the Republican People's Party group to the Assembly as a whole, and a parliamentary motion placed it on the agenda for discussion. Severe criticism was directed at the interior minister. According to Zonguldak deputy Halil Bey, this was a matter of "honor and pride for the country." He spoke of the existence of companies "sticking their noses in abandoned properties affairs . . . [that succeeded in] establishing branches in Ankara," and accused the minister "of not showing sensitivity" on this topic. Halil Bey proposed "the Exalted Assembly's taking action on the affair, [and the establishment of an] investigative committee composed of five or seven people from the honorable members," but the Parliament rejected his proposal.[29]

Interior Minister Ferit Bey, in his speech of response, rejected the accusations and said that "the way the Armenians returned to Istanbul . . . [was in accordance with] the propositions of the laws and regulations." According to the minister, the question was limited to whether abuses had taken place during people's entry into the country. He said that an investigation had been initiated into this.[30] The fierce criticism of the minister, however, continued in the media and, as a reaction, the minister opened a lawsuit against the Istanbul press.[31]

According to newspaper reports, it was Prime Minister İsmet İnönü who saved the minister from being forced to resign.[32] İnönü believed that this entire campaign was "aimed at bringing down the cabinet."[33] Nonetheless, due to the pressure from the press he was forced, in the end, to create an investigatory commission.[34] Ferit Bey, though using another event as an excuse, was unable to withstand the pressure and resigned. The press was very hopeful about the new interior minister, Şükrü Bey, and believed that he would clean things up.[35]

While the investigations were still continuing, the press reported that large sums of money were involved in the matter. Just the bribes distributed by the wealthy Armenian named Sübuhyan exceeded 15,000 liras. Some Armenians were expelled from the country once more because they either were unable to pay the bribes they had promised to give, or the amounts they paid were seen as insufficient.[36] The inspectors conducting the investigation prepared separate reports for each Armenian and Greek entering the country. Only four of these reports were published, and these incompletely. Although much new information emerged, the fact that they were published incompletely led to the raising of some eyebrows. The press was of the opinion that some things were being kept secret, and that it was for this purpose that the reports were intentionally given in an incomplete fashion to the newspapers.[37]

Relying on the first reports many bureaucrats—like the governor-general, police chief of Istanbul, and Ankara prison director Efdaled-din Bey—were removed from office. The reports proposed the initiation of criminal investigations concerning these individuals.[38] The names of several parliamentary deputies were also entangled in this bribery scandal. The government was obliged to directly intervene in the matter and assign it to the assembly. In a decision taken on 29 May 1924, although the assembly was on a break, it wanted the meeting of the "responsible committee of the Parliament as soon as possible" in connection with the topic "from the point of view of the pride of the state." After all, "the honor and pride of the state" were at stake.[39] During this period the report on Sübuhyan, identified as "the most important investigatory report,"[40] was published so public opinion became aware that the issue was not restricted to bureaucrats, but also included some parliamentary deputies.

It was understood from the report, distributed to the press on 20 July 1924, that a network involved in bribery existed in Ankara, led by deputies and the Interior Ministry that was connected to the Istanbul police. The network would obtain the names of rich Armenians applying to the Istanbul police, enter into contact with them, and—promising to obtain clean reports on them—would ask for large sums of money.[41] As we wrote above, those Armenians unable to pay the promised bribes were expelled once more from the country. It was also discovered that some Armenians, who succeeded in entering the country before the news was published in the newspapers, were able to regain their properties.[42]

Moreover, the relationship between the term of office of the Liquidation Commission founded in Istanbul coming to its end and the arrivals to the country is interesting and important. According to the news of 18 April 1924, there were approximately 3,500 cases opened against the Istanbul Liquidation Commission with the goal of regaining properties.[43] The number of Greeks and Armenians who came to Istanbul and wanted to get their properties was about one hundred.[44] The newspapers were correct in writing, "Why There Are No Poor among Those Coming." They stated, "Those coming are all people who are rich merchants and owners of real estate. The coming of any moneyless, poor person among them was not permitted."[45]

At the conclusion of the investigations, over ten people, including high-ranking bureaucrats, were removed from office[46] and in Istanbul five people, the local police chief among them, were arrested.[47] Since it was stated in the final report that many assembly deputies were directly involved in the bribery scandal, the topic was again brought onto the agenda of the assembly and it was decided to hold a secret session. After fierce debates in the 18 February 1925 session, it was decided that investigations of former Interior Minister Ferit Bey, who had resigned by this time, were not necessary.[48]

The entire problem, which was presented as a scandal, concerned the belongings and real estate of Armenians—and the knowledge that, with Lausanne, it would be necessary to return the properties of the Armenians who were present at the latter. In this understanding the truth revealed by this whole series of events called the "bribery scandal" is extremely simple. Lausanne is a turning point. Those surviving Armenians whose financial situation permitted might want to return and obtain their properties, while Turkey was determined not to return these properties. Consequently, Turkey wanted to prevent the entry of the Armenians in any manner possible.

Another truth revealed by these incidents was that security investigations on an individual basis were not sufficient. For this reason, all Armenians who had entered the country in any manner were identified and some were again expelled from the country. Their properties were transferred to the state again. For example, Sübuhyan and Tahtaburunyan, who were the most discussed by name in the bribery scandal, possessed "vast real estate" that was handed over to the administration of the National Property Directorate after these two Armenians were expelled.[49]

The real issue was the existence of a legal problem that had still not been fully solved. How the properties of Armenians who had noiselessly succeeded in entering the country prior to 6 August 1924 would be treated could not be fully clarified. Some newspaper columns pointed to this legal gap.[50] One of the problems was whether the 15 April 1923 law and, in particular, its sixth article would be applicable to the properties of people returning prior to 6 August, since the Lausanne Treaty had not yet gone into effect then. As we shall later see, in order to solve this question legally, some new laws and regulations would have to be issued. Here we will suffice with discussing news from a newspaper of 21 June 1924. According to this news, the 15 April 1923 Liquidation Law was valid for all properties and all transactions conducted after the date that a fugitive fled would be voided.[51]

In other words, even when people considered "fleeing and lost," whose properties had been seized, returned to Turkey the government was determined not to give them back their properties. Moreover, in accordance with an instruction given to the Property Directorate, "a list of abandoned properties in Istanbul belonging to fugitive Ottoman Greeks and Armenians" was going to be produced. In this way, it would be easy to prevent the return of these properties.[52]

In sum, the efforts of American Armenians to enter Turkey in 1923, and the bribery scandal of the spring of 1924, revealed the truth that Armenians and Greeks wanted to come back and regain their properties. Security investigations were not sufficient to stop their coming. A regulation was necessary and, indeed, one was issued.

"To Allow Their Return Means to Waste . . . the Blood We Spilled"

The bribery scandal revealed that it was not only a handful of Armenians who wanted to return. It also higlighted that it is necessary to examine this topic as a part of a generally hostile attitude in the country against the Greeks and Armenians. A brief glimpse at the contemporary press may help readers better appreciate the atmosphere of the period. This will also illuminate the circumstances in which many laws and regulations, especially the *Seyr–i Sefer* (Travel Regulation), were issued. More importantly, it will indicate the pivotal importance of the abandoned properties issue and that public opinion knew of that issue's significance.

The press of the period showed that both the absence of a legal obstacle to the individual return of Armenians and Ottoman Greeks abroad and the possibility of individuals' return to Istanbul according to the Lausanne Treaty led to intense reactions. This was a part of the serious anti-Armenian and anti-Greek hostility dominating the press. For example, *Tevhid-i Efkâr* described non-Muslims as "foreigners in Turkey who are rich."[53] According to the newspaper, "It was absolutely impossible for the non-Muslim elements to be Turkish, to assimilate into Turkishness. . . . They are poisons which have entered Turkey's edifice and must not be assimilated, but gradually must be expelled. There is no other choice for Turkey to live in health and vitality and to be happy."[54]

Hostility to Armenians and Greeks was behind the great reaction to the bribery scandal. It seemed as if the reaction was not to bribes being taken, but to something more important: that the people giving the bribes were Armenians and Greeks and that bribes were made to assist them in entering the country. One newspaper wrote,

There are those appearing among us who in the end, in exchange for a few thousand liras, give the opportunity to those traitors to the homeland and nation who devoted the money they took from the Turk to spill the blood of the Turk, and later in fear of what they had done fled, to again enter among us. This is nothing other than thrusting a poisonous snake into the bosom of our mother or offspring with our own hand. This means treason against the laws of the state. This means betrayal of honor and virtue. This means outright treason of the nation, the homeland.[55]

As the newspaper *Vatan* pointed out, there was a fear that "the issue of the return of the rich Armenians to Istanbul" would lead to the spread of "Armenians to all parts of Istanbul, and maybe of Anatolia, on all kinds of pretexts."[56]

The general opinion on the issue of the returning individuals can be summed up as "rich Armenians having been able to enter the country is a mistake, but their being expelled after this mistake was understood is a good deed."[57] However, even if this action is "praiseworthy, . . . it is not sufficient [because the matter] does not [only] consist of sending the coming Armenians, whose not entering the country is necessary, to the places from which they came." Those who introduced the Armenians into Istanbul must also be sent to court.[58]

The fact that all of Anatolia, after going through World War I, emerged from another war in the 1918–22 period, played a great role in the hostility toward the Armenians and Greeks. A reader from Izmir writing to the newspaper *Tevhid-i Efkâr* expressed the reaction to the return of Armenians and Greeks as thus: "Although Izmir— beautiful Izmir where for years we spilled blood—presented a picture one thousand times more terrible than Istanbul, neither newspapers nor [assembly] deputies [paid] to this issue the importance it deserves." According to this reader, these people, who are "enemies of the Turks, . . . are accused of actual treason and crimes like spilling the blood of our brothers, killing innocent children [and] mothers, [and] burning Turkish villages."[59]

The Travel Regulation was met with similar reactions. The headlines posted by the newspaper *Tevhid-i Efkâr* in connection with this law are very instructional: "Athens and Beyoğlu Are Celebrating: Fugitive Greeks, Armenians, Jews Are Returning to the Country! To Allow Their Return Means to Waste the Value of Our Struggle and the Blood We Spilled!"[60] The newspaper was very sad that the Ottoman Greeks who, "biting like a snake, fearing the encounter of victorious Turkish bayonets," fled Istanbul and "are going to return, cheerful and pleased, through the permission granted by the Travel Regulation."[61]

The newspaper said that there was a very objectionable additional aspect to the return of those who had been pushed "out the door by the victorious kick of the Turkish soldier." Refugees had been given "the property that the fugitive traitors left in the city . . . by the government. . . . After the return of the fugitives," the refugees would have to be removed from the places in which they had settled. The newspaper asked, "In this case, what will we do with the refugees? Are we going to take the houses . . . in which we settled them and return them to the traitors?"[62]

The newspaper, proposing that the properties "they left in Istanbul which they abandoned because they brandished daggers behind the back of the Turkish people," must not be returned to the Christians, added that "if we return them, a *national loss* amounting to an alarming sum" [italics are ours] would arise. The newspaper found that this could not be recuperated, and that "we absolutely must not tolerate" the return of these properties and the expulsion "of our coreligionists from the abandoned properties on which they were settled." The newspaper had an expectation: "We hope very much that the government will pay attention to this point of view and will make the necessary modifications in the regulation."[63] The newspaper *Vatan* complained that "while it was decided that the properties belonging to fugitives were going to be used by the government in order to solve the troubles of occupied regions, such regions remained without any solution; the fugitives [came back and] settled on the properties."[64]

Those who approached the issue rationally were able to see that at the core of the issue were the properties left behind by the Armenians. For example, Mehmet Asım of the newspaper *Vatan* said that "because the abandoned properties of the people who were coming were confiscated by the government, the opening of lawsuits against the government, [and] propounding claims of damage and harm" were feared. According to Mehmet Asım, this situation must be described as a "disaster."[65]

In sum, the confiscated properties of the departed Greeks and Armenians were seen as national revenue, while returning these properties to their true owners was seen as national loss. The laws and regulations of this period were issued in this state of mind.

The Legal Vacuum Created by
Lausanne on Repatriation

There is another fact revealed by the bribery scandal discussions. There were different points of view in Turkey concerning whether

Lausanne permitted Armenians to freely return to the country. This was discussed in the press and the National Assembly throughout the scandal. A close examination of these discussions is extremely important for understanding what the legal situation was and learning how the government wanted to implement the law.

For example, in the secret session of the Grand National Assembly on 3 April 1924, government authorities expressed that Lausanne accepted the individual return of Armenians. Yet they frankly confessed that the policy they followed was to not permit their entry. The reason why they permitted a limited number of entries was to avoid international reaction. Later, even this would be halted through the Travel Regulation.

An interesting discussion on the topic took place in the 3 April 1924 secret session of the Grand National Assembly. Kozan deputy Ali Saip Bey complained that a large number of Armenians were returning to Istanbul. He asked the minister whether these people had the right to return. He also wanted to know whether the provisions of the Abandoned Properties Laws would be applied to their properties. He said, "They say that the property of those leaving the country will be confiscated. Armenian fugitives are continually coming to Istanbul. Will this law be enforced concerning them too? . . . These people previously fled; how is it that they are coming [back] now? How are you going to treat them?"[66] Konya deputy Refik Bey made a pithy comment: "The door was opened. After this, they are going to come."[67]

While Ali Saip Bey was repeating his question, he stressed that the session was a secret one: "Mr. Chairman, sir, as the session is secret, I will ask this of the minister of the interior. The Armenians want to come again and obtain their properties . . . I am asking that since the sitting is secret, let the minister of the interior come and provide us with explanations on this matter." The portion of the response pertaining to the properties was given by Finance Minister Abdülhalik (Renda), who said, "we consider [the properties of these people] abandoned properties." He summed up the policy being followed in one sentence: "We will create as many difficulties as possible for those who are not part of us."[68] The attitude is clear. Even if the Armenians had the right to return as individuals, every sort of obstacle would be placed in their way. This is an important confession.

The problem of the return of the Armenians was also treated in the press. The newspapers *Vatan* and *Cumhuriyet* published articles stating that it was not "absolutely obliged to admit the Armenians who had left." For example, according to Yunus Nadi of *Cumhuriyet*, İsmet

İnönü at Lausanne did not place Turkey under any obligation and even took a stance against the coming of the Armenians.[69]

A deputy speaking to a newspaper concerning the bribery scandal said that the question of the return of the Armenians was one of the most tackled topics at Lausanne. Furthermore, he regarded Interior Minister Ferit Bey's words in the Assembly to the effect of "the coming of the Armenians conforms to the laws" as wrong and said, in order to defend himself, "The Interior Minister spoke very incorrectly of this treaty [Lausanne]."[70]

The issue was also discussed in the 18 February 1925 secret sessions in the Assembly.[71] Some deputies declared that no categorical regulation existed in the Lausanne Treaty about the entry of Greeks and Armenians to Turkey; and "with the proclamation of the general amnesty, consent was absolutely not [given] to the entry of the Armenians who had left the country." Mersin deputy Niyazi Bey's words that "the Turkish government absolutely and categorically is under no obligation concerning the return of Armenians who had left the country" were interrupted by yells of "Bravo."[72]

The former interior minister Ferit Bey, opposing these views, clearly exposed the legal dimension of the issue, declaring, "When we examine the issue from a legal perspective, there is no stipulation of law preventing the return of such fugitives, on condition that they are not subject to the [population] exchange. None of our legal regulations prevent a movement in this manner." He added, "I will go further," and said that in the treaty and protocols signed at Lausanne "the entry of those among such Greek and Armenian fugitives who have not been punished in this country for creating disorder [is] accepted."[73]

In his speech Ferit Bey recalled that the main criticism in the bribery scandal concerned why the Greeks and Armenians were allowed back into the country. He pointed out that the situation concerning the Greeks was very clear and quoted from the second and sixteenth articles of the Convention Concerning the Exchange of Greek and Turkish Populations and Protocol, mentioned above. As for the return of the Armenians, he said that as interior minister he had requested the view of the Foreign Affairs Ministry on 29 April 1924, and the answer arrived on 10 May.

The correspondence between the ministries was secret and Ferit Bey quoted from this exchange. For this reason, it is useful to look into this extremely important discussion, which indicates the legal principles concerning the return of non-Muslims and how the Turkish government wished to violate these principles.

The Foreign Affairs Ministry said that "it is necessary to investigate the situation of Greeks and Armenians who are not subject to [population] exchange and went in various ways to foreign countries and presently evince the desire to return; and it is appropriate to prevent the return of those [of the aforementioned] who could cause serious drawbacks." Continuing, he reminded that during the Lausanne negotiations the Turkish government promised that the "carrying out of this supreme duty through the aforementioned measures would not affect *harmless people and Turkish citizens.*"[74] In other words, after conducting the necessary investigations the ministry repeated the general principle that it was necessary to permit the entry of the Armenians and Greeks.

However, in the same document, the Foreign Affairs Ministry also expressed another very important desire. No matter how many promises were given concerning the Istanbul Greeks, who had been excluded from the population exchange, it wanted to subject these Greeks to the same procedures as the Armenians: "Even though it could be claimed to a certain degree that the Ottoman Greeks were excluded, and the Turkish delegation [at Lausanne] announced repeatedly that the right of originally *Rum* [Ottoman Greek] Turks not subject to [population] exchange to return to Turkey was fully protected by the Exchange of Populations Convention . . . it is apparent that it cannot be suitable to concentrate only on one element."[75] Ferit Bey very properly summarized this complicated proposal of the Foreign Affairs Ministry, which meant open transgression of the Treaty of Lausanne: "In other words, we must work to prohibit the Ottoman Greeks just as we prohibited the others." The Foreign Affairs Ministry felt it necessary to warn about the political line which should be followed: "Because the prevention of the return of non-Muslims without exception who previously left our country could cause objections, the *acceptance of a suitable number of people* from non-Muslims belonging to any race whose return will produce no serious damage and inappropriateness and who have lived inoffensively would be suitable to be taken into consideration to strengthen our position in order to secure the non-admission of the others" [italics are ours].[76]

This position is so clear, it requires no explanation. The ministry was essentially stating that while it did not want to admit any non-Muslims, it had to accept at least a few, just to avoid the unmanagable protests that would otherwise ensue. The goal was not to implement the law but to violate it without creating too much reaction.

Ferit Bey said that the matter arose "based on *the lack of any state law existing to prevent the entry of people into the country*, apart from

people causing disorder" [italics are ours].[77] The former minister repeated that although there was no legal obstacle to the entry into the
country of these Armenians who currently were Turkish citizens, they
were expelled from Turkey. He even confessed that this expulsion was
contrary to the law. His explanation of why this was done is extremely
important. He said, "If I had not expelled them," the impression would
be created that "the Armenians were able to come without being no-
ticed and that they had the right to come." This was something Ferit
did not want to allow.[78]

During the hearings, a very fierce debate took place between Ferit
Bey and Ali Fethi Bey, the prime minister and national defense minister, respectively. The prime minister, referring to the 5 September
1923 decree issued while he was interior minister (which we discussed
above), said "I want to clearly say that . . . in my time, according to
the articles of the 5 September general circular which I issued, no Armenians who obtained foreign passports, cooperated with occupying
forces, or betrayed us entered the country." The words of the prime
minister were greeted with applause.[79]

When Ferit Bey wanted to step into the fray, saying "Unfortunately,
I would like to speak," Prime Minister Ali Fethi Bey interjected, "If
you want to prove the opposite of this," and continued: "Our inspectors
investigated one by one, they reviewed, and in my time were not able
to find and cannot find a decree which was issued for the entry through
our borders of people whose admission into the country was inappropriate. . . . In my time such a decree was not issued."[80]

In reply, Ferit Bey said, "Ali Fethi Bey . . . seems to forget. The records of those who entered by obtaining permission exist." According to
Ferit Bey, there were as many as fifty people who were given permission to enter the country in Ali Fethi Bey's time in office, quoting from
the documents of an Armenian citizen who had been given permission.
Ali Fethi Bey defended himself, saying, "Those who left our country by
obtaining passports can return. However, those who obtained foreign
passports, were in the service of foreign powers in the occupied regions,
or those whose treasons and actions against the Turks are established
by police investigation cannot enter our country. This is the decree,
and this notification is a proclamation completely consistent with the
declaration made by His Excellency İsmet Pasha while the Lausanne
Treaty negotiations were occurring." Those who were given permission for entry into the country in his period were people with Turkish
passports, while, in Ferit Bey's period, they "are people who entered
contrary to this decree."[81]

The discussions continued in this manner and were concluded by a motion to end debate. It was voted that Ferit Bey did not act contrary to the law in giving permission to Armenians to enter, and he was cleared of any blame. The accepted statement read as follows: "We listened to former interior minister Ferit Bey's explanation concerning the entry of the Armenians in question into our country and their being expelled from the country. The commands issued by our friend are within [the scope of] his authority. There was no illegal conduct in his actions."[82] It is significant that, despite all the protests of the assembly, the entries into the country were found to be legal.

The reason why we presented the debate at this length is twofold: first, we wanted to make the legal dimension understandable; and second, we wished to show the mindset behind the political will that must implement the related laws. The matter is clear: Turkey was forced at Lausanne, against its will, to accept the entry of Armenians on an individual basis, but used the laws at its disposal to prevent this from actually taking place. The operation of the bribery network took advantage of the absence of a clear law on the subject, or basically, a legal void. The Travel Regulation issued in 1924 was the direct result of these developments, and its goal was to fill this legal vacuum.

The Travel Regulation: Bans on Entry into the Country and Domestic Travel

In the section "The Prohibition of Domestic Travel and Migration" we presented the decisions of the Kemalist movement pertaining to the prohibitions of domestic migration and travel of Armenians. Until 1923, because the borders were primarily under the control of the Ottoman government, the Ankara government did not deal much with issues of entry and departure from the country, with the exception of the 7 October 1920 Regulation. These issues gained importance when the Ankara government obtained control over the entirety of the country, and especially as a result of the Treaty of Lausanne. The most comprehensive steps on these issues were taken one month prior to the Treaty of Lausanne entering into force, through the Travel Regulation[83] of 2 July 1924, number 663 and the Passport Laws. In fact, the preparations for the Travel Regulation had begun much earlier, and the goal was to prevent Armenians from entering Turkey.

Tevhid-i Efkâr on 29 March 1924, relying on Interior Minister Ferit Bey's words, reported that the ministry was preparing "a legislative bill regarding our lands to the east of a straight line starting from Samsun and stretching along the Mediterranean shore as far as the coast of Silifke as a forbidden zone for Armenians." The newspaper wrote that this prohibition was issued with the goal of "the complete extirpation of the treason and the possibility of the repetition one more time of the Armenians' . . . evil disposition and the thousand and one treasons and disasters, which they perpetrated at the end of the world war and the period of the Armistice." According to the newspaper, by means of this law, "the connection of the Armenians with our homeland will be completely cut." Thus, "we will be forever rid of this injurious mass which while it stayed in our country could not avoid being, like the Greeks, an element of discord and contention." This law "is not at all comparable with the disasters the entire Armenian race perpetrated during the last ten years in the country."[84]

The Interior Ministry announced on 15 June 1924 that "the need was seen for the drawing up of such a regulation on the question of the return to Istanbul of fugitive Armenians."[85] When we look closely at the Travel Regulation, comprising nineteen articles in all, we see that it really was issued to prevent the entry of Armenians into Turkey. The first article prohibited the entry into the country of the *yüzellilikler* (literally, the 150ers), 150 people deprived of their Turkish citizenship. They were members of the imperial family and those who actively opposed the War of Liberation. According to this article, with the exception of the 150, "fearing the consequences of the acts they perpetrated against the country, or the opposition they manifested against the National Movement, *Muslims who are Turkish citizens* who fled to a foreign country in any manner without obtaining a Turkish passport will be able to enter the country by virtue of the right of liberty granted to every citizen by the general amnesty and the constitution" [italics are ours].[86] Thus, the regulation granted permission to enter the country to all (excluding 150) Muslims who were Turkish citizens, no matter how they left the country.

Article 3 concerned Ottoman Greek citizens who remained within the borders of the municipality of Istanbul. According to the second article of the Turkish-Greek population exchange treaty signed on 30 January 1923, the Ottoman Greeks living in Istanbul were excluded from the population exchange. According to its sixteenth article, "No obstacle shall be placed in the way of the inhabitants of the districts excepted from the exchange under Article 2 exercising freely their right to remain in or return to those districts and to enjoy to the full their liberties and rights of property in Turkey and Greece."[87] Thus, there was no obstacle to the free return of the Ottoman Greeks.

Article 3 of the Travel Regulation was related to this issue: "Ottoman Greeks not subject to [population] exchange, having gone with a passport or having fled, who are located in foreign countries, and are of the people of the area the border[88] of which is defined in accordance with the 1328–1912 law of the Istanbul prefecture, and the original inhabitants of the islands of Bozca and İmroz, can come to the aforementioned zones in the recognized way."[89] Again, according to this article, the Ottoman Greeks could live only in Istanbul and the islands of Bozca and İmroz, which were excluded from the population exchange, and their entries and exits would be limited to only this area.

The fourth, fifth, and sixth articles of the regulation concern the Armenians. They state that only those who left with passports issued by the National Government (Article 4), or with an Ottoman passport in the period between 1 July 1922 and the date the National Government gained control over Istanbul (Article 5) could freely return to the country. In other words, Armenians who did not conform to the above-mentioned conditions were prohibited from returning to the country.

According to the seventh article, "Jews leaving Turkey without passports are subject to the procedure of declaration. Jews in transit in Istanbul who are foreign citizens will be expelled."[90] The intention of the procedure of the declaration was that the Jews would apply to Turkish consulates in the places they were residing, complete the relevant documents. If their circumstances were suitable, Jews would permit their return.

According to the eighth article, if Muslims, Ottoman Greeks, Armenians, and Jews who left the country without passports wanted to return, they would have to apply within one year. Applications made after 1 July 1925 would not be accepted.

The rule was clear: only the return of Muslims and Istanbul Ottoman Greeks were permitted. The Ottoman Greeks could return only on the condition that they would live in Istanbul and there was no guarantee that those who left without passports would be accepted. The return of Armenians from abroad was prohibited. This decision shocked the Istanbul Armenians. The Armenian newspapers made a "declaration that it was necessary that in general Turkish citizens profit from any law of the state to the same degree," and they asked for the restrictions in the regulation to be annulled.[91]

However, this expectation was in vain. The regulation continued to be implemented with only a few small changes. The one-year period for applying, mentioned in Article 8, later was continued by being prolonged on an annual basis. For example, on 29 July 1925, as "the applications of our citizens submitting declarations to return to the homeland still have not concluded," and new consulates have been opened and new applications are being made, a regulation of the Council of Ministers extended for one more term the period ending on 1 July 1925.[92] On 6 January 1926 another regulation, number 2987, extended this period for one more year.[93] It is significant that the renewal in 1927 was conducted with the intent "to prevent people who belong to various elements whose circumstances and actions concerning our country in foreign countries are being evaluated and whose return is undesired from freely spreading to every part of the country."[94]

On 17 November 1930 some further changes were made in the Travel Regulation. While preserving its essence, it was reduced from nineteen to ten articles.[95] A change made on 3 October 1931 determined that "visas [could be given] for travel for a two month period . . . to Ottoman Greek Orthodox going to Greece on condition that coming to Turkey they do not settle and . . . do not possess and claim to be the owner of immovable properties in any place in Turkey."[96] The prohibition for the Armenians continued into the 1930s.

Prohibitions on Domestic Travel

The 1 July 1924 Travel Regulation did not only prohibit entry from abroad, but also was used to hinder the travel of non-Muslims within Turkey. It did not contain any explicit provisions preventing such domestic travel, but only prohibited the Greeks of Istanbul from settling and living outside the borders of the municipality. Consequently, a regulation of the Council of Ministers, dated 27 May 1925, admitted that "the Travel Regulation with the exception of Jews inside the country [remained] completely silent concerning the manner of travel of local non-Muslim elements."[97]

Nevertheless, only non-Muslims wanting to go to Istanbul were freely permitted to travel,[98] relying on this same regulation, and in this sense there was a prohibition on domestic travel. In Anatolia there was a serious "crisis of the labor force and experts." For this reason the Council of Ministers, in a December 26, 1924 circular sent to the Istanbul governor-generalship, asked for "permission for the travel of non-Muslim experts and workers." However, these workers "were required to return to the places they came from after finishing their work."[99]

According to newspaper reports, the office of the Üsküdar governor on 2 February 1925, relying on a circular of the government, announced that "the trips to Istanbul of non-Muslims in places like Kartal, Maltepe, and Pendik which are outside of the borders of the prefecture are prohibited." The Armenians and Jews in these neighborhoods "were going down to Istanbul and returning nearly every day due to work." Now this was prohibited. Later the Interior Ministry announced that this travel was dependent on permission.[100] However, it is strange to have to ask Ankara for permission to go to Istanbul from Kartal and Pendik. Thereupon a part of the Armenians in these areas moved to Istanbul.[101]

It can be understood from the newspaper reports that the decisions on this topic created confusion and new arrangements were made.[102] The 26 February 1924 issue of the newspaper *Cumhuriyet*, after stating that "upon a decree given by the office of the Üsküdar governor, it is known that in accordance with the Lausanne Treaty, non-Muslims are not to pass outside of the borders of the prefecture," included a new decree from the Interior Ministry. According to this instruction, "It is confirmed that the travel of *Rums* [Turkish Greeks] outside of the borders of the prefecture are prohibited. However, except for *Rums*, the free travel of non-Muslims in Gebze in Anatolia [and] in Çatalca in Rumeli for a distance as far as the poplars in Boğaz is permitted. No non-Muslim according to the Travel Regulation can travel outside of this boundary."[103]

The prohibition of travel was so important that even bringing an Armenian master craftsman from Istanbul to lay down paving stones on the streets of Ankara was discussed at the Council of Ministers and rejected. It is understood from the decision that the Greek workers laying down paving stones on the streets of Ankara were sent to Greece as a result of the population exchange. The Interior Ministry, on the grounds that the topic was not very clear in the Travel Regulation, applied to the Council of Ministers for "permission to call from Istanbul a fifteen-person group of an Armenian paving master and workers." The Council of Ministers decided, on 27 July 1924, not to give permission for the Armenian craftsmen to come.[104]

On 27 May 1925 another decision was taken on the prohibition of travel. On this date, the Council of Ministers again regulated the issue of domestic travel for non-Muslims. First, the Interior Ministry proposed,

"as the greater prolongation of the restriction of travel of those who go for treatment [or] education from one place to another, or to hot springs, or [for the purpose of a] trial or testimony or who are sent to a place officially by an official or private institution for the determination of procedures pertaining to possession of properties, along with those people who for any reason were separated from their wife or child or parents and wish to visit each other, and those women and men of foreign origin who while primarily possessing foreign citizenship acquired Turkish citizenship through marriage or regulations cannot be seen as appropriate, the taking of a decision should be made in this sense."[105]

The Council of Ministers, discussing the situation, resolved that "procedures [be conducted] in compliance with the communication of the aforementioned minister henceforth concerning non-Muslim elements whose manner of travel is not set forth in the Travel Regulation and possess Turkish citizenship."[106]

It is quite difficult to understand this regulation as giving non-Muslims full freedom of travel. Rather, it must be read as a delineation of the conditions under which their travel might be free, because during that year and the following years, many other special decrees or regulations continued to restrict the freedom to travel of non-Muslims. For example, the prohibition of free travel, which continued to be applied to Armenians and Greeks, was expanded to include Jews beginning on 29 August 1927. However, this prohibition was lifted in March 1928, after a delegation of the Jewish community visited the authorities in Ankara. In the summer of the same year, permission was given to the Armenians, Greeks, and Jews of Istanbul to go as far as Bursa, Yalova, Yakacık, and Izmit in the summer months.[107]

It is extremely significant that the Military Prohibited Zones Law was used to prevent the free travel of non-Muslims. This meant that non-Muslims were being considered not as Turkish citizens, but as foreigners. According to the law, there were two basic categories of prohibited areas. Entry into those areas identified as part of the first prohibited zone was completely banned, while only foreigners were prohibited from entering the areas of the second prohibited zone.[108] Non-Muslim citizens were treated in the same way as foreigners.

A 1929 regulation gave special permission for the travel "freely of non-Muslim Turks without exception and foreigners possessing residence permits, who have the need and health requirement to go in the months of May, June, July, August and September of the year to places of mineral springs and baths like Bursa, Tuzla, Yalova, [and] Çeşme, which are subject to some restrictions according to the law of military prohibited zones."[109] In other words, with the exception of the specified months, non-Muslims were forbidden, just like foreigners, from going to the aforementioned areas.[110]

Travel prohibitions were also on the agenda of the *Serbest Cum-huriyet Fırkası* (Liberal Republican Party).[111] Immediately after its establishment in 1930, founder Fethi Okyar opposed the prohibitions in an interview given to an Armenian newspaper. He said, "It is necessary that all citizens possess equal rights and immunities . . . travel and commerce must be free for all and all must be treated equally."[112]

Passport Laws

The 1918 Passport Law, used to obstruct the entry of Armenians into the country, remained in effect until 1938. According to this law, as readers may recall, those Ottoman citizens, who remained so due to a lack of governmental permission to denaturalize, attempting to enter the country with a foreign passport, would be denied the right to do so. Controlling the borders was very difficult, hence it is possible that the Travel Regulation was issued to rectify this situation. While this regulation prohibited Armenians who left the country without obtaining Turkish passports from returning, it was a problem to identify whether a person entering the country was Armenian. Armenians could obtain passports under different names and attempt to enter the country. In addition, some serious developments at the international level on refugee issues took place, and important treaties were signed.

The most important of these developments was the work done for stateless refugees through the League of Nations. First, in June 1921, the High Commission for Refugees was founded (largely to deal with the refugees fleeing the Russian Bolshevik revolution) and the Norwegian Fridtjof Nansen was appointed as its head. His first important task, apart from dealing with approximately 2 million Russian refugees, was to either ensure the return of the Greeks and Armenians fleeing Turkey, or aid in their settlement in other places. With repatriation not possible, the second alternative constituted a serious problem. In July 1922 the International Governmental Conference was held and an understanding was reached about the creation of an identity and travel certificate, which would be accepted by all countries. These certificates, later named Nansen passports, began to be accepted as official travel documents by twenty-eight states starting at the end of 1922.

As the repatriation of the Armenians was not possible at the conclusion of the Lausanne negotiations, on 31 May 1924 the League of Nations decided to issue travel certificates to Armenians surviving the Genocide and those forcibly expelled from Turkey after 1919. This decision was ratified by thirty-eight states. Henceforth, with this certificate. Armenians who were not citizens of any state would be considered official refugees, able to travel, and would have the right to take sanctuary in any of the signatory countries.

Several difficulties existed in the newly created system. The most important of these were that the certificates were valid for a limited period; and second, that the refugees did not obtain the right to return to the countries from which they had originated. At a meeting, held within the framework of the League of Nations in 1926, a new statute was created for Russian and Armenian refugees in which their certificates were given the status of passports. In a decree prepared in June 1928, Christian communities, other than the Greeks being expelled from Turkey, especially the Assyrians and Assyro-Chaldeans, as well as the Turks known as the 150ers, were given the standing of refugees by the League of Nations.

Every new difficulty was accompanied by new treaties and arrangements. Finally, in April 1931, the Nansen International Office for Refugees was established within the structure of the League of Nations. From 26 to 28 October 1933, a congress was held on the international status of Armenian and Russian refugees, and the foundations of the United Nations Convention relating to the Status of Refugees, which is still in operation today, were laid. In the following years, many new agreements were signed and the recognition of the right of asylum for refugees became the international legal norm. The Armenian refugees and their problems played a central role in the formation of this legal system.[113]

These were all very new developments, and Turkey felt the need to take measures against them. As the Travel Regulation was seen to be insufficient, on 28 June 1938, Turkey issued Passport Law Number 3519, and several new arrangements were made. Article 22 of this law introduced the principle that "by decision of the Interior Ministry, a passport 'bearing the stamp reserved for foreigners,' in order to ensure entering Turkey or leaving Turkey and only entry or exit, on condition that it will be for one time only and that it will be used within 15 days of the date on which it is given, will be given to stateless people if necessary." The most important aspect of the article was that it contained a provision on the passports given by the League of Nations to refugees, known as Nansen passports. According to this provision, "Foreigners carrying the 'Nansen passport' and similar other foreign passports can only make use of transit permission." The coming of such people to Turkey was prohibited, and their coming "subject to the decision of the Council of Ministers."[114]

International law on the subject of refugees countered the problems created by Turkey and the Soviets. To this group Nazi Germany would later be added. After World War II, Turkey, lining up with those supporting the Western world, realized that it had to soften its previous stance on refugees to a certain degree. The first reorganization was done through the Law of 18 April 1949, Number 5370. It appended four articles to the Passport Law, which left members of the Ottoman imperial family free to a limited extent to return to Turkey.[115] This was followed by Law Number 5654 of 24 March 1950. Again, through an article appended to the Passport Law, it gave "permission to come to Turkey in the quality of a tourist to those whose attribute of citizenship in any manner whatsoever fell invalid and who want to come as tourists about whom no objection is seen, to be able to stay at the most four months in a year."[116]

Reports by various ministries during the period of preparation of the law are invaluable for explaining what compelled Turkey to make this change. For example, a report prepared by a commission created in the Interior Ministry revealed these views: "The coming and going to our country of people who for various reasons left Turkey to foreign countries and in any manner lost their Turkish citizenship or had their citizenship annulled, just as tourists for an interim period on condition that they only make use of the rights recognized for tourists, was approved by the majority in this Law Commission . . . in the opinion that it will be useful for our country either for economic reasons or international relations and from the point of view of our participation in the Declaration of Human Rights."[117]

The Interior Ministry commission repeated similar views. According to the commission, which believed in the need "to be going on the path of removing the existing restrictions about which no objections remain after the passing of a period as long as 25 years," the law would ensure "the attaining of an openness which will increase the compatibility of our legislation with contemporary legal understanding abroad from the point of view of human rights considerations in the world."[118]

While Turkey, having chosen to take its place in the Western world, felt the need to make its behavior conform to the changes taking place in the sphere of human rights, was still not very comfortable with this situation. For this reason, the Council of Ministers issued a regulation indicating the manner of implementation of law number 5654 of 4 May 1950. This regulation stated, "Visas cannot be given to the people indicated below," including "the stateless, [and] bearers of Nansen passports and passports or travel documents similar to it." For these people, "the existing provisions will be applied as before."[119] In the months following the issuance of this regulation, a new passport law, Number 5682, was promulgated (on 15 July 1950), and Passport Law 3519 and its addenda were repealed. According to Article 26 of the new law, only if "stateless [people], bearers of Nansen passports and bearers of travel documents (affidavits, laissez-passers, etc.) and bearers of similar documents" possessed visas of the countries they were going to and leaving, could they obtain transit visas. Entry visas to Turkey were subject to permission from the Turkish Interior Ministry. Without this permission, such people could not enter Turkey.[120]

Unfortunately Turkey, in its efforts to become part of the West, allowed for some changes to occur, while not fundamentally changing its attitude.

As it has been seen, the most important goal of the Travel Regulation and the changes later made to it, as well as of the passport laws, was to prevent the entry of the Armenians into Turkey and, if they were in Turkey, to limit their free travel within the country. A political decision was taken to confiscate Armenians' properties and not permit an Armenian presence to flourish once again on the soil of Anatolia. Laws and regulations were accordingly produced. This is what we call the spirit of the laws. Now we can go on to look more closely at the Abandoned Properties Laws issued in the Republican period.

Notes

1. Kardeş, "Tehcir" ve Emval-i Metruke Mevzuatı, 103.
2. Resmi Ceride, No. 68, 7 April 1924. The full name of the law is Hükümet Yedinde Sahipsiz Olarak Mevcut Bulunan Emlâkin, Emvâl ve Emlâki Düşman, Usât ve Hasb-el-lüzum Hükümet Tarafından Tahrip Edilmiş Olanlara Nispet Dâhilinde Tevzii Hakkında Kanun [Law on distributing in proportion ownerless property existing in the hands of the government to those whose belongings and property were destroyed by the enemy, rebels, and the government according to need]. For its full text, see Müdürlüğü, Milli Emlak Muamelelerine Müteallik Mevzuat, 488.
3. Ibid., 434. The full name of the regulation is Emvâl-i Metrukeden Hükümet Konağı İttihazına Elverişli Binaların Devâir-i Hükümete Tahsisi Zımnında Mümkün Olan Suhuletin Gösterilmesi Hakkında Kararname [Regulation on possible facilitation for the purpose of allocation to government departments of suitable buildings from abandoned properties for the adoption of the government building].
4. "High Commissioner Bristol, Constantinople, to the Secretary of State, 6 August 1923," in United States Department of State, Papers Relating to the Foreign Relations of the United States, Vol. 2, 1923, 1191

5. Ibid., 1192.
6. BOA/General Administration of the Interior Ministry 20/21–14/04, Passport Law.
7. "U.S. Secretary of State Hughes to High Commissioner Bristol, 21 August 1923," in United States Department of State, *Papers Relating to the Foreign Relations of the United States,* Vol. 2, 1923, 1192.
8. Ibid.
9. Ibid., 1193–94.
10. Ibid., 1195.
11. Ibid., 1195.
12. Ibid., 1196–99.
13. *TBMM Gizli Celse Zabıtları,* Period 2, Assembly Year 2, Vol. 4, 497. The circular was read by Interior Minister Ferit Bey at the 18 February 1925 session of the Assembly. It is useful to recall here that Armenians coming from America were not allowed into the country despite having the appropriate visas in their passports, but were arrested and sent back.
14. Ibid., 505. Article 5 of the decree was read by Giresun deputy Hacim Muhittin Bey at a secret session of the Grand National Assembly.
15. BCA/TİGMA 030.0.18.01.01.09.27.19.001., Directorate of the Private Secretariat of the Ofice of the Prime Minister, Council of Ministers regulation, 29 May 1924.
16. Ahmet Emin Yalman, *Yakın Tarihte Gördüklerim ve Geçirdiklerim, Cilt 3 (1922–1944)* (Istanbul: Yenilik Basımevi, 1970), 121–24.
17. The first news appeared on 31 March 1924 in the newspaper *Müstakil.* The newspaper *Tevhid-i Efkâr* announced the scandal with titles such as "Did an Armenian Fugitive Come to Istanbul by Spending Ten Thousand Liras?," "An Incomprehensible Puzzle," and "Who Aided the Return of the Fleeing Armenians?". For a treatment of the subject in the press of the era, see Yalman, *Yakın Tarihte Gördüklerim ve Geçirdiklerim,* 114.
18. *Tevhid-i Efkâr,* 2 April 1924.
19. Ibid., 3 April 1924.
20. 4, 5 April 1924. The decision was taken on 4 April and on 5 April they were expelled.
21. *Vakit,* 4 April 1924. Mehmet Asım [Us]'s column.
22. *Tevhid-i Efkâr,* 15 April 1924.
23. *TBMM Gizli Celse Zabıtları,* Period 2, Assembly Year 2, Vol. 4, 501.
24. *Tevhid-i Efkâr,* 14 April 1924.
25. Ibid., 16, 17, 19 April 1924.
26. Ibid., 28 April 1924.
27. *Vatan,* 8 April 1924. Cited by Yalman, *Yakın Tarihte Gördüklerim ve Geçirdiklerim,* 117.
28. *Tevhid-i Efkâr,* 11 April 1924; *Vatan,* 13 April 1924.
29. *TBMM Zabıt Ceridesi,* Period 2, Assembly Year 2, Vol. 8/1, 649 (for the debate, see 648–52).
30. Ibid., 648, 651–52.
31. *Tevhid-i Efkâr,* 29 April 1924.
32. *Tevhid-i Efkâr,* 19 Nisan 1924. A report in the newspaper *Müstakil* stated, "After the matter of the rich Armenian fugitives was discussed in the National Assembly, and ended in the known manner, Izmir deputy Osman Zâde Hamdi Bey asked Urfa deputy Yahya Kemal Bey in the corridors of the Assembly, 'What do you say about this matter?' Yahya Kemal Bey gave this response: 'İsmet Pasha saved the homeland once and Ferit Bey eleven times.'"
33. Quoted from the newspaper *Müstakil* in *Tevhid-i Efkâr,* 15 April 1924.

34. Ibid., 16 April 1924.
35. *Vatan*, 22 July and 23 August 1924, cited by Yalman, *Yakın Tarihte Gördüklerim ve Geçirdiklerim*, 124, 127–28.
36. *Tevhid-i Efkâr*, 15 May 1924.
37. *Tevhid-i Efkâr*, 21 May 1924.
38. Ibid.
39. BCA/TİGMA 030.0.18.01.01.09.27.19.001, Directorate of the Private Secretariat of the Office of the Prime Minister, Regulation of the Council of Ministers, 29 May 1924. The committee mentioned in the regulation is the Parliament Committee for Investigating Government Official. This committee after the Grand National Assembly reopened brought up the issue in the form of a question directed at Interior Minister Ferit Bey after he already had resigned. The National Assembly dealt with this issue in its sessions of 15 and 18 February 1924. These sessions were open to the public and then there were some close sessions followed.
40. Ibid.
41. *Tevhid-i Efkâr*, 21 July 1924.
42. The *Tevhid-i Efkâr* of 17 April wrote that many people returned and obtained their properties prior to the surfacing of the last scandal.
43. Ibid., 18 April 1924.
44. Ibid., 22 April 1924.
45. Ibid., 15 May 1924.
46. Yalman, Yakın Tarihte Gördüklerim ve Geçirdiklerim, 114.
47. *Tevhid-i Efkâr*, 14 February 1925.
48. *TBMM Gizli Celse Zabıtları*, Period 2, Assembly Year 2, Vol. 4, 18 February 1925, 494–514.
49. *Son Telgraf*, 22 January 1925.
50. For example, in the newspaper *Vakit*, Mehmet Asım [Us] in his columns titled "Abandoned Properties," "Difficulties of Abandoned Properties" and "Armenians Abroad" made some proposals for the removal of this legal void (*Vakit*, 31 March, 3 and 5 April 1924.
51. *Cumhuriyet*, 21 June 1924.
52. *Tevhid-i Efkâr*, 30 July 1924.
53. *Tevhid-i Efkâr*, 10 February 1924.
54. *Tevhid-i Efkâr*, 16 February 1924.
55. *Tevhid-i Efkâr*, 5 April 1924.
56. *Vatan*, 8 April 1924. Cited by Yalman, *Yakın Tarihte Gördüklerim ve Geçirdiklerim*, 117.
57. *Cumhuriyet*, 8 May 1924.
58. *Tevhid-i Efkâr*, 5 April 1924.
59. *Tevhid-i Efkâr*, 28 April 1924.
60. *Tevhid-i Efkâr*, 28 July 1924.
61. Ibid.
62. Ibid.
63. Ibid.
64. *Vatan*, 3 April 1924. Cited by Yalman, *Yakın Tarihte Gördüklerim ve Geçirdiklerim*, 115.
65. *Vakit*, 5 April 1924.
66. *TBMM Gizli Celse Zabıtları*, Period 2, Assembly Year 2, Vol. 4, 430.
67. Ibid., 431.
68. Ibid.
69. *Cumhuriyet*, 8 May 1924.

70. *Tevhid-i Efkâr*, 28 April 1924.
71. By decision of the government, the issue was referred to the Parliament Committee for Investigating Government Official. It was discussed in the 15 February 1925 session and a decision for a secret session was taken. At the first secret session, which took place that same day, procedural discussions were conducted, and it was decided to be content with listening to Ferit Bey, the former interior minister. Moreover, the Assembly would not conduct an investigation. Ferit Bey made his defense in the second session of 18 February.
72. *TBMM Gizli Celse Zabıtları*, Period 2, Assembly Year 2, Vol. 4, 507–8. The words of Foreign Affairs Minister Şükrü Bey of the same substance were also interrupted by cries of "Bravo."
73. Ibid., 494.
74. Ibid., 495–96.
75. Ibid., 496.
76. Ibid.
77. Ibid., 497. Contrary to these words of the minister, it is known that Armenians coming from America, despite their having the proper visas in their passports, were not given entry, and after being arrested were sent back to the United States.
78. Ibid., 502.
79. Ibid., 510–11.
80. Ibid., 511.
81. Ibid., 512.
82. Ibid., 513.
83. *Polis Mecmuası* 180, 1 December 1924, 153–57; *Tevhid-i Efkâr*, 28 July 1924.
84. *Tevhid-i Efkâr*, 29 March 1924. The same newspaper included another speech of the interior minister in the news of 14 April. This time it said that there was no question of proclaiming certain areas to be a prohibited zone in the proposed law under preparation.
85. *Cumhuriyet*, 15 June 1924.
86. Ibid.
87. Greece and Turkey–Convention Concerning the Exchange of Greek and Turkish Populations and Protocol, signed at Lausanne, January 30, 1923 [1925] League of Nations Treaty Series 14; 32 LNTS 75; http://www.worldlii.org/int/other/LNT-Ser/1925/14.html.
88. The aforementioned border is as follows.

The first article of the provisional law dated 328 on the organization of the municipality of Istanbul:
    The border of the city of Istanbul is the border which is indicated in the 5 October 1877 dated Istanbul Municipality Law, with the exception of Rumeli Feneri.
    An article of the 5 October 1877 dated Istanbul Municipality Law indicates the border of the Istanbul municipality.
    [According to the way the border of Istanbul is indicated in the map, it includes the places in the line starting from Rumeli Feneri, from in front of Zekeriya and Bahçe Köyleri and passage behind Ayazağa Çiftliği Kâğıthane Alibeyköyü Küçükköy, Rami Davutpaşa Hazinedar Çiftlikleri and Ayastefanos, including Ada; passing to the side of Anatolia, starting from the Bostancıbaşı Bridge behind Erenköy, Kozyatağı Nerdüban Köyü, Libada Çakal Dağı and Göksu Deresi, passing in front of the villages of Akbaba and Kabakuz, [and] ending at Anadolu Feneri.]

89. Ibid.
90. Ibid.
91. *Tevhid-i Efkâr*, 28 July 1924.
92. BCA 030–0-18–01–01–015–49–5-1, regulation of 29 July 1925.
93. *Düstur*, Series 3, Vol. 7 (Ankara: Türk Ocakları Merkez Heyeti Matbaası, 1928), 335–36. The full name of the regulation is Seyrü Sefer Talimatnamesi Ahkâmının Bir Sene Daha Temdîdi Hakkında Kararname [Regulation on the extension for one more year of the provisions of the Travel Regulation].
94. *Düstur*, Series 3, Vol. 8, 2156.
95. *Düstur*, Series 3, Vol. 12 (Ankara: Başvekâlet Müdevvenat Matbaası, 1931), 11–3. The full name of the Regulation is Seyr ü Sefer Talimatnamesinin Tatbiki Hakkında Kararname [Regulation on the implementation of the Travel Regulation].
96. *Düstur*, Series 3, Vol. 13 (Ankara: Başvekâlet Müdevvenat Matbaası, 1932), 3. The full name of the regulation is Seyr ü Sefer Talimatnamesine Bir Madde Tezyili Hakkında Kararname [Regulation on adding an article to the Travel Regulation].
97. BCA 030–0-18–01–01–014–34–12, Regulation of 27 May 1925.
98. Ibid.
99. *Tevhid-i Efkâr*, 26 December 1924.
100. *Son Telgraf*, 3 February 1925.
101. Ibid., 8 February 1925. The newspaper gave the news declaring, "The Travel Regulation Gave Rise to Another Issue."
102. *Son Telgraf*, 3 February 1925.
103. *Cumhuriyet*, 26 February 1925.
104. BCA/TİGMA 030.0.18.01.01.10.36.6.00, Directorate of the Private Secretariat of the Office of the Prime Minister, Regulation of 27 July 1924.
105. BCA 030–0-18–01–01–014–34–12, Regulation of 27 May 1925.
106. Ibid. .
107. The information in this paragraph was derived from Rıfat N. Bali, *Cumhuriyet Yıllarında Türkiye Yahudileri, Bir Türkleştirme Serüveni (1923–1945)* (Istanbul: İletişim Yayınları, 2001), 125–27.
108. *Resmi Ceride*, No. 639, 31 July 1927.
109. BCA 0–18–01–02–3-29–003, Regulation of 8 May 1929.
110. The essence of all the laws and regulations issued during the Republican period concerning non-Muslims was that Jews, Armenians, Greeks, and other Christians were not considered citizens equal to the Turks but were considered foreigners. The policies applied to non-Muslims throughout the Republic period are beyond the scope of this book. For more information on this topic, see Ahmet Yıldız, *Ne Mutlu Türküm Diyebilene: Türk Kimliğinin Etno-seküler Sınırları (1919–1938)* (Istanbul: İletişim Yayınları, 2001); Ayhan Aktar, *Türk Milliyetçiliği, Gayrimüslimler ve Ekonomik Dönüşüm* (Istanbul: İletişim Yayınları, 2006); Soner Çağaptay, *Türkiye'de İslâm, Laiklik ve Milliyetçilik: Türk Kimdir?* (Istanbul: Istanbul Bilgi Üniversitesi Yayınları, 2009); and Murat Koraltürk, *Ekonominin Türkleştirilmesi* (Istanbul: İletişim Yayınları, 2011).
111. This party was established in August 1930 by Fethi Okyar, a close friend of Mustafa Kemal. It was Mustafa Kemal's desire to create an opposition party against the governing Republican People's Party. However, in a very short period Free Republican Party gained unexpected popular support. Kemal, fearing that this party could come to power, asked his friend Fethi Okyar to shut down the party, which he did in November 1930, and Turkey reverted to a one-party state.
112. *Milliyet*, 19 August 1930.

113. For more detailed information on this topic, aside from the references given in footnote 139, the following works can be consulted: Keith David Watenpaugh, "The League of Nations' Rescue of Armenian Genocide Survivors and the Making of Modern Humanitarianism, 1920–1927," *American Historical Review* 115, no. 5 (Dec. 2010): 1–25; Heldref Publication, "Certificates of Identity for Refugees," *Advocate of Peace through Justice* 86, no. 11 (November 1924):597–98; Louise W. Holborn, "The Legal Status of Political Refugees 1920–1938," *American Society of International Law* 32, no. 4 (October 1938):680–703.

114. *Resmi Gazete*, No. 3960, 15 July 1938.

115. *Resmi Gazete*, No. 7190, 25 April 1949. The law did not introduce full freedom, but, making some distinctions between members of the imperial family, left the question of return to the special decision of the Council of Ministers.

116. *Resmi Gazete*, No. 7471, 31 March 1950.

117. Unat, Türk Vatandaşlık Kanunu, 122–23.

118. Ibid., 124.

119. *Resmi Gazete*, No. 7513, 23 May 1950. The full name of the regulation is 3519 Sayılı Pasaport Kanununa Bir Madde Eklenmesine Mütedair Olan 5654 Sayılı Kanunun Tatbik Şeklini Gösterir Yönetmelik [Regulation indicating the manner of application of law number 5654 concerning the addition of an article to Passport Law Number 3519].

120. *Resmi Gazete*, No. 7564, 24 July 1950.

CHAPTER 7

DOMESTIC LEGAL REGULATIONS
DURING THE REPUBLICAN PERIOD

It was necessary to bring domestic legislation into accord with the provisions of the Treaty of Lausanne. This was extremely complicated because, as previously mentioned, according to the 15 April 1923 Liquidation Law, the government was confiscating immovable and movable properties, debits, and credits abandoned by people who had gotten lost, fled to foreign or occupied countries or Istanbul, or, no matter now, had left their places of redicence. It wished to continue this process of confiscation, at least until 6 August 1924. Moreover, the government, without waiting for the date the Treaty of Lausanne entered into effect, began to distribute the abandoned properties it possessed or to use them for the needs of the government by means of the law of 13 March 1924 and the regulation of 3 April 1924.

All the laws and regulations issued with the intent of compliance with the Treaty of Lausanne essentially attempted to solve two difficulties. First, according to the liquidation law, at which date would the properties of those who, no matter how, had left their places of residence no longer be confiscated? Second, the government had already confiscated many properties and it did not wish to give any of them back under any conditions whatsoever. The issued laws and regulations paid special importance to these two matters. In addition to these two fundamental problems, the laws and regulations attempted to resolve certain complications revealed through the bribery scandal.

The First Adjustments

The first step, immediately after the signing of the Lausanne Treaty, was taken through regulation number 711, of 20 July 1924.[1] The regulation contained many technical details and made some important arrangements. To understand it better, it is necessary to remember something. The 15 April 1923 Liquidation Law was being applied to movable and immovable properties of people who, no matter how, left or were driven away from their places of residence. After this law was promulgated, taking into consideration the special conditions of Istanbul, the 29 April 1923 regulation was issued, which was valid only for this city. The 29 April 1923 Regulation took the date of 4 November 1922 as the defining date for the expression "in any manner whatsoever." Accordingly, the properties of those who left Istanbul prior to 4 November 1922, in any manner whatsoever, would be confiscated together with properties of people who left without permission after 4 November 1922. The properties of those who left Istanbul by getting permission of the government after 4 November were outside of the scope of this regulation.

The Treaty of Lausanne was ratified on 23 August 1923 by the Grand National Assembly of Turkey in the form of four separate laws.[2] This ratification created a serious legal problem, though at first glance this might be seen only as a detail. Even though the Lausanne Treaty would enter into effect one year later, the 23 August 1923 laws were special and had to be considered as valid according to domestic law. In other words, the principles of Lausanne had to be implemented as of that date. Legal confusion emerged in two different dimensions. First, according to the special regulation issued for Istanbul, while the property of those leaving their places with the permission of the government after 4 November could not be confiscated, in all other places of Anatolia the property of those who left, even with the permission of the government, could be confiscated. This meant that there were two different practices for two different places. Second, the expression "in any manner whatsoever" was at variance with the provisions of Lausanne.

The 20 July regulation was issued in order to end the different practices in Istanbul and Anatolia and the contradiction with the Treaty of Lausanne. It decreed that after the date of its issuance, the confiscation of the property of those who left Anatolia with the permission of the government would end. In other words, 20 July was defined as the significant date. This meant that henceforth the properties of those who left their places prior to this date—even with the permission of the government—no matter how, would be confiscated.[3] The permission of the government would be a valid criterion after this date. Later, a small rectification would be made to this regulation and the word "Anatolia" would be replaced by "Turkey."[4]

Regulation Number 711 was followed by another regulation dated 18 January 1925.[5] This regulation was issued after the lawsuit opened by a non-Muslim woman, named Mari, in Ankara against the Treasury (a department within the Finance Ministry) concerning the confiscation of her properties by the Treasury during her trips back and forth to Istanbul. The court in Ankara acknowledged Mari to be right and deemed her properties not within the definition of abandoned properties, so that they could not be confiscated. Mari's properties therefore had to be returned to her.

The 18 January 1925 regulation was issued in the fear that the verdict of this court might serve as a precedent for many Armenians in Anatolia. According to the regulation, the verdict of the court was applicable "only in this case" and "legally the possibility of its application in other cases" did not exist. Reference was made to the 20 July 1924 regulation number 711, and the 18 January 1925 regulation underlined that the consideration of "the properties of those who are going in any direction from their place of residence with the permission of the government as [not] being abandoned properties" came into practice as a principle only after 20 July 1924. "In other words," the regulation said, "properties of those who went to other places with the permission of the government prior to 20 July 1340 [1924] [were going to be considered] abandoned properties."[6]

The 18 January 1925 regulation brought clarity to some other issues. It stated that "the implementation of the provisions of the laws in question [Liquidation Laws] concerning the properties of those going and coming temporarily, leaving members of their family in the place they are located with the permission of the government, [is not congruent] with the lawmaker's intent." For this reason, it asked that "if prior to the date the Lausanne Treaty was placed into effect, the properties of those going and coming in this fashion with the permission of the government were not confiscated and no intervention was conducted by the Liquidation Commissions, and after their [the commissions'] abolishment, by the Treasury, no intervention be carried out after this."[7] In other words, in the past if there had been others in Mari's situation whose properties had been seized, nothing was going to be done for them now.

This regulation clarified how the Lausanne Treaty must be interpreted. It stated, "Even though the immovable properties of those going to and returning from other places in the country or to Istanbul with the permission of the government beforehand were confiscated, after the Lausanne Treaty was placed into effect, since the confiscation was annulled by the government [now], if the owners are found today in the places the properties are located, the return of such properties to their owners [is] appropriate to the spirit of the law." The regulation determined that "properties of people who traveled with the permission of the government of the Republic [cannot be considered] abandoned properties."[8]

This is an important regulation because it shows how attentive the government was to even the most minor situation that might develop against its interests concerning abandoned properties, and how carefully it acted.

A 5 February 1925 regulation came after the 18 January one.[9] It was a reorganization of domestic law directly connected with Lausanne and had the date the Lausanne Treaty went into effect at its center. It was issued because the expression "government of the Republic" in the 18 January 1925 regulation had caused confusion. Did this expression mean the date of the proclamation of the republic? If so, then the consideration that the property of those who traveled with government permission was not abandoned property would begin as of 29 October 1923. The Liquidation Law would only be applied to the properties of those who traveled, even with government permission, prior to that date.

The 5 February 1925 regulation elucidated this confusing situation. First, it referred to the 15 April 1923 Liquidation Law, and repeated that, according to the sixth article of this law, the property of those who left the places where they were living, "no matter how," would be confiscated by the Treasury. It stressed that in the 15 April law, "disappearance or separation or escape was mentioned as absolute," and this situation was "generalized" with the expression "in any manner whatsoever." It declared that the 15 April law was valid "on the properties, debts and amounts receivable abandoned by people separating, either with the permission of the government or without permission, in any manner and with any goal whatsoever."[10]

The most interesting aspect of the law is its reminder that no special law had been promulgated concerning those who left with the permission of the government. For this reason, these people could not constitute an exception. In other words, the property of those who left with permission would also be confiscated, according to the law of 15 April 1923.[11] The date of 6 August 1924 remained a potent date here. The regulation, for this reason, referred to the Treaty of Lausanne, repeating that "prior to the placement into effect of the Treaty of Lausanne, if the properties of those temporarily going and coming, leaving their families in the place they were located, were not confiscated and no intervention was taken by Liquidation Commissions, and after their abolishment, by the Treasury, intervention" should not be carried out after the Treaty of Lausanne went into effect. However, if an intervention did occur, it would remain valid: "[if] after the Lausanne Treaty the confiscation of properties were annulled and if their owners today were present at the places the properties were located, such properties [would be returned] to their owners."[12]

In light of these principles, the general rule was presented as follows: "If properties of those temporarily going and returning with the permission of the government prior to the ratification of the Lausanne Treaty were not confiscated by the government, and if today they [the properties] have been taken over [by the owners], [it has been decided that] the properties of such people after this will not be interfered with."[13] All these regulations have only one meaning and interpretation. If the government, in accordance with the Liquidation Law, confiscated some properties, there could never be any question of returning them. After the Lausanne Treaty, even those who remained with their properties would have the right to get them back only if the properties had not been confiscated.

The 13 June 1926 Regulation

The most important regulation issued in the nature of an accommodation to the Treaty of Lausanne was that of 13 June 1926.[14] According to the first article of this regulation properties abandoned after 6 August 1924, the date the Lausanne Treaty entered into force, would be confiscated. The second article said, "If confiscation, that is, the government officially learning that a property was abandoned, took place prior to 6 August 1924, the procedure will be finalized." The return of confiscated property to its owners was never a topic of concern. Once started, the confiscation procedure had to be completed.[15]

The third article concerns what would happen "if the abandoned status of properties is learned of by the government after 6 August 1924."

There were three alternatives: (1) If the owner of this property or his representative was with the property, the property would be returned to him; if not, "it will be managed by the government according to the general provisions of the state in the name of the owners." (2) If these properties had been given to migrants despite the owners being present, the value of the properties at the time they were given to the immigrants would be paid to the owners. (3) If the properties in question had been sold, the owner could obtain only the sale value on the terms of the conditions of the sale.[16]

The fourth article states that "the application of the liquidation laws to properties the owners of which have not fled, disappeared or separated from the place they are located but own property and land in other places is unlawful under any circumstances." If such procedures had taken place, it was necessary to return the properties. Istanbul is specifically mentioned in this article.[17]

A regulation, issued on 17 July 1927, changed the first and second articles of the 13 June 1926 regulation.[18] In the single article, which took the place of the latter, it was repeated that immovable properties considered abandoned according to the Liquidation Laws, prior to the Treaty of Lausanne coming into effect, would continue to be treated as abandoned properties. The important part that was added, stated that "until the date [the Lausanne Treaty] was placed into effect, in the case that they were not quickly taken possession of by the government, there would be no intervention by the government as an administrative measure concerning the abandoned properties which are being occupied and administered by the owners who returned to their properties." This regulation repeated the same principle that there would not be any turning back from already completed procedures, and that "procedures carried out until the date of this regulation in accordance with the regulation dated 13 June 1926 [are considered] valid."[19]

1928: The Distribution of Title Deeds and the Transfer of Revenue to the Treasury Begin

The harmonization with the Lausanne Treaty had been achieved already in great measure. Now a type of second stage began. In this stage, property and land being distributed or sold were registered in title deeds in the names of new owners; in other words, title deeds were given to the new owners and the revenues obtained by sale, rent, or other compensation of the abandoned properties were transferred

to the state treasury as income. This process began in 1928. In this
context, law number 1331, of 28 May 1928, was promulgated. Named
the Assignment (of Deed) Law, it contained twelve articles. The law
related to the registration of the title deeds of real estate being sold
or distributed. If property or land was still in the hands of the state, it
would be registered in the name of the Treasury.[20]

The first article referred to previously existing laws and regulations
concerning the distribution of real estate.[21] It stated that title deed receipts would be given to people to whom the possession of immovable
property was given according to these laws and regulations and who
had transfer of possession documents in their hands. Six months were
granted for the applications of relevant cases to be made. It was planned
that their procedures would be completed within one year.

Another important issue was specified in Article 7 of the law, which
decreed that henceforth properties confiscated in accordance with the
Liquidation Laws would not be given back to their owners, but instead
their equivalent value would be paid. The article stated, "Immovable
properties which were confiscated and are going to be confiscated according to the laws [dated 26 September 1915 and 15 April 1923],
whether they were assigned and handed over to those subject to the
exchange [of population] or found in the charge of the Treasury, would
not be returned to their legally to be established rightful owners, [but]
only the determined values . . . would be paid from the treasury of Finance [Ministry]."[22]

In later years various changes would be made to this law of 28 May
1928, and some new laws related to it would be issued.[23] Of these, the
change made by the Grand National Assembly on 2 June 1929 (number
146) to the interpretation of Article 7 quoted above, is extremely important. It is related to the principle that abandoned properties would
not be given back to their true owners, but only their equivalent values
would be reimbursed.[24]

The Grand National Assembly's amendment concerned two important matters. First, it reiterated Article 7 of the 1928 law. Henceforth,
"since there was no possibility of returning [properties] in accordance
with the law to their owners, permission for returning them to their
verified, or to be verified, rightful owners either prior to the coming
into force of the 28 May 1928 law or after its coming into force" is not
going to be given. The statement contained in this interpretation, that
"immovable properties that were confiscated and are going to be confiscated in accordance with the laws [of 26 September 1915 and 15 April
1923] *are considered to be registered in the name of the Treasury*," is

very important [italics are ours].[25] In later years, this statement would play a central role in property and land lawsuits, and would be specifically mentioned in a 1963 verdict of the Constitutional Court.

Second, the meaning of payment to owners of property of their "determined values" and not the properties themselves, as stated in the law of 28 May, is elucidated. It stated that "the giving of the values recorded at the beginning of 1331 [1915] . . . of these properties to their owners or to the legally being verified or going to be verified rightful holder" was decided upon.[26] In other words, the amount to be paid for the properties would be determined based on their value in 1915. Consequently, the provision of Paragraph A of the third article of regulation number 3753 of 13 June 1926, stating that "abandoned properties will be returned to their owners," was made invalid.

Another piece of legislation connected to the 28 May 1928 law is regulation number 6994, issued on 12 August 1928. This eleven-article regulation contains detailed provisions on how "the registration of immovable [property] documents as title deeds" would be conducted.[27]

An additional important step concerning abandoned properties and their possession was taken again on 28 May 1928, through law number 1349. The law decreed that the "current sum of accumulated money from abandoned properties" in the hands of the Finance Ministry would be registered as revenue in the budget. Another article of the law determined that "after this the same procedure [should be implemented] concerning accruing revenues." Moreover, Article 2 stated that a "sum as great as three hundred thousand liras from . . . various revenues [is] to be" added to the 1928 treasury budget.[28] Here it is natural to ask the following questions: How much was the money assembled in the accounts held in trust by the Finance Ministry? How many properties were sold and how much money was accumulated? What was the ratio between the money amassed and the true value of the property constituting the source of the money? It is possible to ask many more questions, but without complete access to the relevant ministerial documents, we will never know the answers.[29]

While technically not related to the abandoned properties question, the 2 June 1929 law, number 1515, is connected to it for political reasons and is worth discussing. According to this law of five articles, if those who illegally had properties and land that legally were considered closed to private or public use, and that had not been registered in the land registry cadaster, benefited from these properties for a certain period of time, title deeds would be given to them. The first article stated: "Title deed documents will be given and registered by the title deed office in the name of holders keeping in possession free from contention and in good faith as owners vineyards, gardens or plots for fifteen years, and ten years for other land, [with all such types of land] passing in an unofficial manner into the possession of others and closed to [private or public] use until the date the civil law [of 1926] entered into force."[30]

Throughout the history of the Republic (and even today), it was a very widespread practice to appropriate specific kinds of land and property belonging to the state after using them for a certain period of time. In law, this general rule can be defined as follows: "In the case that an immovable property is taken possession of for a certain period of time together with the other conditions called for by the law, the possession of that immovable property will be acquired. The acquisition of property in this manner is called usucapere (attaining through acquisitive prescription)."[31]

In fact, abandoned properties are not considered as part of this category and, because they are registered with title deeds in the name of the Treasury, they cannot in any manner pass into private ownership through possession. However, throughout the history of the Republic of Turkey, it appears that the principle of possession or acquisitive prescription constituted important legal grounds for the continuation of the plunder of Armenian property.[32]

We can make the following observation concerning the process of registering abandoned properties in the names of new owners and the laws and regulations that were issued in this connection: throughout this process, the principle of preservation of the rights of the true owners or other possessors of rights and the payment of the lowest of the value of the properties in 1915 to their owners was observed. No legal decision or practice existed about the owners of abandoned properties losing all rights to their properties, or these rights being expropriated, forcibly seized, and abolished. This means that, based on the existing laws and regulations today, the Armenians have a claim to rights over their properties and can assert such a claim. Even if this right cannot be in the form of regaining the properties themselves, it remains in the form of the right to payment of the properties' equivalent value.[33]

The 22 April 1963 Constitutional Court Decision

The 22 April 1963 decision of the Turkish Constitutional Court is an extremely important legal text of the Republican period for the interpretation of the laws and decrees about abandoned properties.[34] The case concerns abandoned properties belonging to Maryam Urkapyan, who lived in Pangaltı in Istanbul, until her death on 1 March 1942. Upon her death, her property in Üsküdar was confiscated and in 1952 was registered in the name of the Çevri Usta Pious Foundation. After this, Maryam Urkapyan's heir, Boğos Urkapyan, initiated a case with the Danıştay (Council of State) in order to annul the seizure and registration. In the petition, he stated that as his mother was considered "one of the fleeing and disappearing people," and that her property had been seized according to the Liquidation Laws.[35] However, his mother was neither a deserter nor missing and, in fact, was living in Istanbul. For this reason, the confiscation was contrary to law.

In this case, the Eighth Department of the Council of State found Boğos Urkapyan's demand for nullification to be justified and referred it to the Constitutional Court. The Council of State, in the justification for the referral, asserted that the liquidation decision was taken in accordance with the laws of 26 September 1915 and 15 April 1923, which were still in effect. However, it continued, these laws fundamentally abrogated the property and inheritance rights encompassed in the thirty-sixth article of the Constitution, and were also contrary to the tenth and eleventh articles of the Constitution. In its decision of 22 April 1963, the Constitutional Court, after studying the application for review, found the Council of State's request for annulment not to be justified and the laws of 26 September 1915 and 15 April 1923, the legal basis for the confiscation process, not to be contrary to the 1961 Constitution.

The decision is like a summary of the laws and decrees issued in the Republican period on the abandoned properties issue. It underlines that the entry into force on 6 August 1924 of the Treaty of Lausanne was a turning point, and it recalls general rules about the abandoned properties. Accordingly, if a person was physically present as of 6 August 1924 with his property, after this date, "regardless of the actions and actual situations, there is no possibility of the implementation of these laws." The application of "the laws in question" was necessary only for those people who ended up in the position of "fleeing or disappearing prior to the validity of the Treaty of Lausanne." If they were not with their properties at this date, even if they returned to Turkey later, their properties would not be returned to them as they would have been transferred to the Treasury.

One point in the decision is extremely important: the court maintained that whether a decision to confiscate the goods existed was not important in the cases concerning real estate. The reason is that in the way the abovementioned laws were written, the moment that "people who are fleeing or disappearing or being transferred to other places" are in such situations, their goods are considered to have "passed in an automatic manner into the possession of the treasuries of the Finance or Pious Foundations [Ministry]."[36] Although administratively no decision was taken concerning this property, or even if nothing in writing is found in this dossier, "on the date that properties of individuals who fall into the situation indicated by law are found in this situation, they are [considered] transferred to the administration of the Treasury or Pious Foundations [Ministries] according to law."[37]

"Consequently," said the court, prior to 6 August 1924, "the possession of the properties of somebody who entered into the situation of fleeing or disappearing, or was moved to another neighborhood, from the date that he entered into this situation, whether or not there exists a decision for confiscation taken at that date in the dossier, according to its interest, passes to the responsibility of the Treasury or Pious Foundations [Ministry] in accordance with the law." Therefore, "the work of determining whether [he is] fleeing or disappearing" prior to 6 August 1924 "not having begun, and a confiscation decision not having been given prior to this date, basically have no effect on the legal status of properties which were transferred to the responsibility of the relevant treasury according to the law prior to this date."[38]

The interesting aspect of the Constitutional Court decision is that the person who was the subject of the case was in possession of her property on 6 August 1924—and she continued to live as the owner of the property until 1942. Although the court said that the Liquidation Laws could not be applied to cases that arise after 6 August 1924, and although legal regulations in this sense did not exist, the confiscation of the property of Maryam Urkapyan, who lived in Istanbul until 1 March 1942 as its owner, was found to be in accordance with the law.[39]

Another important aspect of the Constitutional Court decision was its indication that decrees about Ottoman Greeks could not be evaluated in the framework of the Abandoned Properties Laws, but had to be acted on in accordance with special statutes included in treaties made with the Greek government.

Although this may be repetitious, we wish to cite two points for emphasis in the Constitutional Court decision published by the Turkish General Directorate of National Real Estate in the comprehensive book entitled *Devlet Malları Mevzuatı* (State Properties Legislation): "3. Even if those who were not with their properties on 6 August 1340 return later, their properties, which in accordance with the law earlier were transferred to the Treasury, are not going to be returned to them. 4. The existence or non-existence in the dossier of the decision to confiscate is not at all important."[40]

The Citizenship Laws of 1928 and 1964

As is known, the Armenians during the deportations and genocide were not denaturalized and remained Ottoman citizens while their wealth was being confiscated. Consequently, it is not possible to establish any type of causal relationship between the Abandoned Properties Laws and citizenship statutes. However, there is a thesis that is frequently proposed, at least on a popular level: even if the Armenians were to claim that they still possessed rights to their properties in accordance with the Abandoned Properties Laws, they would be considered to have lost those rights due to the present citizenship laws. If the Armenians who ended up outside of Turkey after the 1915–24 period today have lost their Turkish citizenships, would they not also have lost their rights to their properties? The reason would be that, according to the Turkish citizenship laws of 1928 and 1964, as we shall see, it is necessary to liquidate the property of those who lose their citizenship.[41]

Before discussing any connection between the denaturalization of Armenians and their rights to their properties, it is necessary to answer the question of what the citizenship status of the Armenians who ended up outside of Turkey was. As we discussed in previous chapters of this book, according to Articles 30–35 of the Treaty of Lausanne, Ottoman Armenians living abroad automatically would lose their Turkish citizenship. However, Turkey did not choose this path. Instead, if the Turkish Council of Ministers did not denaturalize individuals through a special decision, they would continue to preserve their citizenship.

For this reason, as we discussed in detail in the relevant sections above, the signatory countries were required to participate in negotiations on reparations in accordance with the provisions of the Lausanne Treaty. In particular, in the negotiations conducted between Turkey and the United States, the reparation demands of the Ottoman Armenians who had become U.S. citizens amounted to an important sum. The only way for Turkey not to pay these reparations was to claim that these people were still Turkish citizens according to its own laws.

Law number 1041, accepted in 1927, was a one-article law that also regulated the preservation of the Turkish citizenship of Armenians abroad. The article stated, "The Council of Ministers authorizes the expulsion from Turkish citizenship of Ottoman citizens who, not participating in the National Struggle during the independence battles, remained outside of Turkey and did not return to Turkey from 24 July 1923 until the promulgation of this law."[42] In other words, the government if it wished could annul the citizenship of an individual, but if it did not, the individual would continue to possess his Turkish citizenship.

The rule "if the government wishes, it can annul citizenship," was preserved in the Turkish Citizenship Law (number 1312) accepted on 23 May 1928. This was regulated in Articles 9 and 10 that specified in detail who the government could expel from citizenship, if it so desired, and under what circumstances.[43] We see many people in the 1930s and 1940s being removed from citizenship by decisions of the Council of Ministers based on each of these two laws.[44]

A study on this topic demonstrates, based on data concerning ethnic-religious roots and names, that there were significant numbers of Greek Orthodox, Jews, Arabs, and even Kurds among those denaturalized. Based on this information, it is possible to conclude that the government, presumably for the reasons noted above, was very attentive to the issue of denaturalizing Armenians.[45] The number denaturalized, in comparison with the approximately 1.8 million Armenians who were Ottoman citizens in 1915, was extremely miniscule.

We understand from the laws concerning citizenship, that Ottoman Armenians continued to possess Turkish citizenship until 1964. Their citizenship was ended by the temporary supplemental article titled "Lost People," appended to Citizenship Law number 403, issued that year. This Temporary Article 1 stated, "After the National Struggle, people having left Turkey until the end of the year 1930 with passports given by the government of the Grand National Assembly or the Istanbul representatives of the occupying states containing the annotation 'return is illicit' or without documents, and at present about whom it is not known whether they are dead or alive and who only are registered in the population registers, are considered to have lost their Turkish citizenship on the date that this law enters into force. The necessary procedures will be carried out by the Ministry of Internal Affairs."[46]

The second temporary article regulated the applications of these people for regaining citizenship. If people "who are Turkish citizens by birth, whose citizenship was annulled according to the provisions of the Turkish Citizenship Law numbered 1312 and the Ottoman Law [of 1869]" so desired, they could apply within the period of one year to once more obtain Turkish citizenship. The final decision would, of course, be made by the Council of Ministers.[47]

On 1 July 1964, a regulation was issued on how the Citizenship Law should be applied. Its sixtieth article concerned the temporary article on lost people. It said, concerning the procedures pertaining to people "who lost their Turkish citizenship on the date of 22/5/1964 when law number 403 entered into force" that "all population registry offices, after searching for such people in the registers and conducting the necessary investigations, will give the annotation 'lost his citizenship according to the temporary first article of law number 403' on the line of the identity cards of those whose circumstances fit this article, and will send the list by means of the offices of the governors-general to the Interior Ministry."[48]

The second paragraph of the same article of the regulation repeats that if those removed from citizenship in accordance with the provisions of citizenship law number 1312 wish, they can apply within a period of one year to obtain citizenship again. It then mentions a general principle that is extremely important: "As law number 403 . . . stipulated . . . not denaturalizing *those who are Turkish citizens by birth* together with all citizens within the country, and the subjection to the procedure of losing [citizenship] according to the provisions of law number 1312 and the Ottoman Citizenship Law left to the decision of the competent authorities" [italics are ours].[49] As can be seen, Turkey adopted the principle of not denaturalizing people who are Turkish citizens by birth and, for this reason, it recognized the right of those previously denaturalized to citizenship again.

Consequently, the supplement added in 1981 to the Supplemental Temporary Article declares, "People who are Turkish citizens by birth, denaturalized according to the provisions of the Turkish Citizenship Law numbered 1312 or who *for some other reason lost their citizenship*, who within a period of two years commencing from the date of effectiveness of this law want to again assume Turkish citizenship and are in a situation in which no drawback is seen for their naturalization" [italics are ours] can regain their citizenship.[50] In other words, the period set in 1964 was again extended.

Article 46 of the Citizenship Law, numbered 403, abolished the laws of 1927 and 1928. Later, this citizenship law itself was abolished by the Citizenship Law, numbered 5901, of 29 May 2009.[51] In this last citizenship law, there is no provision concerning lost people. It is not possible here to conduct a technical discussion about what the legal status would be of people who lost their citizenship—in the case of this study, Armenians and their children—through this temporary article, when Law number 403 and its temporary article were annulled. Nevertheless, it is worth paying attention to this interesting dimension.

The underlying tendency to act in accordance with the principle of not denaturalizing those who were Turkish citizens by birth and naturalizing again those who, in the past, had been denaturalized, can be observed in all the changes that were made. For this reason, the desire for restoration of their citizenship of so-called lost people and their children—the Armenians—whose citizenship was preserved until 1964, remained a technical detail that could easily be solved according to the existing laws. There is no need to add anything about the symbolic value of the topic in connection with genocide and the question of reparation.

Those Removed from Citizenship and the Liquidation of Their Properties

The 1928 and 1964 laws introduced some regulations concerning how and under what conditions the properties of people who were denaturalized would be liquidated.[52] For example, according to the 1928 Citizenship Law, the properties of people whose citizenship is annulled had to be liquidated. Its twelfth article said, "In the case that those whose citizenship is being annulled are located inside the country, they will be expelled outside of Turkey. In general, the return to Turkey of those being denaturalized is prohibited. Their property will be liquidated by the government."[53]

How the word "liquidation" must be interpreted, whether the intent is seizure and, for this reason, whether people removed from citizenship lose all their rights to their properties, have been subjects of serious debate among jurisprudents. However, "there is doctrinal consensus on the matter that it is not correct for liquidation to be understood in the form of a confiscation, [as] after the properties of people who are being denaturalized are sold by the state, and their debts paid, after reduction by the expenditures carried out as a result of the liquidation, the remaining sum belongs to them."[54] In other words, revenue of the liquidated property must be preserved by the state in order to be paid to the owner.[55]

Law number 403, which took the place of the 1928 law in 1964, regulated removal from citizenship and the right of ownership in a much more detailed manner. It contained a very important difference from the 1928 law. While the 1928 law decreed the liquidation within one year of the properties even of people who with special permission, withdrew from Turkish citizenship (Article 8), the 1964 law stipulated liquidation only under specific conditions. It explained, in connection with various circumstances of denaturalization, how the liquidation would be conducted in its Articles 33 and 35. According to Article 33, the annulment decision had to specify whether the properties of those whose citizenship "was being annulled" would be subject to liquidation. If liquidation was necessary, such people "at the latest within one year liquidating their properties in Turkey . . . are obliged to leave the country. If they did not do this, their properties would be sold by the Treasury, their equivalent values would be deposited in a national bank in their names and accounts, and they would be expelled abroad." According to Article 35, "the properties located in Turkey of people denaturalized in conformity with Article 26 will be liquidated by the Treasury. And their values will be deposited in a national bank in their names and accounts."[56]

What is important here is that the liquidation was not defined as sequestration or confiscation. The person whose property was liquidated possessed rights over the property and the price obtained from the liquidation had to be deposited in a bank account in his or her name in order to be given to him or her. The provisions in the 1964 Citizenship Law, as well as the later one in 2009, are quite clear on this point. A person who lost his citizenship would not lose his rights over his property.

The matter that attracts our interest is that Temporary Article 1 of the 1964 law was not mentioned in these articles dealing with liquidation. In other words, the law, while saying that fugitive and lost people would lose their Turkish citizenship, did not contain any provisions concerning the liquidation of their property and possessions. A similar situation was true for the regulation of 1 July 1964, which was concerned with how the law would be implemented. There, too, was no mention of what would happen to the properties of those who deserted or fled and were denaturalized according to Temporary Article 1.

In fact, this absence is very normal. As specified in the decision of the Constitutional Court of Turkey, the properties of deserters and disappeared people were already subject to the liquidation laws; even if they were not distributed or sold, they still would be registered in the

Treasury. For this reason, there was no need for a special provision. In conclusion, even if it were possible for Armenians (fleeing and deserting, and lost people) to claim rights over their properties in accordance with the Abandoned Properties Laws, there is no legal foundation to the idea that the Armenians had lost their rights to their properties because they lost their citizenship.

The Abandoned Properties Laws and the Present Situation

The laws known as the Abandoned Property Laws were in time repealed. The one that must be considered the most important of them, the 15 April 1923 Liquidation Law, was repealed on 27 November 1988 by law number 3488.[57] The law known as the *Temlik* (Assignment of Possession) Law of 28 May 1928, number 1331, was repealed by law number 4796 of 1945,[58] while the regulation of 13 June 1926 was repealed in 2006 by regulation number 10933.[59]

Apparently, as of 1988 it was believed that the task the 1923 Liquidation Law had to fulfill, concerning the properties of the Armenians, had been completed. An interesting point to mention is that Salâhaddin Kardeş, who compiled and published the law and regulations as a publication of the Finance Ministry, argued that even if the law had been repealed, its provisions were still valid: "In particular, because on the date that the Abandoned Properties Laws, which prescribed the provision of transferal to the Treasury, entered into force, its provisions were put forward, these provisions of those [laws] which are being repealed are still valid."[60] It does not make any sense why these provisions can still be valid if the law in which they are contained is repealed. Our understanding is that Kardeş, through this interpretation, wanted to maintain the validity of whatever acts this law accomplished up until this date; in any case, its interpretation remains an issue for legal scholars.

The various practices concerning abandoned properties in the present legal system constitutes a separate topic. Here we wish to mention a political dimension that we find to be important. As far as we understand, the plunder of Armenian properties continued throughout the Republican period, and is one of the legal issues causing the most trouble to the state. The reason for continuation of the plunder of Armenian properties throughout the Republican period is apparently the acceptance of the acquisition of immovable property through *usucapere* (acquisitive prescription) by the Turkish Civil Code. Articles 639 of the old civil code and 713 of the new one guaranteed that right. According to this general rule, if a person keeps a real estate property that is not registered in the title deed registry for twenty years in his possession, he can obtain the right to register it in his name.[61]

The laws introduced the rule that "not being registered in the title deed registry" was a requirement for taking advantage of this right.[62] As the abandoned properties were essentially registered in the name of the state, they had to be excluded from this procedure.[63] That is to say, it was not possible, according to Turkish law, for abandoned properties to be acquired through acquisitive prescription. However, on the local level through various means—like coming to an understanding with state officials, bribery, and taking advantage of gaps in laws showing that abandoned properties supposedly were not registered, and "possession which secures improvement, amelioration and gaining"—appropriation became an extremely widespread practice.[64]

As a result, through this mechanism the real estate and properties that belonged to the Ottoman Christians and passed to the ownership of the state in accordance with the Abandoned Properties Laws, and became registered in title deeds, in a real sense were subject to plunder. Legally, this procedure that amounted to the state plundering its own properties became so widespread that the state felt it was necessary to take precautions against it through the Preliminary Step Law of Land Agrarian Reform (TTRÖTK, in Turkish) of 19 July 1972; through its thirty-third article, the provision was created that "according to the laws the properties remaining with the state—whether registered with title deeds or not—cannot be acquired through acquisitive prescription."[65]

According to legal scholars, until the date of validity of this new law, the Court of Cassation, relying on Article 639 of the Civil Code of 1926, gave verdicts in favor of acquisitive prescription. After the TTRÖTK came into force, however, it pronounced such decrees to be null and void.[66] After this date the Court of Cassation acted, in its decisions, on the principle that "according to the laws, the acquisition through possession of real estate remaining with the state is not possible."[67]

The transferal in various ways of the abandoned properties to individual possession still constitutes a serious legal issue.[68] For this reason, some steps had been taken on this issue before the Liquidation Law was repealed in 1988. Aside from the law enacted in 1972, many other laws addressed this issue and their restrictive provisions were very clearly written. The most important of them is the Cadaster Law of 21 June 1987, number 3402. The eighteenth article of this law introduced the principle that "real estate remaining with the state in accordance with the laws, whether or not registered with a title deed, cannot be acquired by means of acquisitive prescription."[69]

Another protective provision was introduced through Article 12 of the same Cadaster Law. According to this, in the cadastral records, "ten years after the date of finalization of the records indicating rights, restrictions and determinations, objections relying on reasons prior to the cadaster cannot be made and lawsuits cannot be initiated. Old title deed documents remaining in the sphere of work completed by the cadaster will lose the characteristic of documents subject to procedures. Transactions cannot be carried out relying on these records in the cadaster and title record registry directorates."[70] As far as we know, lawmakers did not see any problem in the annulment of the Liquidation Law in 1988, especially after changes were made in Cadaster Law in 1972 and 1987.

The most important aspect of this change is that the true owners of the abandoned properties were prevented from claiming their rights. Thus, thinking that there were some gaps in Cadaster Law Number 3402, in 2009 further changes were made in order to completely eliminate the possibility of abandoned properties changing hands.[71] The circulars of 1983 and 2001, which we cite below, were intended for this goal of so-called protection.

The 1983 and 2001 Circulars of the General Directorate of Land Registry and Cadaster

The last official documents that we wish to discuss are the circular(s) bearing the signature of State Minister Şuayip Üşenmez, dated 31 October 1983 and 29 June 2001.[72] The circulars, in order to solve problems arising from requests for information on Armenian properties, were sent to all the provincial and district governments, the regional directorates of land registries and cadasters, title deed registry offices, and cadaster directorates in every part of Turkey. For this reason, they are of great significance. They provided directives as to what had to be done when requests were made concerning title deed records dated prior to 6 August 1924.

The language of the circulars is very convoluted. Throughout the text, it could not be stated that applicants lost their rights to their properties. Consequently, administrative offices were requested to hide the information possessed by the state, show it to no one, and ignore requests for title deed information. The circulars form an important foundation to our thesis asserted throughout this work, that tension and contradictions abound in the legal system. They began by reminding that "the real estate of exchanged, disappeared or fleeing . . . individuals passed to the state, [and] the necessity of not conducting any title deed transaction based on these records, and not giving any information, document, or title deed record" had been announced. However, they continued, "it was ascertained from [the news of] events reaching the center that some flaws existed on this issue."[73]

The circulars tried to bring clarity to the issue of abandoned properties: "As is known, the immovable property of people who prior to 6 August 1924 were fleeing our country, getting lost, leaving the country, being subject to [population] exchange, and at that date were not with their real estate, whether or not at that same date an expropriation decision existed, passes to the responsibility of the State." For this reason, the former owners and heirs of these properties, according to Article 928 of the Civil Code, cannot be considered "relevant people" with respect to the properties and "it is necessary not to accept the request for any title procedure, including the granting of title deed documents" from these people.[74]

"In this respect," the circulars continued, if there is a request for any procedure "connected with documents prior to 1924," it is necessary that "requests for title deed procedures, including the provision of information and documents concerning title deed documents of those exchanged, disappearing, fleeing or departing individuals not be met in any way, and these requests be sent to the General Directorate. . . . Directions for procedures according to instructions" will be given from the latter place.[75] In other words, the circulars warn that if you encounter any issues pertaining to the period prior to 1924, do not give any information, but immediately notify the State Ministry.

The circulars also asked for some investigations to be conducted. The first, concerning the document being requested, was "researching whether or not it was applied to any parcel or subject to the cadaster." If work was going to start, or already had begun, on documents in the cadaster, it was necessary that "no procedure in connection with showing their places or similar requests be accepted." "If it were not applied to a parcel, then the rescission of the document" is requested.[76] It is clear as to why such great importance is paid to the Cadaster Law. If a piece of immovable property has entered the cadaster and a ten-year period has expired, no right to demand this property can exist.

The entire language of the circulars is an attempt to hide something, and is a silent confession that the true owners of the properties being hidden are still Armenians. If according to the existing laws the Armenians had lost all their rights to their properties, the circulars could have easily recalled this issue. For example, it could be easily argued that according to the 1923 Liquidation Law and the 1963 verdict of the Constitutional Court the Armenians could not claim any rights to their confiscated properties. However, the circulars did not say this, or were unable to say this.

In sum, we want to note the existence of a deep fear pervading throughout the circulars. It is for this reason that the State Ministry desired that no documents be given to applicants who lost their rights to their properties pertaining to the period prior to 6 August 1924 and that, by passing them to the cadaster and doing other similar procedures, the door to any objections be closed. Turkey's main problem is this reality that exists in its legal system—that the Armenians still possess rights to their properties—and the desire to cover this reality up. This situation leads to the creation of a profound fear and the consideration of the entire matter as an issue of state security.

Profound Fear: Title Deed Registries

The provisions of the Civil Code are extremely clear: "The register of title deeds is open to everyone. Everyone who makes their interest credible can make the relevant page and documents in the land register shown to them or copies given to them in front of the title deed officer. No one can claim not to know a record in the title deed registry."[77] Despite this clear provision, title deed documents connected to the events of 1915 are kept secret in Turkey. In 2006 Turkey's National Security Council found that title deed documents converted to electronic media were transferred to archives and being accessed there by researchers, which was contrary to national security interests. Hence, it prohibited the transfer of title deed documents to archives.[78]

Perceiving title deed documents as a threat to the existence of a country is not a view limited to a single political authority. Such ideas are advocated in law faculties and scholarly articles are written on the subject. Attempts are made to explain why the disclosure of title deed documents is a threat to security. It is useful to give an excerpt from an article written for this purpose here, despite its lengthiness:

> There is no doubt that the opening of access to title deed documents belonging to juridical personages is also going to cause significant problems from

a political point of view. Especially during recent times when the Armenian Question which has become a current issue of public opinion has reached an advanced stage, it can open the way for abuse by individuals whose immovable property fall within the scope of the "Abandoned Properties Laws" and pay no attention to the provisions of the aforementioned laws. In particular, law suits being initiated with the demand of the return to their old owners of immovable properties which are passing to others in accordance with the provisions of the Treaty of Lausanne and other Laws accepted during Republic period such as the "Law on the Liquidation of Those Title Deed Documents which Have Lost Their Legal Values" numbered 1515, the provisions of the Turkish Civil Code numbered 743, the laws numbered 2613, 5602 and 766, and the provisions of the Cadaster Law number 766, are going to be the cause of endless demands being brought up; and this is going to radically shake up the public order formed on the topic being discussed and concomitantly create a legal chaos not seen in the history of the Republic.[79]

It is almost as if an entire society is trying to hide a "secret," including scholars and the National Security Council. It is as if Turkish national existence depends on keeping title deeds connected with the events of 1915 hidden. Is it conceivable that due to national security anxieties a country still keeps title deeds hidden that are connected to something one century old? What does it mean to be a society that fears the disclosure of the owners of immovable properties of a century ago and considers the disclosure of these title deeds to be a question of national security? This is what we have in Turkey. The absence of the Armenians, or hiding of their existence, is the prerequisite for the existence of the Turks. Every reference to the existence of the Armenians is a threat to the Turks' existence. Perhaps it is necessary, first and foremost, to liberate this nation from such a state of mind.

Notes

1. Kardeş, *"Tehcir" ve Emval-i Metruke Mevzuatı*, 131. The full name of the regulation is Anadolu'da Mukîm Bulunduğu Mahalden Hükümetin Müsaadesini Alarak Azîmet Edenlerin Emvâlinin, Emvâl-i Metrukeden Addedilmemesi Hakkında Kararname [Regulation on the properties of those departing, getting the permission of the government from the place in Anatolia in which they reside, not being considered abandoned properties].
2. *Resmi Ceride*, No. 22, 10 September 1923.
3. In other words, the 29 March 1923 regulation issued for Istanbul cancelled the importance of the date of 4 November 1922. The property of those leaving Istanbul to go abroad between 4 November 1922 and 24 July 1924 with the permission of the government could also be confiscated. The same situation was also valid for the 15 April 1923 law. Henceforth, the property of those leaving Anatolia between 15 April

1923 and 24 September 1924 with the permission of the government could also be confiscated.

4.   This change was made of the word "Anatolia" so to avoid any misunderstanding that the regulation would not be applicable in Trakya (Thrace). For the full text of the 12 November 1924 regulation, see Kardeş, *"Tehcir" ve Emval-i Metruke Mevzuatı*, 133.

5.   Ibid., 134–36. The full name of the regulation is Hükümet-i Cumhuriyetin Pasaportuyla Seyahat Etmiş Olanların Emvâlinin Emvâl-i Metruke'den Addolunamayacağına Dair Kararname [Regulation concerning the properties of those who travelled with the passport of the government of the republic [which are] not going to be able to be considered abandoned properties].

6.   Ibid., 135.

7.   Ibid., 135–36.

8.   Ibid., 136.

9.   Ibid., 136–39. The full name of the regulation was Lozan Muahedenamesinin Kabul Edildiği Tarihten Sonra Gitmiş Olanların Gayr-ı menkullerine Müdahale Edilmemesi Hakkında Kararname [Regulation on non-intervention concerning immovable properties belonging to people who left after the date of acceptance of the Lausanne Treaty].

10. Ibid., 137.

11. Ibid., 137–38.

12. Ibid., 138.

13. Ibid., 138.

14. Ibid., 164–65. The 13 June 1926 regulation, number 3753, and the changes it brought remained in force for more than eighty years. They were finally annulled in 2006 by regulation number 10933. *Resmi Gazete*, No. 26310, 5 October 2006.

15. Kardeş, *"Tehcir" ve Emval-i Metruke Mevzuatı*, 164.

16. Ibid., 165.

17. Ibid.

18. Ibid., 141–42. The full name of the regulation is 13 Haziran 1926 Tarihli Talimatnamenin Bazı Maddelerini Muaddil Talimatnamenin Mer'iyet Mevkiine Konulmasına Dair Kararname [Regulation on the placing into a position of effect the regulation modifying several articles of the 13 June 1926 dated regulation].

19. Ibid., 142.

20. Müdürlüğü, *Milli Emlak Muamelelerine Müteallik Mevzuat*, 430–31. The full name of the law is Mübadil, Gayrimübadil, Muhacir ve Saireye Kanunlarına Tevfikan Tefviz veya Âdiyen Tahsis Olunan Gayrimenkul Emvalin Tapuya Raptına Dair Kanun [Law concerning to registration of the title deeds of immovable properties being handed over or customarily assigned in accordance with the laws of [population] exchange, non-exchange, refugee and other laws].

21. These are the 16 April 1340 [1940] law number 488 named Mübadeleye Tabi Halka Verilecek Emvali Gayrimenkule Hakkında Kanun [Law on immovable properties to be given to people subject to [population] exchange]; the 8 November 1339 [1923] law number 368 called Mübadele, İmar ve İskân Kanunu [Exchange, public works and settlement law], and the 13 March 1926 regulation number 781. The first two laws basically concern the population exchange being conducted with Greece, and as can be surmised from their names, gave all types of abandoned property to the people coming to Turkey through the population exchange.

22. Müdürlüğü, *Milli Emlak Muamelelerine Müteallik Mevzuat*, 175. Also see Kardeş, *"Tehcir" ve Emval-i Metruke Mevzuatı*, 108–9.

23. The change made to the sixth article through the 18 March 1929 commentary, numbered 142 (*Resmi Gazete*, No. 1151, 26 March 1929), or the "Appended Law" of 23

March 1929, numbered 1407 (*Resmi Gazete*, No. 1154, 30 March 1929), each can serve as an example. The 28 May 1928 law was abrogated in 1945.

24. Kardeş, *"Tehcir" ve Emval-i Metruke Mevzuatı*, 117–18. See also *Resmi Gazete*, No. 1210, 8 June 1929.
25. Ibid., 117–18.
26. Kardeş, *"Tehcir" ve Emval-i Metruke Mevzuatı*, 117–18.
27. Müdürlüğü, *Milli Emlak Muamelelerine Müteallik Mevzuat*, 431–34.
28. *Resmi Gazete*, No. 902, 30 May 1928.
29. The poser of these questions, Nevzat Onaran, also attempts to find answers to them. See Onaran, *Emvâl-i Metrûke Olayı*, 267.
30. *Resmi Gazete*, sayı: 1211, 9 Haziran 1929.
31. Ali Rıza Düzceer, *Kazandırıcı Zamanaşımıyla Taşınmaz İktisabı* (Tescil Davası-MK.m. 639) (Ankara: Yetkin Basımevi, 1994), 1.
32. This topic will be discussed in more detail in the section "The Abandoned Properties Laws and the Present Situation."
33. Here a decision of Grand General Assembly of the Court of Appeals connected with the topic from 1935 can be mentioned. In this decision, the Appeals Court said that if the person who claimed to be the owner of the abandoned property was one of those who were "fleeing and disappearing" there was no merit to be found in his claim. If it were proven that he was not "fleeing and disappearing," then it would be necessary to give not the property itself but its value to him. Of course this legal rule was based on the Lausanne Agreement. However, the rule that a person found "fleeing and disappearing" is going to lose all right to his possessions does not seem very logical. First of all, Turkey is already attempting to prevent such people from coming back to their country in all possible ways, and thus forcibly is placing them in the situation of "fleeing and disappearing." Second, the laws at hand are not cutting off the connection between the owner of the property and his possessions. This would mean an outright confiscation and as far as the authors can see no such step has been taken concerning the abandoned properties. The authors thank lawyer Cem Murat Sofuoğlu for providing the decision. For its text, see Yargıtay İçtihadı Birleştirme Büyük Genel Kurulu [Grand General Assembly of the Court of Appeals], File No. E:1935/18, K:1936/30, T:25.11.1936.
34. For the full text and interpretation of the Supreme Court decision, see Salâhaddin Kardeş, *"Tehcir" ve Emval-i Metruke Mevzuatı*, 10–11, 169–80; Onaran, *Emvâl-i Metrûke Olayı*, 375–91.
35. Salâhaddin Kardeş, *"Tehcir" ve Emval-i Metruke Mevzuatı*, 169.
36. Ibid., 171.
37. Ibid., 171.
38. Ibid., 171.
39. Six out of a total of fifteen members of the court lodged statements of dissent to the decision.
40. *Devlet Malları Mevzuatı Kitabı* (State Properties Legislation Book, a publication of Milli Emlak Genel Müdürlüğü), 129–30 (http://www.milliemlak.gov.tr/Sayfalar/KurumsalBilgiler/calismalarimiz/yayinlarimiz.aspx).
41. The latest Citizenship Law is numbered 5901, and was issued on 29 May 2009. This law says that there is no general rule in the sense that the properties of people who annul their citizenship are liquidated; only "in situations where it is seen necessary" is the circumstance indicated in the annulation decision. This volume does not discuss this law because it falls outside of its scope. For the text of the law, see *Resmi Gazete*, No. 27256, 12 June 2009.
42. *Resmi Ceride*, No. 598, 31 May 1927.

43. *Resmi Gazete*, No. 904, 4 June 1928. According to Article 9, those who without obtaining special permission accepted another country's citizenship, or served in the army of another country of their own desire, "can be dismissed from citizenship by decision of the Council of Ministers." According to Article 10, "Of those who undertook service in the soldiery of a foreign state . . . those not conform[ing] to the order being given [to leave this service]"; those continuing in the service of an enemy state; those who during mobilization deserted and "fled to foreign countries . . . or, high ranking military authorities who by means of leave and change of scene or official duty" being outside of the country and not returning in time, "are remaining as fugitives," or those who "while living in a foreign country for a period of longer than five years" did not register themselves with Turkish embassies, could be removed from citizenship "if the government desires." Basically these articles are found in the 3 April 1917 law that supplements Article 6 of the 1869 Citizenship Law. See *Takvim-i Vekayi* No. 2861, 22 April 1917.

44. On some Armenians who were denaturalized according to the 1928 Citizenship Law for adopting American citizenship without informing Turkey, see Hatice Mumyakmaz, "Osmanlı'dan Cumhuriyet'e Vatandaşlık," doctoral thesis, Gazi University, Ankara, 2008, 191–92.

45. Soner Çağartay, "Erken Cumhuriyet Dönemi Vatandaşlık Rejimi Üzerine Bir Çalışma," *Toplum ve Bilim* 98 (Autumn 2003), 171–74.

46. *Resmi Gazete*, No. 11638, 22 February 1964.

47. Ibid.

48. *Resmi Gazete*, No. 11742, 1 July 1964, Article 60.

49. Ibid.

50. For changes, see http://mirekoc.ku.edu.tr/sites/mirekoc.ku.edu.tr/files/turk_vatandaligi_kanunu.pdf. There were changes to law number 403 made in 1981, 1989, 1992, and 2003.

51. *Resmi Gazete*, No. 27256, 29 May 2009.

52. The connection between denaturalization and ownership, and in particular with inheritance rights, lies outside of the scope of this volume and requires serious legal knowledge. Here only some views of legal experts can be briefly expressed. For more detailed information on the topic, see Ergin Nomer, "Yabancı Devlet Vatandaşlığını Kazanan (Eski) Türk Vatandaşlarının Mirasçılığı," *İ.H.F. Mecmuası* 55, no. 3 (1997):169–178; Sargın; "Yabancı Gerçek Kişilere Ait Taşınmaz Malların Tasfiyesi," 31–72; Tuğrul Arat, "Türk Vatandaşlığından Iskat Edilen Kişilerin Mülkiyet ve Miras Hakları," *A.Ü.H.F Dergisi* 31, no. 1–4 (1974):279–360; İlhan Unat, "Türk Vatandaşlığından 'koğulanlar' Miras Hakkından Yoksun mudur?," *S.B.F. Dergisi* 20, no. 3 (1965):179–226; Hicri Fişek, "Türkiye'de Yabancıların Aynî Haklardan İstifadesi," *A.Ü.H.F. Dergisi* 7, no. 3–4 (1950): s. 426–440; Gülören Tekinalp, *Türk Yabancılar Hukuku* (Istanbul: Beta Basım Yayım, 2002); Duygu Sürer, "Türkiye'de Yabancıların Taşınmaz Edinmesi," master's thesis, Marmara University, Istanbul, 2008.

53. *Resmi Gazete*, No. 904, 4 June 1928. In this law, a distinction is made between relinquishing citizenship with special permission and annulment. Articles 7 and 8 regulate relinquishing citizenship with permission while Articles 10 and 11, with the joint title Reasons for the Annulment of Citizenship regulate annulment. Essentially the points expressed in these articles were regulated on 3 April 1917 in a law issued as a supplement to Article 6 of the 1869 Ottoman Citizenship Law. For this law, see *Takvim-i Vekayi* No. 2861, 22 April 1333 [1917].

54. Arat, "Türk Vatandaşlığından Iskat Edilen Kişilerin Mülkiyet ve Miras Hakları," 292–93.

55. Jurists view the Caliphate Law and the topic of the 150ers as exceptional situations. The eighth and ninth articles of the 3 March 1924 Repeal of the Caliphate Law (number 431), stating that properties belonging to the throne "were transferred to the nation." Similarly, the second article of the 28 May 1927 number 1064 Law on the Removal from Turkish Citizenship of People Whose Names Are Written in the List of One Hundred and Fifty People in Question in the Announcement and Protocol of General Amnesty Concluded at Lausanne stated, "The aforementioned people henceforth in Turkey are deprived of the right of acquistion and the right of inheritance." This law was abrogated on 29 June 1938, though not retroactively. For more detailed information, see Resmi Gazete, No. 19983, 8 November 1988. The full name of the law: "Uygulama İmkanı Kalmamış Olan Kanunların Yürürlükten Kaldırılmasına Dair Kanun."

56. *Resmi Gazete*, No. 11638, 22 February 1964. For more detailed information on this subject, see Rona Aybay, *Yurttaşlık (Vatandaşlık) Hukuku* (Ankara: A.Ü.S.B.F. Yayını, 1982), 104–22.

57. *Resmi Gazete*, No. 19983, 8 November 1988. The full name of the law is "Law on Repealing Laws of which the Possibility of Application No Longer Remains."

58. *Resmi Gazete*, No. 6059, 17 July 1945. The full name of the law is "Law Concerning the Accurate Liquidation of Matters of [Population] Exchange and Delegation."

59. *Resmi Gazete*, No. 26310, 5 October 2006. The full name of the regulation is "Regulation Concerning the Repeal of Some Regulations."

60. Kardeş, *"Tehcir" ve Emval-i Metruke Mevzuatı,* 10.

61. For Article 639 of the 1926 Civil Code, see http://www.mevzuat.gov.tr/MevzuatMetin/5.3.743.pdf; for Article 713 of the 2001 code, see http://www.tbmm.gov.tr/kanunlar/k4721.html.

62. Ibid.

63. The reason is that through the Assignment of Possession Law of 28 May 1928, number 1331, and the 12 August 1928 decree, number 6994, issued in connection with how this law would be implemented, theoretically, the matter of "the registration of real estate through title deeds" (in the names of their new owners) legally was concluded.

64. The ways through which various kinds of real estate and property belonging to the state can be turned back into private property, and the question of what the relationship is between real estate considered as abandoned properties and the principle of acquired prescription, are extremely technical legal issues requiring a special expertise. For more information, see Düzceer, *Kazandırıcı Zamanaşımıyla Taşınmaz İktisabı,* 96–130, 519–46.

65. *Resmi Gazete*, No. 14257, 26 July 1972.

66. Düzceer, Kazandırıcı Zamanaşımıyla Taşınmaz İktisabı, 103–30.

67. Kemal Tuncay, *Emval-i Metruke ile İlgili İçtihat Özetleri,* http://www.bahum.gov.tr/etkinlikler/seminerler/sunumlar/emvaliMetrukeIctihatOzetleri.pdf.

68. A matter that complicates this issue is that, for example, although some meadows and summer pastures fall in the category of abandoned properties, their registration in the treasury is a problem. It seems that the legal scholars have not sufficiently studied the legal status of such lands. See Yaşar Karayalçın, "Kanunlarımız, Doktrin ve Uygulama Açısından Mer'a ve Yaylaklar 'Emval-i Metruke,'" *Ankara Üniversitesi Hukuk Fakültesi Dergisi* 32, No. 1–4, 1975, 41–70, http://auhf.ankara.edu.tr/dergiler/auhfd-arsiv/AUHF-1975–32–01–04/AUHF-1975–32–01–04-Karayalcin2.pdf.

69. *Resmi Gazete*, No. 19512, 9 July 1987.

70. Ibid.

71. The Court of Cassation's General Assembly issued a decision that during a period of ten years real estate that is claimed to be under command and possession of the state cannot be used, and even after the ten year period ends, such a property registered with a title deed can always be the object of a suit, and its title deed can be annulled. Upon the courts taking some decisions in this direction, on 25 February 2009 an additional sentence was added to Article 12 in a law numbered 5481. By saying "this provision will be applied irrespective of claims, the attributes of the property, or the nature of the parties, including the state or other public entities" all doors to objections were definitively closed (*Resmi Gazete*, No. 27169, 14 March 2009).

72. In fact, it would be more appropriate to speak of only a single circular. The same text was issued on two different dates. For this text, see Kardes, *"Tehcir" ve Emval-i Metruke Mevzuati*, 183–84. .

73. Ibid.

74. Ibid.

75. Ibid.

76. Ibid.

77. Turkish Civil Code, Article 1020, http://www.tbmm.gov.tr/kanunlar/k4721.html.

78. *Hürriyet*, 19 September 2006, http://www.hurriyet.com.tr/gundem/5109117_p. asp; and *Radikal*, 20 September 2006, http://www.radikal.com.tr/haber.php? haberno=199165. Moreover, see http://bianet.org/bianet/ bianet/85432-osmanli-arsivleri-acilirsa-resmitez-zayiflar.

79. Veysel Başpınar, "Elektronik Tapu Sicili Düzenlenirken Tapu Sicilinin Aleniyeti ve Diğer Alanlarla İlgili Alınması Gereken Tedbirler," *Ankara Üniversitesi Hukuk Fakültesi Dergisi* 57, No. 3, 2008, 120–21.

CONCLUSION

It is worth recalling that Lemkin introduced the concept of genocide through the regulations published by the Nazis on how to administer the areas they had occupied; he preferred this method, even though he knew of the crimes that the Nazis had committed. He did not choose to present the concept of genocide through the description of Nazi barbarism. For this reason, his identification of the concept of genocide in the form of a set of laws and regulations, which perhaps under war conditions could be considered as "normal," is extremely meaningful. Lemkin reminds us that we must conceive of genocide as a phenomenon situated inside the legal system. We attempted to do this in this book, to show that the Armenian Genocide consists not only of barbaric displays carried out against Armenians, but also of a series of ordinary legal texts issued in the Ottoman and Republican periods.

To sum up what we have said in a few sentences, if it is necessary to formulate it in legal terms, the Ottoman Committee of Union and Progress Party deported the Armenians for various reasons and, while deporting them, promised that the government would look after their properties and give them their equivalent values in the new places where they would be settled. All the promulgated laws and regulations repeated that the Armenians were the true owners of their properties and the state only undertook their administration in the name of the owners. However, later, the same laws and regulations were used to eliminate the existence of the Armenians in Anatolia.

The same practice continued in the Republican era. The Armenians' right to their properties, which they left behind, was repeated in the international treaties signed in this period. Turkey promised to give back properties to owners who, as of 6 August 1924, were at their properties. Afterwards, Turkey's borders were fortified like a fortress and not even one single Armenian was able to enter the country. Those Armenians who were not allowed back were declared to be "fugitive and missing" and the process of confiscation of their properties continued.

Furthermore, while doing all this in the Ottoman and in the Republican period, it was not said, and it could not be said, that the Armenians had no rights to their properties. Legislation repeated that the Armenians possessed rights to their properties, so that if properties could not be returned their equivalent values must be paid; but the same legislation was simultaneously used to prevent this. This was because the goal was to completely remove the Armenian presence in Anatolia. What was occurring was a legal operation of theft.

As readers can see, we are not discussing any mass extermination of Armenians. We are only listing the promises made by the state to the Armenians and showing how these promises were instilled in the legal system. We are also indicating which policies the government later put into practice, relying on this same legal system. There is only one clear meaning to this legal system: it is an unmistakable type of "legal" robbery and a substantial part of the genocidal process. This shows very clearly that the Armenian Genocide was not only a chaotic, barbaric event, but that it also was carefully and legally institutionalized. These laws demonstrate the ongoing eliminationist intent of successive Ottoman and Turkish governments.

We believe that behind the great uproar caused by successive Turkish governments over the decades on the Armenian Genocide lies this simple truth. Independent of the killing and annihilation, the state, which was conscious of having stolen Armenian properties illegally, raised a racket in order to obscure the truth. This was because no matter what it might call the events of 1915, it was and still is aware that a serious disgrace exists. It is aware that the moment the uproar dies down it will be obligated to give back the usurped Armenian properties or pay their equivalent values.

There is an inherent tension and conflict in the laws and regulations. Even though Turkey used these laws to complete the genocidal process, the same laws and regulations today can force Turkey to compensate Armenian losses.

Why all this took place, why a state and a society would place itself in such a shameful situation of course has a cause, an explanation. The Ottoman regime and its Republican successor saw the existence of the

Christians as a future threat, and founded all their policies on the erasure of the traces of the Christians in Anatolia. They saw the absence of the Christians as the condition for their own existence. This stance, which is the truest expression of Talat Pasha's words, "to eliminate the existence" of the Armenians, gives the main spirit of the policy implemented towards Armenian properties throughout the Ottoman and Republican periods.

The essence of all the laws and regulations issued concerning the Armenians was the erasure of all traces of them on Anatolian soil to prevent them from appearing again. Perhaps the physical annihilation of the Armenians was necessary to achieve this goal, but it was not sufficient in and of itself. The use of the legal system was as important as, and perhaps even more important than, this physical annihilation. The law, in particular the Abandoned Properties Laws, became the most important means for the removal of the Armenians' economic existence and the erasure of their traces from Anatolia. The Abandoned Properties Laws are among the most important laws of the Republic of Turkey. In this sense, we can say that the Republican regime arose based on a legal system intended to eliminate the existence of a people, and internalized this practice of law. This is the reason why we call it a genocidal society, a society that established its existence on the laws and regulation of the genocidal process.

The last thing that we can add is that, without changing this legal structure, the political and social democratization of Turkey will be very difficult. A society based on a mentality that views the absence of the other as the condition for its own existence, and on a legal system created as the product of this mentality, cannot be democratic. A future respecting human dignity and honor cannot be established. We have written these lines in the spirit and hope that this will be understood and changed one day.

BIBLIOGRAPHY

Ottoman and Turkish Archives

Ottoman Prime Ministry Archives (Başbakanlık Osmanlı Arşivi; BOA)

Office of Tribal and Immigrant Settlement of the Interior Ministry (Dahiliye Nezareti İskân-ı Aşâir ve Muhâcirîn Müdüriyeti [İAMM])

Office of Tribes and Immigrants of the Interior Ministry (Dahiliye Nezareti Aşair ve Muhacirin Müdiriyeti Umumiyesi [AMMU])

Cipher Office of the Interior Ministry (Dahiliye Nezareti Şifre Kalemi [BOA/DH.ŞFR])

Interior Ministry Public Security Directorate (Dahiliye Nezareti Emniyet-i Umumiye Müdürlüğü [BOA/DH.EUM])

Third Department of Public Security of the Interior Ministry (Dahiliye Nezareti Emniyet-i Umumiye Üçüncü Şube [BOA/DH.EUM. 3.Şb])

Legal Counsel Office of the Interior Ministry (Dahiliye Nezâreti Hukuk Müşavirliği [BOA/DH.HMŞ])

Record Office of the Public Security Directorate of the Interior Ministry (Dahiliye Nezareti Emniyet-i Umûmiye Müdüriyeti Memurin Kalemi [BOA/DH.EUM.MEM])

Political Division of the Ministry of the Interior (Dahiliye Nezareti Siyasî Kısım [BOA/DH.SYS])

General Administration of the Ministry of the Interior (Dahiliye Nezâreti İdâre-i Umumiye Belgeleri [BOA/DH.İUM])

Record Office Responsible for Foreigners of the Ministry of the Interior Public Security Directorate (Dahiliye Emniyet-i Umumiye Ecanib Kalemi [BOA/DH.EUM.ECB])

Minutes of the Council of Ministers (Meclis-i Vükela Mazbataları [BOA/MV])

Ministry of Foreign Affairs Political Division (Hariciye Nezareti Siyasî Kısım [BOA/HR.SYS])

Foreign Affairs Ministry Legal Counsel Office of Consultation (Hariciye Nezareti Hukuk
    Müşavirliği İstişare Odası [BOA/HR.HMŞ.İŞO])
Sublime Porte Documents Office (Bâb-ı Âlî Evrâk Odası [BOA/BEO])
Yıldız Palace Collection (Yıldız Esas Evrakı [BOA/Y.EE])

Published Archival Documents

Ottoman Prime Ministry Archives

Arşiv Belgeleriyle Ermeni Faaliyetleri, 1914–1918. Cilt 1. Ankara: Genelkurmay Basım
    Evi, 2005.
Osmanlı Belgelerinde Ermenilerin Sevk ve İskanı. Ankara: Osmanlı Arşivi Daire
    Başkanlığı Yayını, 2007.
Osmanlı Belgelerinde Ermeniler (1915–1920). Ankara: Osmanlı Arşivi Daire Başkanlığı
    Yayını, 1994.

Prime Ministry Republican Archives

General Directorate of Land Settlement Archive (BCA/TİGMA; [Toprak İskan Genel
    Müdürlüğü Arşivi])

Parliamentary Proceedings

T. B. M. M. Zabıt Ceridesi, Period 1, Assembly Year 1, Vol. 1. Ankara: TBMM Matbaası,
    1940.
T. B. M. M. Zabıt Ceridesi, Period 1, Assembly Year 3, Vol. 25. Ankara: TBMM Matbaası,
    1960.
T. B. M. M. Zabıt Cerideleri, Period 1, Assembly Year 3, Vol. 29. Ankara: T.B.M.M
    Matbaası, 1961.
T. B. M. M. Gizli Celse Zabıtları, Period 1, Assembly Year 3, Vol. 3. Ankara: Türkiye İş
    Bankası Kültür Yayınları, 1985.
T. B. M. M. Gizli Celse Zabıtları, Period 2, Assembly Year 2, Vol. 4. Ankara: Türkiye İş
    Bankası Kültür Yayınları, 1985.
T. B. M. M. Zabıt Ceridesi, Period 2, Assembly Year 2, Vol. 8/1. http://www.tbmm.gov.tr/
    tutanaklar/TUTANAK/TBMM/d02/c008/tbmm02008037.pdf.
T. B. M. M. Zabıt Ceridesi, Period 2, Assembly Year 4, Vol. 1. 16 May 1927. Ankara:
    TBMM Basımevi, 1957.
Meclis-i Ayan Zabıt Ceridesi, Period 3, Assembly Year 2, Vol. 1. Ankara: TBMM
    Basımevi, 1990.
Meclis-i Mebusan Zabıt Ceridesi, Period 3, Assembly Year 5, Vol. 1. Ankara: TBMM
    Basımevi, 1992.

Legislation

Düstur, Series 1, Vol. 1. Istanbul: Matbaa-ı Amire, 1289.
Düstur, Series 2, Vol. 7. Dersaadet: Matbaa-i Âmire, 1920.
Düstur, Series 3, Vol. 1. Istanbul: Milliyet Matbaası, 1929.

Düstur, Series 3, Vol. 2. Istanbul: Milliyet Matbaası, 1929.
Düstur, Series 3, Vol. 7. Ankara: Türk Ocakları Merkez Heyeti Matbaası, 1928.
Düstur, Series 3, Vol. 8. Ankara: Türk Ocakları Merkez Heyeti Matbaası, 1928.
Düstur, Series 3, Vol. 12. Ankara: Başvekâlet Müdevvenat Matbaası, 1931.
Düstur, Series 3, Vol. 13. Ankara: Başvekâlet Müdevvenat Matbaası, 1932.

United States National Archives

Nielsen, K. Fred. *American-Turkish Claims Settlement under the Agreement of December 24, 1923, and Supplemental Agreements between the United States and Turkey, Opinions and Report.* Washington: U.S. Government Printing Office, 1937.
U.S. Department of State, *Papers Relating to the Foreign Relations of the United States, 1923,* Vol. II. Washington: U.S. Government Printing Office, 1939; http://digital.library.wisc.edu/1711.dl/FRUS.FRUS1939v02.

Reports of the League of Nations

League of Nations: Council. *Return to Turkish Armenian Refugees in Greece of their Deposits in Foreign Banks at Smyrna and Their Property Left in Asia Minor (The Essayan Petition).* Geneva: n.p., 1925.

Official Correspondence

Exchange of Notes between His Majesty's Government in the United Kingdom and the Government of the Turkish Republic concerning the Liquidation of Unexecuted Judgments of the Anglo-Turkish Mixed Arbitral Tribunal, Ankara 23 March 1944, Treaty Series No. 48 (1946). London: His Majesty's Stationery Office, 1946.

Published Court Verdicts

T.C. Şişli İkinci Asliye Ceza Mahkemesi [Şişli Second Criminal Court of the First Instance of the Republic of Turkey], E:2006/1208, K:2007/1106, T: 11.10.2007.
U.S. District Court, C.D. California. Varoujan Deirmenjian, Aris Aghvazarian, Robert Dabaghian, Marguerid Jeredjian, Katia Kermoyan, Paylig Kermoyan, and Raffi Bakian, on Behalf of Themselves and All Others Similarly Situated, as Well on Behalf of the General Public and Acting in the Public Interest, Plaintiffs, v. Deutsche Bank, A.G., Dresdner Bank, A.G., and Does 1–100, Defendants. No. CV 06–774 MMM (CWx).
Yargıtay İçtihadı Birleştirme Büyük Genel Kurulu [Grand General Assembly of the Court of Appeals], E:1935/18, K:1936/30, T:25.11.1936.

Other Documents Published in Turkish

Kardeş, Salâhaddin. *"Tehcir" ve Emval-i Metruke Mevzuatı.* Ankara: T.C. Maliye Bakanlığı Strateji Geliştirme Başkanlığı, 2008.
T.C. Maliye Vekaleti Milli Emlak Müdürlüğü, *Milli Emlak Muamelelerine Müteallik Mevzuat.* Ankara: Başvekalet Matbaası, 1937.

T.C. Devlet Malları Mevzuatı, http://www.milliemlak.gov.tr/Yaynlarmz/Devlet_
Mallar%C4%B1_Mevzuat%C4%B1_Ekli.doc.

Newspapers

Takvim-i Vekayi Nos. 2189 (1 June 1915); 2303 (27 September 1915); 2343 (10 November
    1915); 2481 (15 March 1916); 2861 (22 April 1917).
Resmi Ceride Nos. 22 (10 September 1923); 68 (7 April 1924); 598 (31 May 1927); 639
    (31 July 1927).
Resmi Gazete Nos. 902 (30 May 1928); 904 (4 June 1928); 1151 (26 March 1929); 1154 (30
    March 1929); 1210 (8 June 1929); 1211 (9 June 1929); 2896 (2 January 1935); 3960
    (15 July 1938); 6059 (17 July 1945); 7190 (25 April 1949); 7471 (31 March 1950);
    7513 (23 May 1950); 7564 (24 July 1950); 11638 (22 February 1964); 11742 (1 July
    1964); 14257 (26 July 1972); 19512 (9 July 1987); 19983 (8 November 1988); 26310
    (5 October 2006); 27169 (14 March 2009); 27256 (12 June 2009).
Newspapers in the 1918–30 period: Ati Gazetesi, Cumhuriyet, Jamanag, Memleket
    Gazetesi, Milliyet, Müstakil, Polis Mecmuası, Sabah, Son Telgraf, Tevhid-i Efkâr,
    Tercüman-ı Hakikat, Vakit, Vatan.

Newspaper Reports

Bianet, 19 September 2006 http://bianet.org/bianet/ bianet/85432-osmanli-
arsivleri-acilirsa-resmi-tezzayiflar.
Bugün, 25 June 2012.
Hürriyet, 19 September 2006, http://www.hurriyet.com.tr/gundem/5109117_p.asp.
Milliyet, 19 February 2009.
Radikal, 20 September 2006, http://www.radikal.com.tr/haber.php?haberno=199165.
Radikal, 11 February 2009.

Online Documents and Internet Sites

HANSARD 1803–2005; the Official Report of debates in Parliament; http://hansard.
    millbanksystems.com/written_answers/1928/may/23/turkey-british-claims#
    S5CV0217P0_19280523_CWA_84; http://hansard.millbanksystems.com/commons/
    1933/may/16/turkey-british-claims.
Official Web Site of Nobel Prize, Nansen International Office for Refugees—History;
    http://www.nobelprize.org/nobel_prizes/peace/laureates/1938/nansen-history.html.
Turkish Citizenship Laws; http://mirekoc.ku.edu.tr/legalframework.
Turkish Civil Law; http://www.mevzuat.gov.tr/MevzuatMetin/5.3.743.pdf; http://www.
    tbmm.gov.tr/kanunlar/k4721.html

Turkish Language Published Works

Akçam, Taner. Ermeni Meselesi Hallolunmuştur, Osmanlı Belgelerine Göre Savaş
    Yıllarında Ermenilere Yönelik Politikalar. Istanbul: İletişim Yayınları, 2008.
————. İnsan Hakları ve Ermeni Sorunu, İttihat ve Terakki'den Kurtuluş Savaşı'na. An-
    kara: İmge Kitabevi, 1999.
Aktar, Ayhan. Türk Milliyetçiliği, Gayrimüslimler ve Ekonomik Dönüşüm. Istanbul:
    İletişim Yayınları, 2006.

Armaoğlu, Fahir. *Belgelerle Türk-Amerikan Münasebetleri*. Ankara: Türk Tarih Kurumu, 1991.

Atnur, Ethem İbrahim. *Türkiye'de Ermeni Kadınları ve Çocukları Meselesi (1915-1923)*. Ankara: Babil Yayıncılık, 2005.

Aybars, Ergün. *İstiklâl Mahkemeleri*. Ankara: Bilgi Yayınevi, 1975.

Aybay, Rona. *Yurttaşlık (Vatandaşlık) Hukuku*. Ankara: A.Ü.S.B.F. yayını, 1982.

Bali, N. Rıfat. *Cumhuriyet Yıllarında Türkiye Yahudileri, Bir Türkleştirme Serüveni (1923-1945)*. Istanbul: İletişim Yayınları, 2001.

Baykal, Bekir Sıtkı. *Heyet-i Temsiliye Kararları*. Ankara: Türk Tarih Kurumu, 1974.

Bilsel, Cemil. *Lozan, İkinci Kitap*. Istanbul, Ahmet İhsan Matbaası, 1933.

Çağaptay, Soner. *Türkiye'de İslam, Laiklik ve Milliyetçilik: Türk Kimdir?* Istanbul: Istanbul Bilgi Üniversitesi Yayınları, 2009.

Dadrian, Vahakn, Akçam, Taner. *Tehcir ve Taktil Divan-ı Harb-i Örfi Zabıtları, İttihat ve Terakki'nin Yargılanması (1919-1922)*. Istanbul: Bilgi Üniversitesi, 2009.

Düzceer, Rıza Ali. *Kazandırıcı Zamanaşımıyla Taşınmaz İktisabı* (Tescil Davası-MK.m. 639). Ankara: Yetkin Basımevi, 1994.

Erim, Nihat. *Devletlerarası Hukuku ve Siyasi Tarih Metinleri Cilt 1: Osmanlı İmparatorluğu Andlaşmaları*. Ankara: Türk Tarih Kurumu, 1953.

Goloğlu, Mahmut. *Erzurum Kongresi*. Ankara: Nüve Matbaası, 1968.

————. *Sivas Kongresi*. Ankara: Başnur Matbaası, 1969.

Gökbilgin, Tayyib. *Milli Mücadele Başlarken, II, Sivas Kongresinden Büyük Millet Meclisinin Açılmasına (4 September 1919-23 April 1920)*. Ankara: Türk Tarih Kurumu, 1965.

Halaçoğlu, Yusuf. *Ermeni Tehciri*. Istanbul: Babıali Kültür Yayıncılığı, 2001.

İnönü, İsmet. *Hatıralar, 2. Kitap*. Ankara: Bilgi Yayınevi, 1987.

Kurban Dilek, Hatemi, Kezban. *Bir 'Yabancı'laştırma Hikayesi: Türkiye'de Gayrimüslim Cemaatlerin Vakıf ve Taşınmaz Mülkiyet Sorunu*, Istanbul: TESEV, 2009.

Koraltürk, Murat. *Ekonominin Türkleştirilmesi*, Istanbul: İletişim Yayınları, 2011.

Meray L. Seha. *Lozan Barış Konferansı, Tutanaklar-Belgeler*, Cilt 1–9. Istanbul: Yapı Kredi Yayınları, 1993.

Onaran, Nevzat. *Emvâl-i Metrûke Olayı, Osmanlı'da ve Cumhuriyette Ermeni Mallarının Türkleştirilmesi*. Istanbul: Belge Yayınları, 2010.

Reyna, Yuda, Zonana, M. Ester. *Son Siyasal Düzenlemelere Göre Cemaat Vakıfları*. Istanbul: Gözlem Gazetecilik Basın ve Yayın A.Ş, 2003.

Sağlam, Hakkı Mehmet. *II. Tertip Düstur Kılavuzu, Osmanlı Devlet Mevzuatı (1908-1922)*. Istanbul: Tarih Vakfı Yurt Yayınları, 2006.

Sarıhan, Zeki. *Kurtuluş Savaşı Günlüğü, Erzurum Kongresinden TBMM'ye*, Cilt 2. Ankara: Öğretmen Dünyası Yayınları, 1984.

Soysal, İsmail. *Tarihçeleri ve Açıklamaları ile Birlikte Türkiye'nin Siyasal Antlaşmaları, 1. Cilt (1920-1945)*. Ankara: Türk Tarih Kurumu, 2000.

Sürmeli, Serpil. *Milli Mücadele'de Tekalif-i Milliye Emirleri*. Ankara: AKDTYK Atatürk Arzştırma Merkezi, 1998.

Süslü, Azmi. *Ermeniler ve 1915 Tehcir Olayı*. Van: Yüzüncü Yıl Üniversitesi Rektörlüğü, 1990.

Şimşir, N. Bilal. *Lozan Telgrafları I (1922-1923)*. Ankara: Türk Tarih Kurumu, 1990.

————. *Lozan Telgrafları II (Şubat—Ağustos 1923)*. Ankara: Türk Tarih Kurumu, 1994.

Unat, İlhan. *Türk Vatandaşlık Kanunu*. Ankara: S.B.F. Yayınları, 1966.

Tekinalp, Gülören. *Türk Yabancılar Hukuku*. Istanbul: Beta Basım Yayım, 2002.

Tunaya, Zafer Tarık. *Türkiye'de Siyasi Partiler, Cilt II, Mütareke Dönemi*. Istanbul: Hürriyet Vakfı Yayınları, 1986.

Yalman, Emin Ahmet. *Yakın Tarihte Gördüklerim ve Geçirdiklerim, Cilt 3 (1922-1944)*. Istanbul: Yenilik Basımevi, 1970.

Yeghiayan, Vartkes. *Malta Belgeleri, Türk Savaş Suçluları Hakkında İngiltere Dışişleri Bakanlığı Belgeleri.* İstanbul: Belge Yayınları, 2007.
Yıldız, Ahmet. *Ne Mutlu Türküm Diyebilene: Türk Kimliğinin Etno-seküler Sınırları (1919–1938).* İstanbul: İletişim Yayınları, 2001.

Works Published in Languages Other than Turkish

Aftandilian, Gregory. *Armenia Vision of a Republic, The Independence Lobby in America 1918–1927.* Boston: Charles River Books, 1980.
Gidel, Gilbert. *Recueil des décisions des Tribunaux Arbitraux Mixtes instituts par les Traites de Paix,* 10 vols. Buffalo, NY: William S. Hein & Co., 2006.
Hayes, Peter. "Plunder and Restitution." In *The Oxford Handbook of Holocaust Studies,* edited by Roth, John K., Edward J. Sexton, Hayes, Peter, Theodore Z. Weiss, 540–59. Oxford and New York: Oxford University Press, 2010.
Kaprielian Churchill, Isabel. *Like Our Mountains, A History of Armenians in Canada.* Montreal: McGill-Queen's University Press, 2005.
Karagueuzian, Hrayr S., and Yair Auron. *A Perfect Injustice, Genocide Theft of Armenian Wealth.* New Brunswick, NJ: Transaction Publishers, 2009.
Lemkin, Raphael. *Axis Rule of Occupied Europe, Laws Of Occupation, Analysis Of Government, Proposals For Redress.* Washington, DC: Carnegie Endowment, 1944.
———. *Axis Rule of Occupied Europe, Laws Of Occupation, Analysis of Government, Proposals for Redress.* Clark, NJ: The Lawbook Exchange, 2008.
McDogall, M. Errol. *Reparations, 1930–31. Special report upon Armenian claims.* Ottawa: F.A. Acland, Printer to the King, 1931.
McNair, Arnold D., and Hersch Lauterpacht, eds. *International Law Reports, Annual Digest of Public International Law Cases, Years 1927 and 1928,* Volume 4, UK, Cambridge: Grotius Publications, 1981.
Migliorino, Nicola. *(Re)constructing Armenia in Lebanon and Syria: Ethno-cultural Diversity and the State in the Aftermath of a Refugee Crisis.* New York, Oxford: Berghahn Books, 2008.
Psomiades, J. Harry. *Fridtjof Nansen and Greek Refugee Crisis 1922–1924.* Bloomingdale, IL: The Asia Minor and Pontos Hellenic Research Center, 2011.
Trask, Roger. *The United States Response to Turkish Nationalism and Reform 1914-1918.* Minneapolis: University of Minnesota Press, 1971.
Üngör, Uğur Ümit, and Mehmet Polatel. *Confiscation and Destruction, The Young Turk Seizure of Armenian Property.* London and New York: Continuum International Publishing, 2011.
Weis, Paul. *Nationality and Statelessness in International Law.* Netherlands, Alphen aan den Rijn Sijthoff and Noordhoff International Publishers B.V., 1979.
Yeghiayan, Vartkes (ed.), *British Reports on Ethnic Cleansing in Anatolia, 1919–1922: The Armenian-Greek Section.* Glendale, CA: Center for Armenian Remembrance, 2007.

Articles in Turkish and English

Aktan, Gündüz. "Ermeni Sorununun Tarihsel Boyutu: Lozan Barış Antlaşması ve Ermeni Sorunu." *Avrasya Stratejik Araştırmalar Merkezi Ermeni Araştırmaları Enstitüsü,* http://www.eraren.org/bilgibankasi/tr/index1_1_2.htm.
Arat, Tuğrul. "Türk Vatandaşlığından Iskat Edilen Kişilerin Mülkiyet ve Miras Hakları." *A.Ü.H.F Dergisi* 31, No. 1–4 (1974): 279–360.

Atnur, Ethem İbrahim. "Osmanlı Hükümetleri ve Tehcir Edilen Rum ve Ermenilerin Yeniden İskanı Meselesi." *Atatürk Yolu* 4, No. 14 (November 1994): 121–39.

Başpınar, Veysel. "Elektronik Tapu Sicili Düzenlenirken Tapu Sicilinin Aleniyeti ve Diğer Alanlarla İlgili Alınması Gereken Tedbirler." *Ankara Üniversitesi Hukuk Fakültesi Dergisi* 57, No. 3, (2008): 98–132.

Çağaptay, Soner. "Kim Türk? Kim vatandaş? Erken Cumhuriyet Dönemi Vatandaşlık Rejimi Üzerine Bir Çalışma." *Toplum ve Bilim* 98 (Autumn 2003): 166–85.

Çiçek, Kemal. "The 1934–1935 Turkish-American Compensation Agreement and its Implication for today." *Review of Armenian Studies*, No. 23 (2011): 93–146. For a description of Kemal Çiçek's topic, see http://www.dunyabulteni.net/index.php?aTy pe=haber&ArticleID=125395.

Davis, Uri. "Citizenship Legislation in the Syrian Arab Republic." *Arab Studies Quarterly* 28 (1996): 29–47.

Efiloğlu, Ahmet, and Raif İvecan. "Rum Emval-i Metrukesinin İdaresi." *History Studies* (2/3, 2010): 125–46.

Fişek, Hicri. "Türkiye'de Yabancıların Aynî Haklardan İstifadesi." *A.Ü.H.F. Dergisi* 7, Nos. 3–4 (1950): 426–40.

Freeman, Michael. "Genocide, Civilization and Modernity." *British Journal of Sociology* 46, no. 2 (June, 1995): 207–23.

Gordon J., Leland. "The Turkish American Controversy over Nationality." *The American Journal of International Law* 25, no. 4, (October 1931): 658–69.

Güzel, Şükrü Mehmet. "Anayasal Düzen, Hukuk, Adalet, Diaspora Ermenilerinin Türkiye Cumhuriyetine Toplu Geri Dönebilmeleri Mücadelesi." http://www.21yyte.org/ tr/yazi6103-Diaspora_Ermenilerin_Turkiye_Cumhuriyetine_Toplu_Geri_Done-bilme_Mucadelesi__.html.

Heldref Publication. "Certificates of Identity for Refugees." *Advocate of Peace through Justice* 86, no. 11 (November 1924): 597–98.

Hill, W. H. "The Anglo-Turkish Mixed Arbitral Tribunal." *Juridical Review* 47, no. 3 (1935): 241–52.

Holborn, W. Louise. "The Legal Status of Political Refugees 1920–1938." *American Society of International Law* 32, no. 4 (October 1938): 680–703.

Jaeger, Gilbert. "On the History of the International Protection of Refugees." *International Review of the Red Cross* 83, no. 843 (September 2001): 727–37.

Karayalçın, Yaşar. "Kanunlarımız, Doktrin ve Uygulama Açısından Mer'a ve Yaylaklar 'Emval-i Metruke'." *Ankara Üniversitesi Hukuk Fakültesi Dergisi* 32, nos. 1–4 (1975): 41–70, http://auhf.ankara.edu.tr/dergiler/auhfd-arsiv/AUHF-1975-32-01-04/AUHF-1975-32-01-04-Karayalcin2.pdf.

Lutz, E. Russell. "Claims against Turkey." *The American Journal of International Law* 28, No. 2 (April 1934): 346–49.

Moses, Dirk. "Toward a Theory of Critical Genocide Studies." Edited by Jacques Semelin, *Online Encyclopedia of Mass Violence*, 18 April 2008. http://www.massviolence. org/IMG/article_PDF/Toward-a-Theory-of-Critical-Genocide-Studies.pdf.

Nomer, Ergin. "Yabancı Devlet Vatandaşlığını Kazanan (Eski) Türk Vatandaşlarının Mirasçılığı." *İ.H.F. Mecmuası* 55, no. 3 (1997): 169–78.

Sargın, Fügen. "Yabancı Gerçek Kişilere Ait Taşınmaz Malların Tasfiyesi." *Türkiye Barosu Dergisi* 1 (1992): 31–72.

Tachjian, Vahé. "The expulsion of non-Turkish ethnic and religious groups from Turkey to Syria during the 1920s and early 1930s." Edited by Jacques Semelin, *Online Encyclopedia of Mass Violence*, 25 March 2009. http://www. massviolence.org/IMG/article_PDF/The-expulsion-of-non-Turkish-ethnic-and-religious-groups.pdf.

Tashjian [Tachjian], Vahe [Vahé]. "Recovering Armenian Properties in Turkey through the French Authorities in Syria and Lebanon in the 1920s." *The Armenian Genocide: From Recognition to Compensation*, Presentation at 23–25 February 2012 international conference in Beirut.

Theriault, Henry. "The Global Reparations Movement and Meaningful Resolution of the Armenian Genocide." *Armenian Weekly* (6 May 2010). http://www.armenianweekly.com/2010/05/06/reparations-2/.

Tuncay, Kemal. *Emval-i Metruke ile İlgili İçtihat Özetleri*. http://www.bahum.gov.tr/etkinlikler/seminerler/sunumlar/emvaliMetrukeIctihatOzetleri.pdf.

Unat, İlhan. "Türk Vatandaşlığından 'koğulanlar' Miras Hakkından Yoksun mudur?" *S.B.F. Dergisi* 20, no. 3 (1965):179–226.

Watenpaugh, David Keith. "The League of Nations' Rescue of Armenian Genocide Survivors and the Making of Modern Humanitarianism, 1920–1927." *American Historical Review* 115, no. 5 (December 2010): 1–25.

Unpublished Doctoral and Master's Theses

Atnur, Ethem İbrahim. "Tehcirden Dönen Rum ve Ermenilerin İskanı." Master's thesis, Erzurum University, Erzurum, 1991.

Eroğlu, Tayfun. "Tehcirden Milli Mücadeleye Ermeni Malları (1915–1922)." Master's thesis, Dokuz Eylül Üniversitesi, İzmir, 2008.

Günaydın, Adem. "The Return and Resettlement of the Relocated Armenians (1918–1920)." Doctoral thesis, Orta Doğu Teknik Üniversitesi, xx, 2007.

Marashlian, Levon. "The Armenian Question from Sèvres to Lausanne: Economic and Morality in American and British Policies, 1920–1923 (Volume 1)." Doctoral thesis, University of California, Los Angeles, 1992.

Mumyakmaz, Hatice. "Osmanlı'dan Cumhuriyet'e Vatandaşlık." Doctoral thesis, Gazi University, Ankara, 2008.

Özdemir, Mustafa. "I. Dünya Savaşı Sırasında Osmanlı Ülkesinde Yaşanan Göç Hareketleri." Doctoral thesis, Dokuz Eylül Üniversitesi, İzmir, 2007.

Sofuoğlu, Adnan. "Kuvay-ı Milliye Döneminde Kuzey-Batı Anadolu (1919–1921)." Doctoral thesis, Erzurum University, Erzurum, 1993.

Sürer, Duygu. "Türkiye'de Yabancıların Taşınmaz Edinmesi." Master's thesis, Marmara University, Istanbul, 2008.

INDEX

Index of Place Names

Adana, 20, 33, 47, 51,
Adapazarı, 28
Aleppo, 28, 30, 32, 33, 34, 85
Alexandrapol/Alexandropol (Gyumri), 4,
    88
Amanos, 33
Amasya, 28
Anatolia, 11, 16, 17, 20, 28, 31, 39, 43, 45,
    46, 47, 53, 58, 63, 71, 73, 75 107, 114,
    118, 119, 126, 127, 128, 132, 134,
    135, 154, 155
Ankara, 47, 49, 50, 51, 70, 71, 73, 74, 90,
    92, 95, 97, 98, 114, 115, 116, 124,
    128, 129, 135,
Antep, 85
Ardahan, 89
Armenia, 90
Artvin, 89
Athens, 107, 119
Aydın, 30, 31, 32, 33, 43, 58

Bafra, 28
Batum, 34, 89
Berlin, 104
Beyoğlu, 119
Beirut, 93
Bilecik, 28
Bitlis, 28, 30, 33, 34
Boğaz, 128
Boğazlıyan, 28

Bulgaria, 11, 43
Bursa, 28, 33, 129

Canik, 30, 32, 33, 34, 43
Caucasus, 33, 39
Cebel-i Bereket, 28
Cebel-i Lübnan (Mount Lebanon) 32
Cilicia, 9, 47, 48
Çarşamba, 28
Çatalca, 32, 33, 34, 128
Çeşme, 129
Çorum, 28
Çukurova, 47

Damascus, 33
Develi, 28
Diyarbakır (Diyarbekir) 12, 28, 30, 33, 34

Edirne, 28, 31, 32, 33, 34
Egypt, 107
Erzincan, 33, 34
Erzerum (Erzurum) 28, 30, 32, 33, 34, 42,
    43, 45, 46, 50, 57
Eskişehir, 28, 30, 31, 32, 33, 34

Fatsa, 28
France, 4, 15, 72, 83, 90, 91, 92, 93,
94, 95, 96, 103, 104, 106, 108

Gebze, 128

Gemlik, 28
Giresun, 51, 113
Germany, 9, 12, 29, 66, 103, 104, 131
Great Britain, 15, 40, 66, 72, 83, 104
Greece, 10, 11, 20, 43, 44, 48, 51, 52, 62,
    73, 83, 100, 103, 107, 125, 127, 128
Gümüşhacıköy, 28
Gyumri (see Alexandrapol/Alexandropol)
    4, 88

Hanak, 89
Havza, 28
Hüdavendigâr (Hüdavendigar) 33

İçel, 32, 33, 34
İmroz, 126,
India, 73,
Iraq, 20, 72, 73
Ireland, 73
Iskenderun (İskenderun; Alexandretta),
    20
Istanbul (Constantinople) 4, 8, 11, 12, 32,
    39, 43, 45, 46 47, 48, 50, 51, 53, 54,
    60, 72, 73, 75, 82, 94, 98 104, 109,
    110, 111, 113, 114, 115, 116, 117, 118
    119, 120, 122, 125,126, 127 128, 129,
    134, 135, 136, 138, 142, 143, 145
Izmir (İzmir/Smyrna) 4, 47, 56, 57, 58, 59,
    100, 104, 106, 107, 119,
Izmit (İzmit/Nicomedia) 28, 30, 32, 33,
    34, 129

Kale-i Sultaniye, 32, 33
Karacabey, 28
Karahisar-ı Sâhib (Afyon) 28, 30, 31, 32,
    34, 59
Karamürsel, 28
Karesi, 28, 30, 32, 34
Kars, 4, 87, 88, 89
Kartal, 12, 127, 128
Kastamonu, 31, 32, 33, 34, 43
Kayseri (Caesarea) 27, 28, 30, 31, 32, 33,
    34
Keskin, 28
Kırşehir, 28
Kirmastı 28
Konya, 28, 30, 31, 32, 33, 34, 47, 64, 120
Kozan, 28, 120
Kütahya, 31, 32, 33, 34, 59

Lebanon, 80, 90, 91, 92, 93, 94

Malatya, 8
Maltepe, 127
Marash (Maraş) 20, 28, 30, 31, 32, 33
Menteşe, 32, 33, 34
Mersin, 28, 121
Merzifon, 28
Mihalıççık, 28
Moscow, 4, 71, 87, 88, 89
Mosul, 32, 33, 34

New York, 10, 31, 66, 110, 76, 85, 91
Niğde, 28, 30, 31, 32, 33, 34

Ordu, 28, 51
Orhangazi, 28

Palestine, 73, 104
Pangaltı 142
Pendik, 12, 127, 128

Romania, 51, 104, 107
Rumeli Feneri, 125, 126
Russia, 42, 44, 45, 71, 88, 89

Samsun, 51, 124
Silifke, 124
Sis
Sivas, 12, 28, 30, 31, 32, 33, 34, 46, 47
Sivrihisar, 28
Syria, 9, 20, 31, 48, 80, 90, 91, 92, 93, 94,
    95

Teke, 32, 33, 34, 42
Termen, 28
Tirebolu, 28
Tokat, 28
Trebizond (Trabzon), 28, 29, 30, 32, 35,
    42, 43, 44, 56
Tuzla, 129

United States, 40, 79, 80, 96, 97, 100, 102,
    108, 110, 111
Urfa, 28, 30, 31, 32, 33, 34, 115
Ünye, 28
Üsküdar (Scutari), 58, 127

Van, 21, 30, 32, 33, 34

Yalova, 28, 129
Yozgat, 28

Zor, 30, 32, 33

Index of Personal Names

Adnan Bey, 110
Ahmet İzzet Pasha (İzzet Pasha), 31, 33
Ahmet Rıza Bey, 18
Aktan, Gündüz, 82, 83
Ali Fethi Bey (national defense minister and prime minister), 123
Ali Saip (Saib) (parliamentary deputy of Kozan), 120
Ali Şükrü Bey (parliamentary deputy of Trebizond) ,58
Aras, Tevfik Rüştü (Tevik Rüştü), 95
Atatürk, Mustafa Kemal, 46, 47, 62, 129

Boyacıyan, Kevork, 51
Bristol, Mark Lambert (US high commissioner in Turkey), 110, 111, 112

Cemal Pasha, 9
Chambrun, Charles de, 94

Damat Ferit Pasha, 48
Değirmenciyan, Beton, 113
Demirdjian, Moses Nerces, 85
Dink, Arat, 8
Dink, Hrant, 8
Drummond, Eric, 107

Efdaleddin Bey (director of prisons), 115
Enver Pasha, 32
Ertegün, Münir, 101
Essayan, M., 107

Ferit Bey (minister of internal affairs), 112, 113, 115, 116, 117, 121, 122, 123, 124

Grew, Joseph C. (US ambassador to Switzerland) 97
Gümüşgerdanyan, 113

Hacim Muhittin Bey (parliamentary deputy of Giresun), 113
Hakkı Sami Bey (parliamentary deputy of Sinop), 56
Halil Bey, 114
Hasan Bey (parliamentary deputy of Trebizond), 56
Hasan Fehmi Bey (Fehmi Bey) (minister—treasury minister/first secretary of the treasury), 10, 13, 48, 50, 57, 63

Hüseyin Rıfat, 53

İnönü, İsmet (İsmet Pasha), 64, 67, 68, 69, 70, 71, 72, 73, 74, 76, 77, 79, 90, 97, 98, 115, 121, 123

Jackson, Jesse B. (US consul at Aleppo), 85

Kyriacopoulus, Ahmed Reshid, 107,

Lemkin, Raphael, 8, 9, 10 154

Mehmet Asım, 114, 117, 120
Mehmet Şükrü Bey (parliamentary deputy of Karahisarısahip), 59
Meray, Seha, 64, 67, 68, 70, 72, 73, 74

Nansen, Fridtjof, 48, 78, 130, 131, 132
Nielsen, Fred K. (Nielesen), 99, 100, 101
Niyazi Bey (parliamentary deputy of Mersin), 121
Nordenskjoeld, Baron de, 107
Nurettin Pasha, 57

Okyar, Fethi, 129
Osman Zâde Hamdi Bey (parliamentary deputy of Izmir), 115
Özoğlu, Şuşan, 88

Pelle, General, 90

Ragıp Bey (parliamentary deputy of Kütahya), 59,
Rauf Bey (prime minister), 46, 68, 79, 97
Refik Bey (parliamentary deputy of Konya), 64, 120
Renda, Mustafa Abdülhalik, 64, 121
Rıza Nur, 70
Rumbold, Horace, 70, 73

Salih Efendi (parliamentary deputy of Erzerum), 57
Seropyan, Sarkis, 8
Sofuoğlu, Cem Murat, 19, 142
Sübuhyan, Karnik, 113
Şahin, İbrahim, 8
Şükrü Bey (minister of the interior) 58, 59, 115, 121

Tahtaburunyan, 117
Talat Pasha, 9, 10, 86, 155
Tashjian, Vahe, 48, 93, 94

Urkapyan, Boğos, 142
Urkapyan, Maryam, 142, 143
Üşenmez, Şuayip, 151

Vahdettin, 37, 38, 48, 50, 52, 55, 56

Yahya Galip Bey, 13
Yahya Kemal Bey (parliamentary deputy
   of Urfa) 115

Index of International Agreements (chronological)

Sevres, 107
Lausanne, 3, 4, 5, 13, 15, 16, 17, 39, 40,
   50, 54, 56, 62, 64, 66, 67, 68, 71, 72,
   75, 76, 77, 78, 79, 80, 81, 82, 83, 84,
   85, 87, 88, 90, 91, 92, 93, 94, 96, 98,
   102, 103, 105, 106, 107, 109, 110,
   111, 112, 117, 118, 120, 121, 122,
   123, 124, 125, 128, 130, 134, 135 136,
   137, 138, 141, 142, 144, 147, 153
The Mudros Armistice, 39, 51

The League of Nations, 17, 38, 48, 75, 78,
   87, 103, 107 130, 131
The Mixed Arbitral Tribunal(s) 17, 66, 81,
   82, 83, 87, 103 105, 106, 107
Turkey-US Compensation Treaty, 5, 96,
   101
The Treaties of Alexandrapol (Gyumri),
   Kars and Moscow, 87, 88, 89,
The Ankara Treaty, 90

Index of Laws and Regulations (chronological)

The Deportation Law, 20, 34
The Regulation of, 10 June, 1915, 22, 23,
   26, 29
The Temporary Law of, 26 September,
   1915, 24, 36, 51, 54, 55, 60, 74 109,
   139, 140, 142
The Regulation of, 8 November, 1915, 24,
   25, 36, 54, 55, 60, 61, 109
12 January, 1920, 35, 36, 38, 48, 50, 52,
   55, 58, 59
The, 1869 Law of Citizenship, 40, 41, 67,
   77, 78, 79, 85, 97, 99, 107, 110, 111,
   112, 145

The Passport Laws of, 1911, 1915, 1918,
   41, 42, 124, 130, 133
The, 20 April, 1922, 51, 52, 53, 54, 60
The, 14 September, 1922, 54, 60
The, 15 April, 1923, 10, 54, 60, 74, 117,
   134, 137, 142, 148
The, 29 April, 1923, 54, 60, 134
Tekalif-i Milliye, 62
The, 5 February, 1925, 84, 136, 137,
The, 13 June, 1926, 84, 137, 138, 140, 149

War and Genocide

General Editors: Omer Bartov, Brown University; A. Dirk Moses, European University Institute, Florence/University of Sydney

There has been a growing interest in the study of war and genocide, not from a traditional military history perspective, but within the framework of social and cultural history. This series offers a forum for scholarly works that reflect these new approaches.

"The Berghahn series Studies on War and Genocide has immeasurably enriched the English-language scholarship available to scholars and students of genocide and, in particular, the Holocaust."—**Totalitarian Movements and Political Religions**

Volume 1
The Massacre in History
Edited by Mark Levene and Penny Roberts

Volume 2
National Socialist Extermination Policies: Contemporary German Perspectives and Controversies
Edited by Ulrich Herbert

Volume 3
War of Extermination: The German Military in World War II, 1941–44
Edited by Hannes Heer and Klaus Naumann

Volume 4
In God's Name: Genocide and Religion in the Twentieth Century
Edited by Omer Bartov and Phyllis Mack

Volume 5
Hitler's War in the East, 1941–1945
Rolf-Dieter Müller and Gerd R. Ueberschär

Volume 6
Genocide and Settler Society: Frontier Violence and Stolen Indigenous Children in Australian History
Edited by A. Dirk Moses

Volume 7
Networks of Nazi Persecution: Bureaucracy, Business and the Organization of the Holocaust
Edited by Gerald D. Feldman and Wolfgang Seibel

Volume 8
Gray Zones: Ambiguity and Compromise in the Holocaust and Its Aftermath
Edited by Jonathan Petropoulos and John K. Roth

Volume 9
Robbery and Restitution: The Conflict over Jewish Property in Europe
Edited by Martin Dean, Constantin Goschler and Philipp Ther

Volume 10
Exploitation, Resettlement, Mass Murder: Political and Economic Planning for German Occupation Policy in the Soviet Union, 1940–1941
Alex J. Kay

Volume 11
Theatres of Violence: Massacre, Mass Killing and Atrocity in History
Edited by Philip G. Dwyer and Lyndall Ryan

Volume 12
Empire, Colony, Genocide: Conquest, Occupation, and Subaltern Resistance in World History
Edited by A. Dirk Moses

Volume 13
The Train Journey: Transit, Captivity, and Witnessing in the Holocaust
Simone Gigliotti

Volume 14
The "Final Solution" in Riga: Exploitation and Annihilation, 1941–1944
Andrej Angrick and Peter Klein

Volume 15
The Kings and the Pawns: Collaboration in Byelorussia during World War II
Leonid Rein

Volume 16
Reassessing the Nuremberg Military Tribunals: Transitional Justice, Trial Narratives, and Historiography
Edited by Kim C. Priemel and Alexa Stiller

Volume 17
The Nazi Genocide of the Roma: Reassessment and Commemoration
Edited by Anton Weiss-Wendt

Volume 18
Judging "Privileged" Jews: Holocaust Ethics, Representation, and the "Grey Zone"
Adam Brown

Volume 19
*The Dark Side of Nation-States: Ethnic
Cleansing in Modern Europe*
Philipp Ther

Volume 20
*The Greater German Reich and the Jews:
Nazi Persecution Policies in the Annexed
Territories 1935-1945*
Edited by Wolf Gruner and Jörg Osterloh

Volume 21
*The Spriti of the Laws: The Plunder of
Wealth in the Armenian Genocide*
Taner Akçam and Umit Kurt

Volume 22
*Genocide on Settler Frontiers:
When Hunter-Gatherers and
Commercial Stock Farmers Clash*
Edited by Mohamed Adhikari